The **ACT**
Course Book

ENGLISH, READING, & WRITING

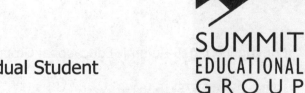

Focusing on the Individual Student

SUMMIT
EDUCATIONAL
GROUP

Copyright Statement

The ACT Course Book, along with all Summit Educational Group Course Materials, is protected by copyright. Under no circumstances may any Summit materials be reproduced, distributed, published, or licensed by any means.

Summit Educational Group reserves the right to refuse to sell materials to any individual, school, district, or organization that fails to comply with our copyright policies.

Third party materials used to supplement Summit Course Materials are subject to copyright protection vested in their respective publishers. These materials are likewise not reproducible under any circumstances.

Ownership of Trademarks

Summit Educational Group is the owner of the trademarks "Summit Educational Group" and the pictured Summit logo, as well as other marks that the Company may seek to use and protect from time to time in the ordinary course of business.

ACT is a trademark of ACT, Inc.

All other trademarks referenced are the property of their respective owners.

ISBN: 978-0-578-16061-0

CONTENTS

TEST-TAKING FUNDAMENTALS

About the ACT   2

Your Commitment   3

ACT Structure   4

Content   5

Scoring   6

Knowing Your Limits   8

General Tactics   10

ENGLISH OVERVIEW

The English Test   14

Format   15

Attractors   17

Setting Your Goal   18

Working Through the English Test   20

General Tips   21

ENGLISH – USAGE AND MECHANICS

Pronouns   24

Subject-Verb Agreement   28

Verb Tense   30

Adjectives versus Adverbs   32

Idioms   32

Diction   34

Fragments   38

Run-Ons   40

Parallelism   42

Modifiers   44

Periods   48

Semicolons   50

Colons   50

Commas   52

Apostrophes   56

ENGLISH – RHETORICAL SKILLS

Main Idea   66

Intent   68

Organization   70

Addition   72

Deletion   74

Transitions   76

Style   80

Wordiness   82

English Practice   88

READING OVERVIEW

The Reading Test   130

Format   131

Attractors   132

Setting Your Goal   134

Working Through the Reading Test   136

General Tips   137

READING

Active Reading   140

Paired Passages   142

Literary Narrative or Prose Fiction Passages   146

Social Science Passages   147

Humanities Passages   148

Natural Science Passages   149

Answering the Questions   152

Anticipating the Answer   153

Process of Elimination   158

Detail Questions   162

Generalization Questions   164

Main Idea Questions   166

Comparative Relationship Questions   168

Cause-Effect Questions   170

Voice Questions   172

Method Questions   174

Contextual Meaning Questions   176

Inference Questions   178

Reading Practice   184

Writing Overview

The Writing Test   218

Format and Scoring   219

Working Through the Writing Test   221

General Tips   222

Writing

Analyzing the Issue   226

Assessing Perspectives   228

Preparing to Write   230

Introduction   234

Supporting Paragraphs   238

Prove   242

Disprove   246

Compare   250

Conclusion   254

Proofread   258

Writing Effectively   260

Writing Practice   268

Answer Key

ANSWER KEY   302

Preface

Since 1988, when two Yale University graduates started Summit Educational Group, tens of thousands of students have benefited from Summit's innovative, comprehensive, and highly effective test preparation. You will, too.

Successful test-takers not only possess the necessary academic skills but also understand how to take the ACT. Through your ACT program, you'll learn both. You'll review and develop the academic skills you need, and you'll learn practical, powerful and up-to-date test-taking strategies.

The *Summit SAT Course Book* provides the skills, strategies, and practice necessary for success on the ACT. The result of much research and revision, this book is the most effective, innovative and comprehensive preparation tool available.

This book's first chapter – Test-Taking Fundamentals – gives students a solid foundation of ACT information and general test-taking strategies. The following chapters cover the verbal content strands of the ACT – English, Reading, and Writing. Each chapter is divided into manageable topic modules. Modules consist of the skills, strategies, and common question types for particular topics, *Try It Out* questions, and *Put It Together* questions. At the end of each chapter, homework questions provide additional practice.

Some English modules include frequencies for specific question types. These are not absolute, but are general trends based on research of many official ACTs.

We are confident that you will not find a more complete or effective ACT program anywhere.

We value your feedback and are always striving to improve our materials. Please write to us with comments, questions, or suggestions for future editions at:

edits@mytutor.com

Your program will give you the skills, knowledge, and confidence you need to score your best.

Good luck, and have fun!

Chapter Summaries

We've reproduced the Chapter Summaries below to give you a preview of what you'll be covering. The Summaries are meant to serve as quick, condensed reference guides to the most important concepts. Obviously, you can't bring them into the test with you, but from now up until the night before the test, use them to preview and review the material covered in this book. Of course, Chapter Summaries also reside at the end of each chapter.

General Test-Taking Summary

❑ Know your limits. Remember: Most students don't need to answer every question to reach their goals.

❑ Pace yourself through each section, and don't get stuck on any one question for too long. You can always skip the question and come back to it.

❑ Don't leave answers blank.

❑ Be aware of attractors.

❑ Carefully read and think about each question. Make sure you know what the question is asking.

❑ Focus on one question at a time. Resist the temptation to think about the 10 questions ahead or the question you did a minute ago.

❑ Use Process of Elimination (POE), and make educated guesses.

English – Usage and Mechanics Summary

Pronouns

❏ A pronoun must clearly refer back to the noun or nouns it represents.

❏ To check for the correct pronoun in a compound phrase, ignore the rest of the group.

❏ Don't use *that* or *which* when referring to people. People are always *who* or *whom*.

❏ The pronoun "who" always refers to the subject. The pronoun "whom" always refers to an object.

Subject-Verb Agreement

❏ Singular subjects require singular verbs, and plural subjects require plural verbs.

❏ To simplify sentences, remove all extra information between the subject and the verb.

❏ Subjects grouped by "and" are plural, even if the "and" joins two singular words.

❏ When the subject follows the verb, flip the sentence to put the subject first.

Verb Tense

❏ Verb tense must be consistent with the timeline presented in the rest of the passage.

Adjectives versus Adverbs

❏ Use adjectives to describe nouns. Use adverbs to describe verbs, adjectives, and other adverbs.

Idioms

❏ On the ACT, idioms typically appear in the form of verbs with certain prepositions.

❏ There are too many idioms to memorize; the key to knowing English idioms is familiarity with the language. The best way to learn idioms is to read regularly.

Diction

❏ Be careful as you consider answer choices – an incorrect answer may sound right if you are used to hearing it in casual conversation.

Fragments

❏ Be careful with verbs ending in *ing*. These are sometimes used as a description of the subject rather than the subject's action.

❏ Unnecessary words or punctuation can create fragments.

Run-ons

❏ Many run-on problems result from using commas improperly or not using conjunctions.

❏ Some run-on sentences are best fixed with transitions.

Parallelism

❏ When a sentence groups ideas, such as in a list, they must be presented in "parallel" form. Make sure that parts of speech are consistent.

❏ When two things are compared, they must be parallel. Consider the logic of the comparison; it must be explicitly clear that the same types of things are being compared.

Modifiers

❏ Descriptions must be placed next to the things they describe.

Periods

❏ Correct period placement will result in logical and complete sentences both before and after the punctuation.

Semicolons

❏ Semicolons, like periods, are used to separate independent clauses.

Colons

❏ Colons can only be used following independent clauses.

❏ Colons are most commonly used to introduce lists, but they may also be used to present noun phrases, quotations, or examples which clarify or elaborate on the independent clause.

Commas

❏ If a sentence begins with a phrase that sets time, place, or purpose, then the phrase should be followed by a comma.

❏ When two independent clauses are joined by a conjunction, such as "and" or "but," there should be a comma placed before the conjunction.

❏ Commas separate items in a list.

❏ Clauses with nonessential information are offset by commas.

Apostrophes

❏ When the possessor is a singular noun, possession can be indicated by adding 's.

❏ When the possessor is a plural noun ending in s, possession can be indicated by adding an apostrophe. Plural nouns that do not end in s can be made possessive by adding 's.

❏ "It's" is always a contraction of "it is." Likewise, "its" is always a possessive pronoun.

English – Rhetorical Skills Summary

Main Idea

❑ Every part of a passage should contribute to the passage's main idea.

Intent

❑ When asked to judge a passage based on the author's goals, pay careful attention to the wording of the question and answer choices.

Organization

❑ When organized properly, an essay's ideas should build upon each other and transition naturally.

Addition

❑ Only choose to add material if it introduces new, useful information to the passage.

Deletion

❑ Sentences should be deleted if they are not relevant to the focus of the passage or do not support and strengthen the passage's ideas.

Transitions

❑ Transitions can be used to show the relationship between sentences or between clauses in a sentence.

Style

❑ Make sure the language of passages is consistent in tone and expresses appropriate ideas.

❑ It is unacceptable to use slang or colloquialisms in the type of writing that appears on the English Test, even if the colloquial or slang word conveys the proper meaning.

Wordiness

❑ Shorter and simpler is usually better. Questions on wordiness require you to eliminate redundancies and irrelevant information.

Reading Summary

Reading the Passages

☐ Stay engaged. While reading, you should be thinking about the information, reflecting on what you have already read, anticipating what will come next, and analyzing how the passage is constructed.

☐ Map the passage. Find the main idea of each paragraph.

☐ Make notes that help you understand the reading.

☐ Treat paired passages as two separate passages.

1. Read the first passage and answer the questions for it.

2. Read the second passage and answer the questions for it.

3. Answer the questions that concern both passages.

Answering the Questions

☐ Questions do not follow the order of the passage, nor do they progress from easy to difficult.

☐ Tackle each passage's questions using the following three steps:

1. Attack the easy and medium questions first.

2. Make a second pass through the questions to work on the problems you skipped and marked, focusing on the ones you think you are most likely to answer correctly.

3. Guess on the remaining questions.

☐ When a question refers to specific line numbers, read a few lines before and after the given lines to get the full context.

☐ Understand the question before you look at the answer choices.

☐ Make sure that you've found the best answer, not just a good one. Reading questions, especially difficult ones, will usually contain at least one or two choices that are "almost right."

Writing Summary

❑ Before you begin your essay, read the assignment carefully and consider the issue and perspectives.

❑ Take a minute to plan your essay. Make a simple outline of the points you want to cover in your essay.

❑ It is usually best to have four or five paragraphs in your essay: the introduction, two or three supporting paragraphs, and a conclusion.

❑ A simple way to organize your essay is to create three body paragraphs: one for defending your thesis, and the other two for assessing the other viewpoints presented in the prompt.

❑ Take time during the last two minutes to read through your essay. You won't have time to make major changes, but you can make some minor improvements. It's easy to skip or misspell words when you're trying to write quickly, so this step is very important.

❑ Make sure each sentence is necessary. Do not try to stuff your essay with irrelevant facts.

Assessment and Objectives Worksheet

Complete this worksheet after the first session and refer back to it often. Amend it as necessary. It should act as a guide for how you and your tutor approach the program as a whole and how your sessions are structured.

The assessment will come from information that you and your parent(s) provide and from your initial diagnostic test. Keep in mind that you know yourself better than anyone else. Please be honest and open when answering the questions.

Student's Self-Assessment and Parent Assessment

- How do you feel about taking standardized tests? Consider your confidence and anxiety levels.

- Work through Table of Contents. Are there particular areas that stand out as areas for development?

- Other Concerns

Diagnostic Test Assessment

- Pacing

  o Did you run out of time on any or all sections? Did you feel rushed? Look for skipped questions or wrong answers toward the end of sections.

  o How will the concepts of Knowing Your Limits and Setting Your Goal help you?

- Carelessness

  o Do you feel that carelessness is an issue? Look for wrong answers on easy questions.

  o Why do you think you make careless mistakes? Rushing? Not checking? Not reading the question carefully? Knowing "why" will allow you to attack the problem.

- Are certain areas for development evident from the diagnostic? Work through the questions you got wrong to further identify areas that might require attention.

Initial Score Goals

Note that score goals should be adjusted as necessary through the program.

Composite Goal: _____   English Goal: _____

Math Goal: _____   Reading Goal: _____

Science Goal: _____   Writing Goal: _____

Program Objectives

Consider your assessment, and define your objectives. Make your objectives concrete and achievable.

Objective*	How to Achieve the Objective

*Sample Objectives

Objective	How to Achieve the Objective
Reduce carelessness by 75%.	Before starting to work on a question, repeat exactly what the question is asking.
Use Active Reading skills to avoid losing focus while reading passages.	Practice reading skills every day. Read novels or magazines at an appropriate reading level. Ask questions and engage the text while you read.
Reduce test anxiety.	Build confidence and create a detailed testing plan. Start with easier questions to build confidence and slowly build toward more challenging questions. Take pride in successes and continue to reach for goals. Try to relax.
Learn how to fully develop an essay example with specific details.	Show models of well-developed sample paragraphs. Develop paragraphs with tutor. Learn effective language for supporting or criticizing other arguments.
Get excited about the test prep.	Stay positive. Know that score goals can be achieved. Learn tricks to beat the test. Make the test like a game. Focus on progress.

SUMMIT
EDUCATIONAL
GROUP

Test-Taking Fundamentals

- ❑ About the ACT
- ❑ Your Commitment
- ❑ ACT Structure
- ❑ Content
- ❑ Scoring
- ❑ Knowing Your Limits
- ❑ General Tactics

About the ACT

❑ What does the ACT measure? According to the ACT folks, it measures your achievement – not IQ – in English, math, reading, science, and writing (if you choose to take the Writing Test). We feel that, to some extent, it measures how good you are at taking standardized tests. Either way, the ACT is an important element in the college admissions process.

Over the course of this program, you are going to learn to master the ACT by developing your test-taking abilities, working on fundamental ACT skills, and practicing with real ACT questions.

❑ Your performance on the ACT is **not** designed to reflect your scores on typical school exams or grades.

You are not expected to achieve a perfect score on the ACT, unlike on a typical school exam. The ACT is designed so that no student is expected to answer every question correctly.

❑ You might need to review and practice skills in one or more topics that appear on the test. You might just be rusty, or the topic might be unfamiliar to you. Your diagnostic will indicate your weak areas. You and your instructor will work to strengthen these weak areas throughout the program.

❑ Your instructor will emphasize both general test-taking strategies and problem-specific strategies, and you will practice these strategies during homework. Our strategies make the ACT less intimidating and more like a challenging game.

You'll practice on ACT-like questions throughout the book, and you'll take official ACT exams. The ACT, like any standardized test, has its own characteristics – from types of questions to timing. There is no more effective practice than working on real tests and simulated ACT questions.

Your Commitment

❑ Your commitment to the program will determine how much you get out of it. Your instructor has made a commitment to your success on the ACT, and you need to make a commitment to helping yourself.

Attend all sessions.

Pay attention during sessions.

Ask questions when you don't understand something.

Complete all homework assignments.

ACT Structure

❑ The ACT is made up of four tests, which appear in the same order on every test: English, Math, Reading, and Science. Some of the tests can be divided into subsections. There is also an optional Writing Test.

Test	English	Mathematics	Reading	Science	Writing
Time	45 min	60 min	35 min	35 min	Optional
Questions	75	60	40	40	1
Sub-scores	Usage / Mechanics Rhetorical Skills	Pre-Algebra / Elementary Algebra Intermediate Algebra / Coordinate Geometry Plane Geometry / Trigonometry	Social Studies / Natural Sciences Arts / Literature	–	Ideas / Analysis Development / Support Organization Language Use

❑ Without the optional Writing Test, the ACT takes 2 hours and 55 minutes. You are given one 10-minute break.

You are given another 10-minute break before the Writing Test, if you do choose to take it.

❑ Occasionally, the ACT will have an experimental section.

The experimental section is used to try out new problems, and it doesn't count towards your score. It shows up at the end of the test, and is shorter than the other sections (about 20 minutes). That said, don't ever assume that the last section is experimental. Do your best on every section!

Content

❑ The English Test requires you to revise and edit pieces of writing, using the rules of Standard Written English.

You don't need to know many grammatical terms, but you do need to understand how they work.

❑ The Math Test covers all topics of high school math: Pre-Algebra, Algebra, Plane Geometry, Coordinate Geometry, and Trigonometry.

❑ The Reading Test evaluates your ability to read, understand, and analyze short reading passages.

The Reading Test is made up of four reading passages of about 750 words each. The passages are always divided into four categories and appear in the same order: Literary Narrative / Prose Fiction, Social Science, Humanities, and Natural Science.

❑ The Science Test asks you to interpret and analyze data, to understand the parts and significance of an experiment, and to recognize the similarities and differences between the views of two scientists.

You don't need to know any scientific facts to do well on the Science Test.

❑ The Writing Test asks you to create a well-structured, well-written essay on a given topic.

Although taking the Writing Test is officially optional, many colleges require a Writing score. Even if you don't think you'll need it, it's a good idea to sign up for the essay. You don't want to have to take the entire ACT again if you find out later that you need the essay score for a specific school.

Scoring

❑ On the ACT, you receive one raw point for each correct answer. All questions in a test are worth the same, regardless of difficulty. Your **raw score** is the number of questions you answered correctly.

There is no penalty for an incorrect answer. <u>You should never leave an ACT question blank, even if you have to guess.</u>

❑ Your raw scores are converted to **scaled scores** using a conversion table. The conversion table makes up for the slight differences in difficulty between different ACT tests, and allows you to compare different versions of the test.

Here is part of a typical conversion table:

Scaled Score	Raw Scores			
	English	Math	Reading	Science
36	75	60	39-40	40
35	-	59	38	39
34	74	58	37	-
33	73	57	36	38
32	72	54-56	35	37
31	70-71	52-53	34	36
30	68-69	50-51	33	-
29	66-67	48-49	32	35
28	64-65	46-47	31	33-34
27	61-63	44-45	30	32
26	58-60	42-43	29	31
25	56-57	40-41	27-28	29-30
24	53-55	37-39	26	28
23	51-52	35-36	25	26-27
22	49-50	33-34	23-24	24-25
21	46-48	31-32	22	23
20	43-45	29-30	20-21	21-22
19	41-42	26-28	19	19-20
18	38-40	23-25	18	17-18

❑ Your four scaled scores are averaged to find your **composite score**, which is on a 1-36 scale. This composite score is rounded to the nearest whole number.

Your Writing score does not factor into your composite score. A different conversion table is used to calculate a Combined English/Writing Test score.

❑ Your score report will also give you scaled subscores for every test except Science. For example, your English score will be split into Usage/Mechanics and Rhetorical Skills.

Knowing Your Limits

❏ During the real test, put your time and energy into the problems you are most capable of answering. If you struggle with difficult problems or with finishing sections in time, spend more of your time on the easy and medium problems and less time on the difficult problems. Here's why:

- You do not need to answer every question correctly to score well.

- You'll minimize mistakes on difficult questions, which often contain "attractor" or trap answers.

- You'll be less hurried, and you'll make fewer careless mistakes.

❏ During your test prep, push your limits.

As you prepare for the ACT, try to learn from the questions that give you trouble. Note your mistakes and make sure that you don't repeat them. Pay attention to the questions that are the most difficult and note what makes them so challenging and how to solve them.

As your skills improve, you will be able to answer more and more of the questions on the ACT. You will learn to recognize tricks and traps and work with more speed and confidence.

These are the results of three students taking the same 12-question section.

Note: This example is not based on an actual test section; it is only for illustration.

Cautious Test-Taker	Completist Test-Taker	Skilled Test-Taker
1 (A) (B) (C) (D)	1 (A) (B) (C) (D)	1 (A) (B) (C) (D)
2 (F) (G) (H) (J)	✗ 2 (F) (G) (H) (J)	2 (F) (G) (H) (J)
3 (A) (B) (C) (D)	3 (A) (B) (C) (D)	3 (A) (B) (C) (D)
4 (F) (G) (H) (J)	✗ 4 (F) (G) (H) (J)	4 (F) (G) (H) (J)
o 5 (A) (B) (C) (D)	5 (A) (B) (C) (D)	✗ 5 (A) (B) (C) (D)
6 (F) (G) (H) (J)	✗ 6 (F) (G) (H) (J)	6 (F) (G) (H) (J)
7 (A) (B) (C) (D)	7 (A) (B) (C) (D)	7 (A) (B) (C) (D)
o 8 (F) (G) (H) (J)	8 (F) (G) (H) (J)	8 (F) (G) (H) (J)
✗ 9 (A) (B) (C) (D)	9 (A) (B) (C) (D)	9 (A) (B) (C) (D)
10 (F) (G) (H) (J)	✗ 10 (F) (G) (H) (J)	✗ 10 (F) (G) (H) (J)
o 11 (A) (B) (C) (D)	11 (A) (B) (C) (D)	11 (A) (B) (C) (D)
o 12 (F) (G) (H) (J)	12 (F) (G) (H) (J)	12 (F) (G) (H) (J)

Raw Score = **7**   Raw Score = **8**   Raw Score = **10**

✗ = wrong answer
o = blank

Cautious test-takers may get most of their answers correct, but they spend too much time checking answers on easy questions and they avoid challenging problems. This approach causes cautious test-takers to run out of time and to miss opportunities for reaching their full potential.

Completist test-takers are so determined to answer every question in time that they rush through the section. This approach causes completist test-takers to make careless mistakes on problems that they could have gotten correct if they had worked at a steadier pace.

Skilled test-takers learn to recognize easy and difficult questions, and they spend their time accordingly. Skilled test-takers finish sections on time without having to rush, and they never leave a question blank, but instead make educated guesses on challenging problems.

General Tactics

❑ Focus on one question at a time.

The ACT is timed, so it's normal to feel pressure to rush. Resist the temptation to think about the 10 questions ahead of you or the question you did a minute ago. Relax and focus on one question at a time. **Patience** on the ACT is what allows you to work more quickly and accurately.

❑ Carefully read and think about each question.

Before you jump to the answers, start scribbling things down, or do calculations, make sure you understand exactly what the question is asking.

❑ Write in your test booklet.

When you're ready to solve the problem, use the space in your test booklet. Cross out incorrect answers, write down calculations to avoid careless errors, summarize reading passages, etc. Write down whatever will help you solve the problem.

❑ Use process of elimination (POE).

If you can legitimately eliminate at least one answer, you should guess. The more answers you can eliminate, the greater advantage you have. Once you have eliminated an answer, cross it out or put an "X" by it.

❑ Memorize the format and instructions before you take the test. At test time, you can skip the instructions and focus on the problems.

❑ The multiple-choice answer to each individual question is independent of the answers to the other questions. For example, sometimes an answer (A) might be correct 2, 3, or 4 times in a row, and that's okay. Don't be afraid to pick any particular multiple-choice answer just because you saw that answer recently. Choose the answer which is best for that particular question.

SUMMIT
EDUCATIONAL
GROUP

English Overview

- ❑ The English Test
- ❑ Format
- ❑ Attractors
- ❑ Setting Your Goal
- ❑ Working Through the English Test
- ❑ General Tips

The English Test

❑ The ACT English Test measures your skill at evaluating and improving short essays. You've likely been practicing most of these skills on school writing assignments for years.

Format	75 questions 5 passages Multiple-choice 4 answer choices
Content	Grammar and Usage Sentence Structure Punctuation Strategy Organization Style

Scoring	English Test Score: 1-36
	Subscores:
	    Usage and Mechanics: 1-18
	    Rhetorical Skills: 1-18

Time	45 minutes

❑ The ACT English Test contains a certain number of questions per topic:

Content Area	Questions	Sample Topics
Usage/Mechanics	40	
Grammar & Usage	12-15	subject-verb agreement, pronouns, idioms
Sentence Structure	15-18	run-ons, fragments, modifiers
Punctuation	8-10	commas, apostrophes, colons, semicolons
Rhetorical Skills	35	
Strategy	12-15	main idea, adding, deleting
Organization	8-12	organization, transitions
Style	12-15	style, wordiness

Format

❑ You are asked to read 5 essays of roughly the same length and answer questions about grammar, style, and strategy. There are usually 15 questions related to each essay.

The essays are consistent in quality with those written by average high-school juniors or seniors, and cover a wide range of topics and tones.

❑ English Test question types are divided into two major content categories: Usage and Mechanics, and Rhetorical Skills.

Usage and Mechanics questions test your understanding of written English conventions, such as grammar and punctuation.

Rhetorical Skills questions test your ability to understand an author's intent and to strengthen the author's ideas and arguments.

❑ The instructions are the same on every ACT. Familiarize yourself with the instructions before you take the test. At test time, you can skip the instructions and focus on the problems.

DIRECTIONS: In the five passages that follow, certain words and phrases are underlined and numbered. In the right-hand column, you will find alternatives for the underlined part. In most cases, you are to choose the one that best expresses the idea, makes the statement appropriate for standard written English, or is worded most consistently with the style and tone of the passage as a whole. If you think the original version is best, choose "NO CHANGE." In some cases, you will find in the right hand column a question about the underlined part. You are to choose the best answer to the question.

You will also find questions about a section of the passage, or about the passage as a whole. These questions do not refer to an underlined portion of the passage, but rather are identified by a number or numbers in a box.

For each question, choose the alternative you consider best and fill in the corresponding oval on your answer document. Read each passage through once before you begin to answer the questions that accompany it. For many of the questions, you must read several sentences beyond the question to determine the answer. Be sure that you have read far enough ahead each time you choose an alternative.

> **Answer the questions as you read through the passage. Although the ACT suggests you should read entire English passages before you begin to answer the questions, this is unnecessary and time-consuming.**

Attractors

❑ Spot and avoid attractor answer choices.

The test writers predict potential mistakes by students and include those mistakes as answer choices. In other words, they set traps for the unsuspecting student. We call these answer choices "attractors." Attractors show up most often on medium and difficult problems.

In the following problems, which answer choices are attractors?

Its' surprising that Academy-Award winning actor Bing Crosby was so influential in the invention and use of magnetic tape recording. Crosby was not only an actor, but also a performer for radio shows across the country. These shows were performed several times for listeners whom live in different time zones, but Crosby used his knowledge from Hollywood to create a simpler solution.

Rather, then perform live radio shows multiple times, he recorded one performance and replayed the show later. To promote his idea, Crosby invested large amounts of money in companies at the cutting edge of recording technology. Crosby's innovation and passion contributed to the development of early computers, VHS, and cassette tapes.

1. A. NO CHANGE
    B. Its
    C. It's
    D. That's

2. F. NO CHANGE
    G. who lived
    H. whom lives
    J. who lives

3. A. NO CHANGE
    B. Rather then
    C. Rather than
    D. Rather,

Setting Your Goal

❑ You receive 1 raw point for a correct answer. You lose nothing for incorrect answers. Your **raw score** is calculated by adding up raw points. Your raw score is then converted to a **scaled score** from 1-36.

❑ You don't have to get every question right to score well.

To score a 21 on the English Test – which is the national average – you need to answer only 45 of the 75 questions correctly. That's only 60%, or just over half of the questions! On your regular school tests, 60% is almost a failing grade, but on the ACT, it's above average!

❑ Use the table below to set a target for the number of questions you need to answer correctly to hit your goal score for the English Test.

English Scaled Score	English Raw Score	Percent Correct
36	75	100%
35	74	99%
34	72-73	96%
33	71	95%
32	70	93%
31	69	92%
30	67-68	89%
29	65-66	87%
28	63-64	84%
27	61-62	81%
26	58-60	77%
25	55-57	73%
24	53-54	71%
23	50-52	67%
22	48-49	64%
21	45-47	60%
20	42-44	56%
19	40-41	53%
18	37-39	49%
17	35-36	47%
16	33-34	44%
15	30-32	40%
14	28-29	37%
13	26-27	35%
12	24-25	32%

❑ For most students, attempting every question on the ACT will prevent them from scoring to their potential. Attempting every question means you'll have to rush, which means you're more likely to make careless mistakes.

Having a realistic goal makes the test more manageable. With less pressure to answer every question, you can spend more time on easy and medium problems and less time on the difficult ones.

Remember, you get one raw point for each question, whether it's the simplest question or the hardest question. Whether it takes you ten seconds or three minutes, it's still one point.

❑ Create a Plan of Attack for the English Test.

Using your goal score and the score table, complete the Plan of Attack below. This will help you determine your best pace while working through the test.

Most of your time and energy should be spent on the questions needed to achieve your goal score. Assume that you will likely miss some of the questions you attempt, and use educated guessing on the rest.

English Test Plan of Attack

My overall ACT Goal: _____

My English Test Goal: _____

How many questions do I need to answer correctly (raw score)? _____

How many questions should I attempt? _____

> Questions you "attempt" are those that you give time and energy to solve. You should still use educated guessing to quickly answer the rest of the questions.

Working Through the English Test

❑ Focus on one passage at a time. Answer all of the questions to a passage before you move onto the next.

❑ Tackle each passage using the following three steps:

Step 1: Answer the questions along with the passage.

Answer each question as you come to it in the passage. If you come across a complicated question, circle it and come back to it later. It will usually be easier to answer when you understand the context of the whole passage.

Step 2: Make a second pass.

Work on the questions you skipped and marked, focusing on the ones you think you have the best chance of answering correctly.

Do as many of these as you can. For some, you might be able to find the right answer. For others, you might be able to eliminate answer choices and make an educated guess.

Step 3: Guess on the remaining questions.

Before you move on to the next passage, guess on any remaining questions. Even if you feel like you really don't know the answer, it will be easier to guess while you're still thinking about the passage.

❑ There is no penalty for guessing, so make sure you answer every question. With about 2 minutes to go, you should answer any remaining questions.

❑ On average, each passage of 15 questions should be completed within 9 minutes.

General Tips

❑ Shorter is often better.

The ACT prefers writing that is direct and simple. Usually, answer choices with complex or redundant writing will be incorrect. On the English Test, the shortest answer choice is often the correct answer.

Carefully consider answer choices that would omit portions of passages. Choose to remove information if it is irrelevant or unnecessary.

❑ If there's more than one error in a question, deal with one at a time. Eliminate all of the choices that contain one error, and then repeat the process with the next error.

❑ Don't always trust your ear. Standard written English may be more formal than what you are used to hearing.

Even if something sounds right the first time you read through it, double check for frequently tested grammatical errors. There are certain things that you might say, hear, or write in everyday life that contain grammatical errors.

❑ Don't find errors where none exist.

Just because something is underlined doesn't mean that it contains an error. The option "NO CHANGE" is correct approximately ¼ of the time – just as frequently as any other answer choice.

❑ Rhetorical Skills marked with a numbered box are usually more time-consuming than Usage and Mechanics questions. If time is short, focus on underlined grammar questions and guess aggressively.

SUMMIT
EDUCATIONAL
GROUP

Usage and Mechanics

- ❏ Grammar and Usage
  - ○ Pronouns
  - ○ Subject-Verb Agreement
  - ○ Verb Tenses
  - ○ Adjectives versus Adverbs
  - ○ Idioms & Diction

- ❏ Sentence Structure
  - ○ Fragments
  - ○ Run-Ons
  - ○ Parallelism
  - ○ Modifiers

- ❏ Punctuation
  - ○ Periods
  - ○ Colons & Semicolons
  - ○ Commas
  - ○ Apostrophes

Pronouns

(3-6 per test)

Pronoun questions often require you to determine whether a pronoun should be singular or plural, and they often test your knowledge of apostrophes. Challenging pronoun questions involve ambiguous pronouns that must be replaced with specific nouns.

❑ Pronouns can be used as subjects, objects, or possessives.

SUBJECT	OBJECT	POSSESSIVE
I	me	my, mine
you	you	your, yours
he, she	him, her	his, her, hers
we	us	our, ours
they	them	their, theirs
who	whom	whose
it	it	its
one	one	one's

❑ A pronoun must clearly refer back to the noun or nouns it represents.

Oscar mentioned that his sisters are older than he is.

❑ If there is no noun or multiple nouns that a pronoun can refer to, use a specific noun instead.

A seat belt should be worn to protect (*it/a passenger*) from potential injuries.

Most pearls aren't found by divers but are cultivated in farms. (*These/Pearls*) vary in price depending on their quality and origin.

❑ To check for the correct pronoun in a compound phrase, ignore the rest of the group.

Incorrect: My father gave presents to my brother and I.
Correct: My father gave presents to…   …me.

(*He/Him*) and his cousin went shopping for stereo equipment.

❑ Don't use *that* or *which* when referring to people. People are always *who* or *whom*.

Mark Twain expressed his belief that politicians were generally frauds (*that/who*) did not know more than a tiny fraction of what they claimed to know.

❑ The pronoun "who" always refers to the subject. The pronoun "whom" always refers to an object.

In order to determine whether a pronoun is a subject or object, try plugging in an easier pronoun (such as "he/him") and see which works best. If the objective-case pronoun ("him") works best, use the objective case for the pronoun in question ("whom"). This is called the "M test," because many object pronouns have the letter *m*.

❑ If a pronoun follows a preposition, such as "to" or "for," it is an object.

Jamie was a respected reporter (*who/whom*) would speak honestly about the facts.

To (*who/whom*) should the committee award the prize if no one deserves it?

Humility is only had by people (*who/whom*) realize and appreciate their own limitations.

PUT IT TOGETHER

On most weekends, Jess's sister visits her, and they gossip and cook. It's usually the same conversations and rumors, and it's always the same recipe. For them, the ritual is key. Flour and lard fill a large bowl on the kitchen table. Jess adds salt and baking powder and then tells her younger sister to help mix. As <u>her</u> and her sister work, the dough seems to come alive under their fingers. Last, they add the warm water: just enough to hold the dough together. The recipe is simple and ancient. Their grandmother used to assure them that anybody has the skills to make something as easy as tortillas.

Jess rolls pieces of dough into balls. As she presses <u>it</u> into a flat circle, Jess can almost feel the ghosts of her grandmother's hands folding around her own, guiding her. She knows, from memory of so many traditional meals at home, the exact thickness the dough should be. Her motions are careful, rhythmic, exactly as the women in her family have always done. Her sister watches and copies, with a bit of clumsiness. Someday, Jess and her sister will become mothers and teach the recipe to <u>its</u> own daughters. For now, they are more

focused on memories of their grandmother, <u>whose</u> cooking had been the symbol of their heritage as they had grown up.

1. A. NO CHANGE
    B. it
    C. she
    D. they

2. F. NO CHANGE
    G. that
    H. this one
    J. one

3. A. NO CHANGE
    B. they're
    C. their
    D. it's

4. F. NO CHANGE
    G. of whose
    H. whom
    J. her

> Try rereading the sentence with each answer choice.

While an iron pan heats on the stove, Jess sips her coffee. She then places two of the raw tortillas in <u>it</u>. In a moment, there is the familiar smell of smoke. She imagines watching her future children as they try to make their own tortillas for the first time. And she feels as though her grandmother is watching over her now, with love and pride.

5. A. NO CHANGE
   B. that
   C. them
   D. the pan

What does "it" refer to?

Subject-Verb Agreement

(1-3 per test)

Subject-verb agreement is not often tested directly on the ACT. However, the skill of determining whether a subject or verb is singular or plural is useful for several types of pronoun and apostrophe questions.

❑ Singular subjects require singular verbs, and plural subjects require plural verbs.

The <u>teacher</u> of the school's chemistry and physics classes <u>assigns</u> too much homework.

The other <u>teachers</u>, whom I prefer, usually <u>assign</u> little or no homework.

❑ To simplify sentences, remove all extra information between the subject and the verb. Then, make sure the subject and verb agree.

The birthday <u>party</u> ~~for my nieces, as well as their twenty friends,~~ <u>was</u> a success.

A whole group of tourists and children (*was*/*were*) gathered around to watch the mime.

❑ Appositive phrases (nonessential details set off by commas or dashes) are not part of the subject, even if the appositive phrases include other nouns.

Vanessa, along with the rest of her class, (*is*/*are*) hoping for a vacation.

❑ Subjects grouped by "and" are plural, even if the "and" joins two singular words.

The wet dog and its muddy owner (*want*/*wants*) to go inside.

You can simplify compound subjects by replacing them with a plural pronoun.

Incorrect: He and my brother <u>goes</u> to school.

Simplified: They ...   ... (*go*/*goes*) to school.

Correct: He and my brother <u>go</u> to school.

❑ When the subject follows the verb, flip the sentence to put the subject first.

Here (*is*/*are*) the <u>source</u> of the problems that have been ruining our budget.

Scattered around the west side of campus (*is*/*are*) a set of paintings and a collection of sculpture installations.

PUT IT TOGETHER

While World War II did aid Boston's recovery from the difficulties of the Great Depression, the <u>effects</u> of the war's end in 1945 is what truly altered the city's economic landscape. The advent of the technology industry, with its demand for new concrete and steel buildings, led to a boom in construction. Unfortunately, some people placed more importance on creating new developments than on preserving older cultural landmarks.

<u>There was</u>, throughout the 1960s, several cities renovated under the banner of "urban renewal." Boston's West End was one of the most well documented of such neighborhoods. The West End consisted mostly of working class families, and the aesthetics and the culture of the <u>community was</u> highly influenced by Eastern Europe. The neighborhood represented a peaceful blending of a wide variety of cultures. <u>That being</u> razed in 1959 and replaced by high-rise apartment and hospital buildings. In the process, an important cultural area, along with historic landmarks and parks, <u>were replaced</u> by monstrosities of concrete and steel.

1. **A.** NO CHANGE
   B. affects
   C. effect
   D. affect

> Subject-verb agreement questions often involve pronouns.

2. **F.** NO CHANGE
   G. It was
   H. It is
   J. There were

3. **A.** NO CHANGE
   B. community were
   C. community, was
   D. community being

4. **F.** NO CHANGE
   G. They were
   H. Those were
   J. It was

5. **A.** NO CHANGE
   B. was replaced
   C. replacing
   D. replaced

> The ACT makes subject-verb errors harder to find by separating the subject and the verb.

Verb Tense

Most verb tense questions test for consistency within and among sentences. These questions may also test subject-verb agreement or sentence structure skills.

❑ Verb tense must be consistent with the timeline presented in the rest of the passage. You may have to check previous or later sentences to find the correct tense.

❑ The most challenging verb tense questions typically require an understanding of the difference between past, past perfect, and present perfect tenses.

> Eliminating the need of fossil fuels (has been/had been) an elusive goal for many years, but we are getting closer to solving this problem.

> Henry (has been/had been) a skeptic of UFO sightings for years, but he finally believed in them when he saw unexplainable lights in the night sky.

PUT IT TOGETHER

In times of inflation, the value of money falls and prices

<u>seemed</u> higher. Most modern economists support a slow,

1

regulated rate of inflation. But economists are also aware of

the potential danger of inflation: if there is too much money

compared to the worth of goods, money <u>would have had</u> very

2

little value. A prime example of this "hyperinflation" occurred

in 1920s Germany. Prior to 1923, 50 German marks <u>had had</u> a

3

value equal to 1 U.S. dollar. In 1923, it <u>had taken</u> more than 4

4

trillion marks to equal the value of a single dollar. German

workers were given a single day's wage in wheelbarrows full

of cash, which was worth less than the material it was printed

on. Such an enormous shift in worth can have harsh, long-

lasting consequences on an economy.

1. A. NO CHANGE
    B. had seemed
    C. seem
    D. seems

2. F. NO CHANGE
    G. will have had
    H. will have
    J. having

3. A. NO CHANGE
    B. has had
    C. having
    D. to have

4. Which of the following alternatives to the underlined portion would NOT be acceptable?

    F. would have taken
    G. would take
    H. take
    J. took

Adjectives versus Adverbs

(1-2 per test)

Deciding between using an adjective or an adverb is usually straightforward if you understand the intent of the sentence. Occasionally, these questions can be solved by eliminating a redundant adjective or adverb.

❑ Use adjectives to describe nouns. Use adverbs to describe verbs, adjectives, and other adverbs.

Adverbs usually end in *ly*.

The puppy is (*delightfully/delightful*) curious and playful.

Baking requires (*carefully/careful*), precise measuring, so following recipes is suggested.

Idioms

(1-3 per test)

Idioms are expressions that mean something other than the literal meanings of their individual words. On the ACT, idioms typically appear in the form of verbs with certain prepositions.

There are too many idioms to memorize; the key to knowing English idioms is familiarity with the language. The best way to learn idioms is to read regularly.

❑ Idioms must be both proper and logical.

Mallory's preoccupation (*with/on*) her school project caused her to overlook the fact that her dog had escaped (*from/of*) its kennel.

❑ Make sure you are familiar with commonly used idioms.

accuse of	agree to	agree with	agree on
apologize for	apply to	apply for	approve of
arrive at	blame for	care about	care for
compare to	compare with	consist of	contribute to
count on	cover with	decide on	depend on
differ from	different from	distinguish from	forgive for
insist on	participate in	prevent from	prohibit from
provide with	rely on	respond to	substitute for

PUT IT TOGETHER

Opossums are quite simple creatures. For their size, they are some of the least intelligent mammals in the world. If you only know of opossums through popular media, you might believe that they are <u>cleverly, rat-like</u> scavengers dangling from trees. The image of the sly opossum is supported by

the phrase "playing 'possum," which <u>referring</u> the common belief that opossums cunningly pretend to be dead when

threatened. In reality, opossums are less <u>vicious and wily</u> than their popular image suggests. When they "play dead," opossums are not being clever or crafty; rather, when an opossum senses danger, it will often experience an

<u>automatically involuntarily</u> reaction. This death-like state is a reflex that opossums cannot control. The opossum's reaction is not any cleverer than sneezing to expel irritants or instinctively flinching to avoid oncoming danger.

1. **A.** NO CHANGE
   B. clever, rat-likely
   C. clever, rat-like
   D. cleverness, rat-likened

2. **F.** NO CHANGE
   G. refers to
   H. refers on
   J. refers

3. **A.** NO CHANGE
   B. viciously and wily
   C. vicious and wile
   D. viciousness and wile

4. **F.** NO CHANGE
   G. automatic, involuntarily,
   H. automatically
   J. involuntary

> Check for unnecessary wordiness. The English Test typically prefers shorter, simpler answers.

Diction

Diction questions test the proper usage of English words that are commonly misused in casual conversation. Be careful as you consider answer choices – an incorrect answer may sound right if you are used to hearing it.

❏ Know the proper usage of the following words.

Accept: to approve or receive (verb)
Except: excluding, besides (preposition)

I like every flavor (*accept/except*) coconut.
I (*accept/except*) your proposal.

Affect: to influence (verb)
Effect: result or consequence (noun)

The lyrics of his songs still (*affect/effect*) me.
That story had a strong (*affect/effect*) on people.

Than: in comparison with
Then: at that time

A kilogram is heavier (*than/then*) a pound.
I exercised, and (*than/then*) I rested.

Lose: to fail or cease to have
Loose: not firm

The bolt had a (*lose/loose*) fit.
We might (*lose/loose*) this game.

Lie: to pause for rest
Lay: to set down

Please (*lie/lay*) the package on the table.
After a marathon, I (*lie/lay*) in bed all day.

Lead: present tense of "to lead"
Led: past tense of "to lead"

Now, the tour guides (*lead/led*) us down the path.
Our bad directions had (*lead/led*) us in circles.

Principle: an accepted rule
Principal: leader

Sincerity is a (*principle/principal*) of good conduct.
The (*principle/principal*) was late to the meeting.

Number: countable quantity
Amount: measurable quantity

A large (*number/amount*) of people had a party.
A large (*number/amount*) of flour is used in cake.

Fewer: a countable difference
Less: an uncountable difference

The express aisle allows 15 items or (*fewer/less*).
After going to the circus, I have (*fewer/less*) fear of clowns and elephants.

Between: in a comparison or in the space separating two objects
Among: in the midst of more than two objects

The only difference (*between/among*) the two refrigerators is how much they cost.
He wants to build a cabin in the wilderness (*between/among*) all those elm trees.

PUT IT TOGETHER

A weathered guitar case, worn from long years on the road,

<u>lays</u> in one corner of the room and gathers dust. Beside it, in a
   1

creaking rocker, sits Smokin' Joe Henderson, sucking

lemonade through a twisty straw his granddaughter brought

him. He has lived <u>more years then</u> any other surviving
                      2

member of the family. The kids come around often to hear

Joe's stories of the old days. <u>Some</u> of them remember when
                                  3

the guitar would come out of its battered case and Joe would

play a few of those legendary licks for them. Now, his arthritis

is too bad to play; it hurts him even to hold the guitar. Over

the years, he began playing <u>less</u> songs and telling more stories,
                              4

which were just as fascinating.

1. A. NO CHANGE
    B. lay
    C. lies
    D. lie

2. F. NO CHANGE
    G. most years then
    H. more years than
    J. most years than

3. Which of the following alternatives to the underlined portion would be LEAST acceptable?

    A. A few
    B. Several
    C. An amount
    D. A number

4. F. NO CHANGE
    G. least
    H. lesser
    J. fewer

> **Don't always rely on what sounds good. Know the proper diction rules.**

Checkpoint Review

William James Sidis may have been the <u>smartest</u> man to
have ever lived. His incredible mind was a wonder, a project,
and a burden. The legacy William has left behind is
complicated. While his intellect is a matter of research and
respect, his parents are <u>general criticized</u> for raising William
in a way that brought too many social hardships.

Before he was even born, William's father, Boris, was
determined to raise a genius. Boris, <u>whom</u> had gained a
reputation for his use of hypnosis in psychological treatment,
enforced an intense curriculum of language arts and
mathematics. Boris believed that a child's mind can hold an
unlimited amount of knowledge, and so William's childhood
development <u>becoming</u> an experiment for proving this theory.

At the age of eighteen months, William could read the
New York Times. At age six, he was fluent in English, French,
Latin, German, Russian, Turkish, and Hebrew. At age eight,
he published his second book, which described a language he
had invented, a complex blend <u>to</u> several Romance languages
he called Vendergood. Boris carefully documented his son's
progress and regularly published academic papers boasting the
<u>successful effects</u> of his teaching methods. In one update of
William's progress, he wrote, "You must begin a child's
education as soon as he displays any power to think. I do not
mean by this that the child should be deprived of play. Get the
child so interested in study that study will truly be play."

1. **A.** NO CHANGE
   B. very intelligent
   C. more smart
   D. smarter

2. **F.** NO CHANGE
   G. general critical
   H. generally critically
   J. generally criticized

3. **A.** NO CHANGE
   B. who
   C. which
   D. OMIT the underlined portion.

4. **F.** NO CHANGE
   G. becomes
   H. became
   J. being

5. **A.** NO CHANGE
   B. at
   C. on
   D. of

6. **F.** NO CHANGE
   G. successfully affects
   H. affective success
   J. effectively success

Checkpoint Review

William entered Harvard University at age eleven. He quickly attracted media attention, which frustrated him. The constant attention from reporters and peers <u>were</u> a source of anxiety for young William. Because of his age and social inexperience, he was teased by his fellow students. At his graduation at age 16, he told reporters "I want to live the perfect life. The only way to live the perfect life is to live it in seclusion. I have always hated crowds."

7. **A.** NO CHANGE
   B. was
   C. are
   D. is

Once William had attained his degree, the brilliant achievements in his future <u>was seemingly</u> certain. His colleagues and professors predicted he would become an influential pioneer of mathematics or physics, a genius in the league of Einstein or Newton. But for all the brainpower he had developed, William did not want to stay in the academic world he had been forced into since birth. Rather than remain a scholar, he <u>choose</u> to live a simpler life. William spent the rest of his life moving from one city to the next, changing his name to remain anonymous. <u>Him and his parents</u> no longer spoke to each other. Journalists continued to search for him, reporting that he was working simple jobs and living a lonely, disappointing life. When asked about why he abandoned his studies, William replied, "The very sight of a mathematical formula makes me physically ill. All I want to do is run an adding machine." It seemed that he was exhausted from a lifetime of constant studying, and he merely wanted the chance to let his mind relax.

8. **F.** NO CHANGE
   G. was seeming
   H. were seemingly
   J. seem

9. **A.** NO CHANGE
   B. would of chose
   C. chose
   D. chooses

10. **F.** NO CHANGE
    G. He and his parents
    H. Their parents
    J. They

SUMMIT
EDUCATIONAL
GROUP

Fragments

(4-6 per test)

A complete sentence must have a subject (who or what does the action), a predicate (the action), and a complete idea. Any sentence missing one of these elements is a fragment.

Fragment questions are usually solved by choosing the proper verb or using proper punctuation.

❑ Be careful with verbs ending in *ing*. These often indicate a fragment.

Incorrect: Cape Cod providing a pleasant break from Boston's summer heat.

Correct: _____

❑ Unnecessary words can create fragments.

Incorrect: The journalist who traveled to faraway lands.

Correct: _____

Incorrect: The editor, a stern man, if he were to censor the profane article.

Correct: _____

❑ Unnecessary punctuation can split an otherwise complete sentence into fragments.

Incorrect: Achilles' mother held him by the heel; and dipped him in the river Styx.

Correct: _____

PUT IT TOGETHER

Although viruses share some of the distinctive properties

of living <u>organisms that</u> are not technically alive. They are
¹

unable to grow or reproduce in the same way that living

creatures do. Instead, they act like parasites in order to

reproduce. After locating and making contact with the right

kind of cell, a virus <u>injecting</u> its genetic material. To replicate,
²

<u>for which it then uses</u> the host cell, which is unable to
³

distinguish the virus' genes from its own. This process kills

the <u>cell, creating</u> a new virus organism.
⁴

1. A. NO CHANGE
    B. organisms, and that
    C. organisms, they
    D. organism

2. F. NO CHANGE
    G. which has injected
    H. injected
    J. injects

3. A. NO CHANGE
    B. it uses
    C. by using
    D. using

4. Which of the following is NOT acceptable?

    F. cell and creates
    G. cell. The process also creates
    H. cell; creating
    J. cell, yet creates

> **Fragment questions often involve using proper punctuation.**

Run-Ons

Because run-on errors are fixed with the proper use of punctuation or transition words, it is important to have strong skills with periods, semicolons, commas, and transitions.

❑ Run-on sentences result when multiple independent clauses are improperly joined.

Incorrect: They were best friends they haven't spoken to each other in years.

Correct: They were best friends. They haven't spoken to each other in years.

Correct: They were best friends; they haven't spoken to each other in years.

Correct: They were best friends, but they haven't spoken to each other in years.

❑ Many run-on problems result from using commas improperly or not using conjunctions.

Incorrect: My history professor is brilliant, I've learned a lot from her.

Correct: My history professor is brilliant _____.

❑ Some run-on sentences are best fixed with transitions.

Incorrect: The traffic court's docket was full of <u>cases, the judge must hear</u> within a single afternoon.

Correct: The traffic court's docket was full of <u>cases, all of which the judge must hear</u> within a single afternoon.

PUT IT TOGETHER

Rachel Carson's 1962 book *Silent Spring* reported that chemicals had been found in the bodies of animals and that these products stayed in the soil for <u>years. In addition,</u> she
₁
revealed that synthetic pesticides were more harmful than naturally derived products. Carson warned that chemicals could be hazardous to our bodies' natural processes. Many people dismissed her as <u>reactionary, in the end,</u> however, she
₂
was vindicated, and in 1972 laws established stricter standards for pesticides. A new federal agency, the EPA, was created to educate the <u>public the agency enforces</u> laws protecting
₃
humans and the environment.

> Look for run-on errors when transitions are underlined.

1. **A.** NO CHANGE
   B. years, in addition,
   C. years in addition,
   D. years in addition

2. Which of the following alternatives to the underlined portion would NOT be acceptable?

   F. reactionary. In the end,
   G. reactionary; in the end,
   H. reactionary in the end
   J. reactionary;

3. **A.** NO CHANGE
   B. public and enforce
   C. public, and it also was given the power to enforce
   D. public. Enforcing it with

Parallelism

(1-3 per test)

Parallelism questions are easiest to spot when they appear with a list. Trickier questions will involve comparisons which must be made parallel so the same types of things are being compared.

❑ When a sentence groups ideas, such as in a list, they must be presented in "parallel" form. Make sure that parts of speech are consistent.

> Incorrect: The actors' clothes appear elegant, stylish, and cost a lot, but in fact, the costumes are drab, awkward, and being quite cheap.

> Correct: The actors' clothes appear _____,
>
> but in fact, the costumes are _____.

❑ Conjunctions used on pairs (e.g., not only... but also, both... and, neither... nor) require that the words following each conjunction be parallel.

> Incorrect: As a governor, Carlotta's responsibility was not only responding to the needs of the citizens but also to be aware of the limits of her office.

> Correct: As a governor, Carlotta's responsibility was not only responding to the needs
>
> of the citizens but also _____.

❑ When two things are compared, they must be parallel. Consider the logic of the comparison. It must be clear that the same types of things are being compared.

> Incorrect: Every year, more tourists travel to Disney World than the Louvre.

> Correct: Every year, more tourists travel to Disney World than to the Louvre.

> Incorrect: Joanne goes to the movie theater more than Tanya.

> Correct: _____

❑ When checking grouped ideas for parallelism, also make sure that the ideas are distinct. Repeated ideas should be removed to prevent unnecessary wordiness.

PUT IT TOGETHER

Some flowers that grow in tropical environments share several odd traits: large size, brief blooms, and <u>release a corpse-like odor</u>. The titan arum is a tropical plant with the world's largest inflorescence, which is made up of a plant's stem and flowers. The inflorescence of the titan arum can reach a startling ten feet <u>in height and two feet thick</u>. Its flowers bloom for only forty-eight hours, during which they release a terrible stench. The odor is described as a blend of rotten meat, garlic, sweat, and fish. The awful smell attracts insects, which help pollinate the flowers.

> Look for parallelism errors when you see a list.

1. A. NO CHANGE
    B. an odor like that of a corpse
    C. releasing a corpse-like odor
    D. release like a corpse an odor

2. F. NO CHANGE
    G. high and two feet thickness
    H. highly and two feet thickly
    J. in height and two feet in thickness

Modifiers

A modifier is a descriptive word or phrase.

Modifier questions require careful consideration of the logic of sentences. Make sure that modifiers are properly placed so they describe the right things.

❑ Descriptions must be placed next to the things they describe.

> Incorrect: <u>Biking to school</u>, the wind nearly blew me over.
>
> Correct: Biking to school, I was nearly blown over by the wind.
>
> Correct: As I biked to school, the wind nearly blew me over.
>
> Correct: The wind nearly blew me over as I biked to school.

❑ A dangling modifier is a modifier that typically appears at the beginning of a sentence and is usually punctuated by a comma. The subject that directly follows the modifier should be what the modifier describes.

> Incorrect: Tired and homesick, Mike's vacation was not as fun as he had hoped.
>
> Correct: Tired and homesick, _____.

❑ When a modifier is misplaced, the entire sentence can become illogical.

> Incorrect: He skipped a rock over the surface of the river <u>that was perfectly round</u>.
>
> Correct: He skipped a rock <u>that was perfectly round</u> over the surface of the river.

❑ Some modifiers questions will require you to rewrite a modifier in order to eliminate modifier errors.

> Incorrect: Looking at the horizon, ominous clouds warned me of a storm approaching.
>
> Correct: _____, ominous clouds warned me of a storm approaching.

PUT IT TOGETHER

On his way to his grandmother's home, <u>the sight of</u>
<u>something by Matthew who</u> stopped his bike suddenly. A
$_1$
rattlesnake was stretched out on the pavement in front of him.

Nervous but curious, <u>Matthew's bike stood</u> between him and
$_2$
the deadly creature.

<u>An examination of</u> the rattling end of the snake's tail, an
$_3$
animal control officer was kneeling near the edge of the road.

Trying to coax it into a container, <u>using the officer's tool</u> that
$_4$
looked to Matthew like a large fishhook. He knew enough not

to get close, but he asked why she was helping the poisonous

creature.

"He doesn't know it," she said, "but if this guy stays on

the asphalt, he'll bake." She laughed, as the snake finally

slipped into the carrier. "In the old west, he would've been the

deadliest thing around. We'd have shot him on sight."

<u>Because he was already late for dinner,</u> Matthew was
$_5$
afraid to come closer. He waited for the officer to carry it

away <u>on his bike</u>, and then got back and continued to his
$_6$
grandmother's home.

1. A. NO CHANGE
    B. Matthew saw something and
    C. Matthew's sight of something
    D. something seen by Matthew

2. F. NO CHANGE
    G. Matthew standing his bike
    H. Matthew stood his bike
    J. standing Matthew's bike

3. A. NO CHANGE
    B. Examining
    C. A study of
    D. DELETE the underlined portion.

4. F. NO CHANGE
    G. the tool being used by the officer
    H. the officer was using a tool
    J. use of the officer's tool

> **Look for modifier errors when you see a descriptive phrase at the beginning of a sentence.**

5. A. NO CHANGE
    B. Even though the snake was safely caged,
    C. As his grandmother had warned him,
    D. Leaning on his handlebars,

6. The best placement for the underlined portion would be:

    F. where it is now.
    G. after the word *officer*.
    H. after the word *back*.
    J. after the word *home* (and before the period).

Checkpoint Review

In Ethiopian society, communal eating is the cultural norm. Injera, a soft, porous, and pancake-like flatbread, taking[1] the place of utensils, providing a vessel for delivering food to the mouth. Due to the fermentation process, it has a tangy, sourdough taste that complements the spices found in many sauces and stews in Ethiopian cooking.

Injera is made from teff; being a[2] tiny grain similar in size to poppy seeds, less than 1milimeter in diameter. Native to Ethiopia, recognizing teff[3] as a highly nutritious grain. It can vary in color, ranging from pale white to yellow to deep brown. Those who can afford the expense will pay more for the pure white variety, known as manga, then other varieties.[4] Many will buy the less expensive red or mixed varieties or will blend the teff with cheaper grains, such as sorghum, barley, and maize.

From the plateaus of the highlands to the plains of the lowlands, teff adapts well to the lands of Ethiopia. It can survive through droughts and floods, grows[5] more efficiently in higher temperatures than wheat and other grains can. Its optimal growth occurs at altitudes of 1800-2100 meters, but it can be grown at sea level to as high as 3000 meters. Over 6 million farmers harvest teff, producing a quarter of the cereal production in the country. Scattering a handful of the grain can sow a large area. Only one pound of seed is needed to grow

1. A. NO CHANGE
   B. having taken
   C. it takes
   D. takes

2. F. NO CHANGE
   G. teff, being a
   H. teff. A
   J. teff, a

3. A. NO CHANGE
   B. recognized teff
   C. one recognizes teff
   D. teff is recognized

4. F. NO CHANGE
   G. than other varieties
   H. then do other varieties
   J. than for other varieties

5. A. NO CHANGE
   B. floods and grow
   C. floods grow
   D. floods; grows

Checkpoint Review

an acre of the <u>crop and lending</u> well to the seminomadic
₆
lifestyles of some Ethiopian tribes.

The process of making injera from teff flour is passed
down from generation to generation in Ethiopian culture.
Before it ferments, <u>the flavor of teff is sweet and mild</u>. It is
₇
high in protein, calcium, vitamin C, amino acids, dietary fiber,
and iron. The iron content comes from the soil particles that
are <u>processed: some</u> soil cannot be separated from the grain
₈
due to its small size. The grain is ground into flour and mixed
with water to form a dough. Then, the leaven, or ersho, is

added and it is left to ferment for several <u>days once</u> the dough
₉
has fermented, a yellow layer will appear on the top. This will
be removed. The dough is cooked on a flat iron or clay pan,
called a mitad.

In Ethiopia, injera is central to many customs. There is a
tradition, called gursha, in which one scoops food with injera
and feeds it to another person at the table. This is a symbol of
Ethiopian hospitality, companionship, and <u>being loyal</u>. The
₁₀
use of injera promotes a more intimate bond between one and
his or her food or loved ones.

6. **F.** NO CHANGE
   G. crop, and lending
   H. crop, lending
   J. crop. Lending

7. **A.** NO CHANGE
   B. teff's flavor is sweet and mild
   C. the sweet and mild flavor of teff
   D. teff is sweet and mild in flavor

8. Which of the following alternatives would
   NOT be acceptable?

   F. processed; some
   G. processed, because some
   H. processed, some
   J. processed. Some

9. **A.** NO CHANGE
   B. days. Once
   C. days, once
   D. days; once,

10. **F.** NO CHANGE
    G. is loyal
    H. loyalty
    J. to be loyal

Periods

(2-4 per test)

The correct use of periods is tested on many questions involving fragments, run-ons, semicolons, colons, and commas. Understanding the relationship between sentence structure and punctuation is key for many questions on the English Test.

❑ Complete sentences end with a period. A complete sentence must have a subject (who or what does the action), a predicate (the action), and a complete idea.

Correct period placement will result in logical and complete sentences both before and after the punctuation.

Incorrect: My cat Moxie likes chasing the laser pointer yesterday she ran into a wall.

Incorrect: My cat Moxie likes chasing. The laser pointer yesterday. She ran. Into a wall.

Correct: _____

❑ The use of a period tells the reader that the two sentences are separate and distinct ideas. If two ideas are closely related, they can also be linked within one sentence by semicolons or commas and transition words.

Incorrect: More than fifty million buffalo once roamed North America by 1900, fewer than a thousand remained.

Correct: More than fifty million buffalo once roamed North America. By 1900, fewer than a thousand remained.

Correct: More than fifty million buffalo once roamed North America, but by 1900, fewer than a thousand remained.

SUMMIT
EDUCATIONAL
GROUP

PUT IT TOGETHER

The so-called "sweet science" of boxing has long

captured the nation's <u>imagination, every few years, a</u> celebrity

[1]

like Muhammad Ali or Sugar Ray Robinson grabs the national

spotlight. For a time, these people are the public faces of

<u>boxing. Gain worldwide recognition.</u> Although even the

[2]

greatest of pugilists eventually leave the spotlight, the sport

will endure as it has for thousands of years.

1. A.   NO CHANGE
    B.   imagination. Every few years, a
    C.   imagination: every few years that a
    D.   imagination every few years. A

2. F.   NO CHANGE
    G.   boxing; gain worldwide recognition.
    H.   boxing. Gaining worldwide recognition.
    J.   boxing, and they gain worldwide recognition.

> Period questions usually involve fragments or run-ons.

Semicolons

(0-2 per test)

Most semicolon questions will test your skills with fragments and run-ons. These questions usually ask you to choose whether a semicolon, comma, or no punctuation should be between certain clauses.

❑ Semicolons, like periods, are used to separate independent clauses. A semicolon indicates that two ideas are related.

> Incorrect: Mark's job was monotonous, it involved doing the same tasks over and over.
>
> Correct: _____

Colons

(0-2 per test)

The key to correcting most colon errors is determining whether the clauses before and after the punctuation are independent or dependent. What comes after a colon, unlike a semicolon, does not have to be an independent clause.

❑ Colons can be used only after independent clauses.

> Incorrect: Before I leave the house, I make sure I have my: keys, phone, and wallet.
>
> Correct: Before I leave the house, I make sure I have three important things: my keys, my phone, and my wallet.

❑ Colons are most commonly used to introduce lists, but they may also be used to present noun phrases, quotations, or other examples which clarify or elaborate on the independent clause.

Although colons can be used to separate independent clauses, a semicolon or period is usually used instead.

> Correct: I brought only my favorite book: *To Kill a Mockingbird*.
>
> Correct: I brought only my favorite book: *To Kill a Mockingbird* is all I need.

PUT IT TOGETHER

Since the early 1900s, science fiction has been fascinated

with lasers. Like bolts of neon-colored <u>lightning: these</u>

devastating energy beams are often shown as the weapon of

future. But where are our phasers, blasters, and plasma guns?

The unfortunate reality is that science-fiction lasers may never

become science fact. Making a destructive laser would require

incredibly massive energy stores. Also, lasers don't work

<u>immediately they</u> do damage through heat over time. For now,

with our current scientific knowledge, the dream of laser

battles will remain just that: a dream.

1. **A.** NO CHANGE
   B. lightning these
   C. lightning, these
   D. lightning;

> Check for independent clauses before and after colons and semicolons.

2. **F.** NO CHANGE
   G. immediately, they
   H. immediately; they
   J. immediately

Commas

(5-8 per test)

Many questions on the ACT English Test involve commas. Questions that involve other skills will often ask you to make a decision about proper comma placement as well.

Most comma questions involve nonessential clauses. These questions also often involve correcting fragment or run-on errors.

❑ If a sentence begins with a phrase that sets time, place, or purpose, then the phrase should be followed by a comma.

Incorrect: At the end of the street, I saw a group of kids playing basketball.

Correct: _____

❑ Incorrect comma placement can change the logical structure of the sentence and create a fragment or run-on error.

Incorrect: After a leisurely breakfast, we took, a walk on the beach.

Incorrect: After, a leisurely breakfast we took a walk on the beach.

Correct: _____

❑ When two independent clauses are joined by a conjunction, such as "and" or "but," there should be a comma placed before the conjunction.

Incorrect: My dog appears to want to play, but he really just wants you to pet him.

Correct: _____

❑ Commas separate items in a list. This is sometimes called the "serial comma," because it separates each of the items in a series.

Incorrect: During lunch, we talked about my parents, Elvis, and Michael Jackson.

Correct: During lunch, we talked about _____.

If multiple adjectives describe a noun, those adjectives form a list and the commas separate the adjectives from each other but not from the noun.

Incorrect: Mr. Kamin's speech was profound, reflective, and emotional.

Correct: _____

❑ Clauses with nonessential information are offset by commas. *Which* is often the proper pronoun for these clauses.

Nonessential clauses can also be offset by parentheses or dashes.

Correct: The new findings, which seem to disprove the modern understanding of the universe, confused the astronomers.

Correct: The new findings (which seem to disprove the modern understanding of the universe) confused the astronomers.

Correct: The new findings – which seem to disprove the modern understanding of the universe – confused the astronomers.

PUT IT TOGETHER

The Amazon river dolphin is the largest, in size, of the world's freshwater dolphins. It lives in the <u>Amazon, and Orinoco,</u> River systems in South America, which run through

Colombia, Brazil, Ecuador, Bolivia, Peru, and <u>Venezuela, and is</u> commonly known as the "boto."

<u>Besides, their natural habitats</u> there are several differences between Amazon river dolphins and marine dolphins. River dolphins have broad flippers and flukes to help them maneuver through flooded forests and marshes during the wet season. Rigid hairs found on their beaks are like a sensory <u>organ. Assist</u> them when they search for prey on the muddy river bottom. The most noticeable difference relates to their physical appearance, particularly their color. The boto are called the "pink dolphins" because their skin can be varying <u>shades, of pink,</u> depending on age. As they mature, parts of

their <u>bodies, usually the flanks and the ventral body</u> turn pink. Overall, despite the few peculiarities of Amazon river dolphins, they do closely resemble their ocean-dwelling cousins.

Due to its curious nature, the Amazon river dolphin will interact with <u>humans, leading</u> to mixed outcomes. Local

1. **A.** NO CHANGE
   B. Amazon and Orinoco
   C. Amazon, and Orinoco
   D. Amazon and Orinoco,

2. **F.** NO CHANGE
   G. Venezuela. And is
   H. Venezuela, is
   J. Venezuela is

3. **A.** NO CHANGE
   B. Besides, their natural habitats,
   C. Besides their natural habitats,
   D. Besides their natural habitats

> Comma questions often involve fragments, run-ons, and transitions.

4. **F.** NO CHANGE
   G. organ, assist
   H. organ, assisting
   J. organ assist

5. **A.** NO CHANGE
   B. shades of pink,
   C. shades, of pink
   D. shades of, pink

6. **F.** NO CHANGE
   G. bodies usually the flanks and the ventral body,
   H. bodies, usually the flanks and the ventral body,
   J. bodies, usually the flanks and the ventral body

7. **A.** NO CHANGE
   B. humans leading
   C. humans, lead
   D. humans

<u>legends, about this animal</u> have led to the belief that they
8
possess various magical powers; therefore, they are typically

respected and protected by the locals. However, they have

been hunted in the past and also killed in recent years, because

they are seen as competition for the fish supplies in the rivers.

8. F. NO CHANGE
   G. legends, about this animal,
   H. legends about this animal
   J. legends about this animal,

Apostrophes

(2-4 per test)

Apostrophes are used to express possession or to take the place of missing letters in contractions.

The most common type of apostrophe questions test between *its* and *it's* and between *they're* and *their*. For these questions, it is important to understand how apostrophes are used in contractions. These questions may also require subject-verb agreement and pronoun skills.

❑ When the possessor is a singular noun, possession can be indicated by adding *'s*.

> Correct: Is that <u>Bob's</u> dog or is it <u>James's</u>?

❑ When the possessor is a plural noun ending in *s*, possession can be indicated by adding an apostrophe. Plural nouns that do not end in *s* can be made possessive by adding *'s*.

> (*Children's/Childrens'*) joy often comes from not having to handle many responsibilities.

❑ Pronouns do not require apostrophes to indicate possession. Rather, pronouns have their own possessive forms.

> Incorrect: The apple tree may be her's, but the fruit is now their's.
>
> Correct: The apple tree may be _____, but the fruit is now _____.

There is one exception to this rule: the possessive form of the indefinite pronoun *one* requires an apostrophe

> Incorrect: It is not in <u>ones</u> best interest to throw rocks at a beehive.
>
> Correct: It is not in <u>one's</u> best interest to throw rocks at a beehive.

❑ "It's" is always a contraction of "it is." Likewise, "its" is always a possessive pronoun.

Similarly, "who's" means "who is" and "whose" is a possessive pronoun.

Incorrect: It's raining again, and that poor dog doesn't have a roof over it's head.

Correct: _____ raining again, and that poor dog doesn't have a roof over _____ head.

❑ There are many contractions in English, all of which require apostrophes.

The following is a short list of common contractions.

It's = It is   She'll = She will

You're = You are   He'd = He had; He would

They've = They have   Who's = Who is

They're = They are   Won't = Will not

PUT IT TOGETHER

Over the years, thousands of manuscripts had taken <u>its'</u>
                                                        ¹
turn on Marlena's desk, and most got tossed away. She had

become a publisher to help artists, but she rejected far more

than she accepted.

Her office was humble, with only two pictures on the wall.

They had been gifts from Jon Mitchell, her mentor. The first

was of a starving child. It focused on the <u>boy's face</u>, showing
                                              ²

<u>it's thinness and the eyes intense colors</u>. When Jon gave her
                    ³
the photo, he had asked, "How does this make you feel?"

"Awful," she said. "Anybody would feel bad, looking at

someone suffer like that."

"Exactly," Jon said. Then he gave her the second photo,

which showed the same boy beating another child with a stick.

At the time, Marlena wasn't sure what the point of this

was. "They had a fight, probably over food," she guessed.

Jon seemed pleased by her answer. "I took these

photographs while I toured southeast Asia. The one with the

stick, he got angry because his brother called him ugly. That is

why <u>their</u> fighting. Now, how does the photo make you feel?"
       ⁴

"I don't know," she admitted. Suddenly, the image was too

complex to summarize in a single feeling.

1. A. NO CHANGE
   B. they're
   C. their
   D. it's

2. F. NO CHANGE
   G. boys' face
   H. boys faces
   J. boys' face's

3. A. NO CHANGE
   B. its thinness and the eyes' intense colors
   C. its thinness and the eye's intense color's
   D. it's thinness and the eyes intense colors'.

4. F. NO CHANGE
   G. its'
   H. it's
   J. they're

"The development of a <u>novels'</u> story should be similar," he explained. "A good story affects you in ways you can't understand. Good stories are powerful, but not simple."

Now, as an experienced publisher, she keeps the two photos on her wall as a reminder.

5. **A.** NO CHANGE
    B. novels
    C. novel's
    D. novels's

Checkpoint Review

The Minstrel's Story

Minstrels were common professional entertainers during medieval times. The minstrels were usually instrumentalists, but some also juggled, did stunts, or told stories. Most of them mixed a couple of these skills at once. Minstrels' traveled
[1]
from town to town, putting on performances, but some minstrels were employed by wealthy families and provided entertainment to the upper classes.

Minstrels had many different names and were present in many countries. A French minstrel for example was called a
[2]
troubadour, while a Viking minstrel was called a skald. Minstrels in different countries had different methods. Troubadours, usually, sang poems about love, politics, God,
[3]
and death. Many times these performers were accompanied by fiddle and lute players called jongleurs. Scottish and Irish minstrels; called bards, usually sang poems about national
[4]
pride and heroism. Bards used alliteration and rhyme scheme as their primary poetic devices.
[5]

Minstrels were popular because they provided a source of news and entertainment. Before modern media, people often had no way to know of what was happening in another town or another culture. Furthermore, they had little access to new
[6]
stories and folktales. Minstrels, who traveled from town to town, were often an important source of information and entertainment for people. In addition to providing

1. **A.** NO CHANGE
    B. Minstrels
    C. Minstrel's
    D. Minstrels's

2. **F.** NO CHANGE
    G. minstrel, for example
    H. minstrel for example;
    J. minstrel, for example,

3. **A.** NO CHANGE
    B. Troubadours, usually sang
    C. Troubadours usually sang,
    D. Troubadours usually sang

4. **F.** NO CHANGE
    G. minstrels, called bards
    H. minstrels called bards;
    J. minstrels, called bards,

5. **A.** NO CHANGE
    B. they're
    C. there
    D. its

6. **F.** NO CHANGE
    G. culture, furthermore, they
    H. culture, furthermore. They
    J. culture furthermore they

Checkpoint Review

amusement for audiences, minstrels served a more practical

<u>purpose educating the people.</u>
⁷

    Minstrels are no longer common. Sometimes, bards can

be seen playing at fairs or folk festivals, but this is more a

novelty than it is the continuation of a tradition. As forms of

mass media have become increasingly prevalent and available,

the modern role of minstrels has <u>changed: once</u> a necessary
⁸

source of news, they are now a rare source of entertainment.

While poetry is still an important component of all developed

societies, <u>its</u> transmission through minstrels has all but died
⁹

out. Today, it is hard to imagine a time when a minstrel could

be found in every town square, singing his songs of love,

death, and <u>philosophy; while</u> the captivated townsfolk
¹⁰

watched with rapt admiration.

7. **A.** NO CHANGE
   B. purpose. Educating the people.
   C. purpose; educating the people.
   D. purpose: educating the people.

8. **F.** NO CHANGE
   G. changed, once,
   H. changed once,
   J. changed once

9. **A.** NO CHANGE
   B. it's
   C. its'
   D. that's

10. **F.** NO CHANGE
   G. philosophy. While
   H. philosophy, while
   J. philosophy: while

English – Usage and Mechanics Summary

Pronouns

❑ A pronoun must clearly refer back to the noun or nouns it represents.

❑ To check for the correct pronoun in a compound phrase, ignore the rest of the group.

❑ Don't use *that* or *which* when referring to people. People are always *who* or *whom*.

❑ The pronoun "who" always refers to the subject. The pronoun "whom" always refers to an object.

Subject-Verb Agreement

❑ Singular subjects require singular verbs, and plural subjects require plural verbs.

❑ To simplify sentences, remove all extra information between the subject and the verb.

❑ Subjects grouped by "and" are plural, even if the "and" joins two singular words.

❑ When the subject follows the verb, flip the sentence to put the subject first.

Verb Tense

❑ Verb tense must be consistent with the timeline presented in the rest of the passage.

Adjectives versus Adverbs

❑ Use adjectives to describe nouns. Use adverbs to describe verbs, adjectives, and other adverbs.

Idioms

❑ On the ACT, idioms typically appear in the form of verbs with certain prepositions.

❑ There are too many idioms to memorize; the key to knowing English idioms is familiarity with the language. The best way to learn idioms is to read regularly.

Diction

❑ Be careful as you consider answer choices – an incorrect answer may sound right if you are used to hearing it in casual conversation.

Fragments

❑ Be careful with verbs ending in *ing*. These are sometimes used as a description of the subject rather than the subject's action.

❑ Unnecessary words or punctuation can create fragments.

Run-ons

❑ Many run-on problems result from using commas improperly or not using conjunctions.

❑ Some run-on sentences are best fixed with transitions.

Parallelism

❑ When a sentence groups ideas, such as in a list, they must be presented in "parallel" form.

❑ When two things are compared, they must be parallel. Consider the logic of the comparison; it must be explicitly clear that the same types of things are being compared.

Modifiers

❑ Descriptions must be placed next to the things they describe.

Periods

❑ Correct period placement will result in logical and complete sentences both before and after the punctuation.

Semicolons

❑ Semicolons, like periods, are used to separate independent clauses.

Colons

❑ Colons can only be used following independent clauses.

❑ Colons are most commonly used to introduce lists, but they may also be used to present noun phrases, quotations, or examples which clarify or elaborate on the independent clause.

Commas

❑ If a sentence begins with a phrase that sets time, place, or purpose, then the phrase should be followed by a comma.

❑ When two independent clauses are joined by a conjunction, such as "and" or "but," there should be a comma placed before the conjunction.

❑ Commas separate items in a list.

❑ Clauses with nonessential information are offset by commas.

Apostrophes

❑ When the possessor is a singular noun, possession can be indicated by adding 's.

❑ When the possessor is a plural noun ending in *s*, possession can be indicated by adding an apostrophe. Plural nouns that do not end in *s* can be made possessive by adding 's.

❑ "It's" is always a contraction of "it is." Likewise, "its" is always a possessive pronoun.

SUMMIT
EDUCATIONAL
GROUP

- ❑ **Strategy**
  - ○ Main Idea
  - ○ Intent

- ❑ **Organization**
  - ○ Addition
  - ○ Deletion
  - ○ Transitions

- ❑ **Style**
  - ○ Wordiness

Main Idea

(2-4 per test)

The main idea is the central point, opinion, or purpose of a passage or a portion of a passage. Every part of a passage should contribute to the passage's main idea.

Many Rhetorical Skills questions will require an understanding of the passage's main idea. These questions often ask you to make revisions to the passage, and these edits should reinforce and be relevant to the main idea.

❑ Before you can answer a main idea question, you may need to reread part of the passage.

Steroids have been a controversial topic in baseball for a while now. The recent discovery of steroid use in baseball has had a distinct, negative effect on the way the game is being played. The data accumulated over recent years, along with the rising number of athletes who admit to using steroids, suggest a direct connection between steroids and rising home-run totals. As players continue to set new records, <u>the achievements of older athletes are forgotten to history</u>. The popularity of steroid use has cast doubt on many professional baseball players. This hurts the reputation of the players and the sport, and it is discouraging to fans. However, despite the problems with steroids, is there any way to effectively prevent their usage?

Given that all the choices are true, which one best indicates the focus of this paragraph?

A. NO CHANGE
B. baseball becomes more popular as a sport.
C. there is debate over the legitimacy of athletes' accomplishments.
D. it gets harder to keep track of the numbers.

What is the main idea of the paragraph?

Which answer choice is most closely related to this main idea?

PUT IT TOGETHER

In the wilderness of Africa, an odd little bird is admired by local people. This bird, the honeyguide, is one of the few that can digest beeswax. It has a fondness for bee larvae, but it is unable to break through the exterior of a hive. ☐1 Honeyguides search the savannahs, mapping out every hive in a range of hundreds of kilometers. These birds will try to attract the attention of humans and guide them to a beehive. In exchange for the guidance, honey-hunters will make sure to leave some wax comb for the bird to eat. <u>Thus, the honey-hunters and the honeyguides have developed bonds of cooperation.</u>
2

[1] There are rumors of honeyguides also cooperating with ratels, a fierce type of badger. [2] The ratel is nicknamed the "honeybadger," and it is known for being fearless, willing to brave numerous bee stings to burst into a hive. [3] Once the ratel consumes its fill of honey, the honeyguide will venture into the opened hive for its own share of wax and larval grubs. [4] Some researchers dismiss the claims of honeyguide interactions with ratel as exaggerated legends. ☐3

Whether with humans or badgers, the honeyguide has adopted a behavior that is as fascinating as it is unique. Its dependence on communication with other species is a wonderful testament to the complexity of the natural world.

1. Which of the following sentences, if added here, would best reflect the point made in this paragraph?

   A. These aren't the only creatures who seek bee hives; humans and badgers treasure hives as stores of food.
   B. In order to satisfy its hunger, the honeyguide relies on humans, which the bird leads to the hives.
   C. Another major source of nutrients for honeyguides is waxworms, which are actually moth larvae.
   D. Surprisingly, honeyguides do not seem to feed on the stores of honey in hives.

2. Which of the choices, all true, would best support the claim made in the preceding sentence while remaining consistent with the focus of the paragraph?

   F. NO CHANGE
   G. But the fact remains that it is more efficient to keep bee yards than rely on finding wild bee colonies.
   H. Honeyguides also leave their eggs in other bird species' nests and depend on these other birds to raise their young.
   J. Honeyguides are also sometimes called "indicator birds."

3. Which of the following sentences in this paragraph is LEAST relevant to its main focus and, therefore, could be deleted?

   A. Sentence 1
   B. Sentence 2
   C. Sentence 3
   D. Sentence 4

Intent

Intent questions ask you to consider what the author is hoping to achieve in the passage. Some of these questions will appear at the end of passages and ask you to consider whether the author was successful with creating a specific argument or idea. These require a broad understanding of the passage's main idea. Other questions ask you to create or judge a sentence based on the author's goals.

❑   When solving intent questions, read the question and answer choices carefully. The difference between a correct and incorrect answer is often a specific aspect of the author's goal.

Throughout the 1990s and early 2000s, the sport of baseball was surrounded by controversy. Now dubbed the "steroid era," these years saw the rise of Mark McGwire, Sammy Sosa, and Barry Bonds, whose record-breaking homerun streaks brought in masses of fans. Despite the incredible achievements of these players, the members of the Baseball Writers Association of America have decided not to induct these athletes into the Hall of Fame. This decision has brought nods of approval from those fans who fondly think of baseball as a traditional, simple sport. It has also brought harsh criticism from fans who just want to see endless streams of bat-cracking homeruns. The latter point to earlier eras, such as the 1960s, when players used performance-enhancing amphetamines without any scandals or backlash. [?]

Suppose the writer had decided to write an essay exploring in detail the career of a home-run hitter in the 1960s. Does the given essay successfully fulfill the writer's goal?

A. Yes, because it discusses famous baseball players from the 1960s who had many home runs.

B. Yes, because the entire essay is about home-run hitters and the various factors that contribute to their success.

C. No, because the essay does not discuss specific players' careers.

D. No, because it focuses on players from the 1990s and 2000s, and only mentions players from the 1960s for context.

What is the main idea of the paragraph?

Does this main idea match with the intent described in the question? Why or why not?

PUT IT TOGETHER

[1] It may be impossible for us to understand the impact of President Franklin D. Roosevelt's radio-broadcasted "fireside chats." In the 1930s, radio was one of the main connections to the outside world. Though most Americans had never seen the president, they felt a deeply personal connection by being able to hear his voice.

At the height of the Great Depression, with incredible odds stacked against him, President Roosevelt took office. In 1933, one in four Americans was out of work and nearly 10,000 banks had closed. <u>As he bravely battled polio and the resulting paralysis,</u> Roosevelt brought his confidence and calm
2
to the living room of every American family. Through radio broadcasts, he reassured the American public by explaining the complicated American banking system and why it had failed. Roosevelt used simple language and a confident tone as he eased the concerns and frustrations of struggling Americans and explained his solutions.

In addition to the humble charm and compelling rhetoric of Roosevelt's broadcasts, a key to the power of his "fireside chats" was that they brought an entire nation together in one moment. Sadly, this is much less possible today, as people do not want to be restricted by broadcast schedules.

---

1. The writer wants to add a description here that would further illustrate why it is hard for a modern audience to imagine the effects of Roosevelt's radio broadcasts for 1930s Americans. Assuming capitalization would be adjusted as needed, which choice would best accomplish this intention?

   A. Because new technologies have allowed for stronger radio broadcast signals,
   B. Because our culture is slow to adopt some new technologies,
   C. Since previous presidents had not been so open and personable with the public,
   D. America in the 1930s was radically different from what we know today, so

2. At this point, the writer would like to emphasize the extent of people's hardship in the 1930s. Given that all the choices are true, which one best accomplishes this purpose?

   F. NO CHANGE
   G. Promoting the tenets of his New Deal plan,
   H. Relying on a "brain trust" of advisors to help solve the economic crisis,
   J. In the midst of widespread despair, with millions suddenly jobless and homeless,

> Question 3 asks about the preceding passage as a whole.

3. Suppose the writer's goal had been to write an essay chronicling the evolution of radio broadcasts. Would this essay successfully accomplish writer's goal?

   A. Yes, because the essay explains why modern audiences may not appreciate Roosevelt's "fireside chats" in the same way that 1930s audiences did.
   B. Yes, because the essay details how economic status affects the rate at which technology develops.
   C. No, because the essay addresses more than one time period in its analysis of radio.
   D. No, because the essay limits itself to describing Roosevelt's broadcasts and their historical context.

> You may need to skim through the whole passage again to answer this type of question.

Organization

(3-5 per test)

Organization questions ask you to order ideas so there is a clear progression from topic to topic. When organized properly, an essay's ideas should build upon each other and transition naturally.

❑ When you see numbered sentences or paragraphs, be prepared for an Organization question. A few questions on each test will ask you to move one sentence to a different part of a paragraph, to rearrange all of the sentences in a paragraph, or to move a paragraph to a different part of the essay.

[1] Recently, Mark McGwire, Sammy Sosa, and Barry Bonds were deemed too unethical to enter the Hall of Fame, and so it would seem that there is no honor given to cheaters. [2] However, history shows that this isn't completely true; players whose greatness was partly due to cheating are in the Hall now. [3] The famous pitcher Gaylord Perry was known for his "spitball," a technique involving the application of petroleum jelly to the ball and which was banned because it gave the pitcher an unfair advantage. ⟨?⟩ [4] Several of baseball's modern record holders have been denied their spot in the Baseball Hall of Fame because of their steroid usage. [5] Despite his acknowledged cheating, Perry was elected into the Hall of Fame and was widely respected for his great (but illegitimate) pitching skills.

For the sake of logic and coherence, Sentence 4 should be placed:

A. where it is now.
B. before Sentence 1.
C. after Sentence 2.
D. after Sentence 5.

What are the two main ideas that the paragraph discusses?

Which of these ideas does Sentence 4 match up with best?

PUT IT TOGETHER

[1] Alfred of Wessex, who would become the "Great" king, was born into a time of war. [2] After nearly a decade of commanding the English armies, his skill in leadership and combat finally led to a treaty with the Vikings. 1 [3] For many years before his reign, Vikings had been raiding the coasts of England for plunder. [4] As a prince, Alfred had led his brother's army in the Battle of Ashdown, a critical victory that would set a precedent for his future glory. [5] By the time Alfred had assumed the role of king, Wessex was the only Anglo-Saxon kingdom that had not been conquered by the Viking invaders. [6] During his reign, he turned the tide against the Vikings and began to reconquer the lands of England. [7] He rallied a great army, strengthened defensive settlements, and established a powerful navy. 2

[1] During the following era of peace, Alfred did more than fortify the military; he also strengthened his people through education. [2] In order to preserve knowledge and unite the people of England, Alfred encouraged literacy in the English language. [3] Thanks to Alfred, England became much stronger and safer. [4] It is because of these great accomplishments that Alfred is the only English king to earn the title of "the Great." [5] For this purpose, he personally commissioned English translations of several Latin texts, and even performed some of these translations himself. 3

1. For the sake of the logic and coherence of this paragraph, Sentence 2 should be placed:

   A. where it is now.
   B. after Sentence 3.
   C. after Sentence 5.
   D. after Sentence 7.

2. The writer wants to divide the previous paragraph into two in order to separate Alfred's reign from the time before he was king. The most logical place to begin the new paragraph would be at the beginning of sentence:

   F. 3
   G. 4
   H. 5
   J. 7

> Rather than rearrange the whole paragraph at once, focus on one sentence at a time. Which sentence should be followed by sentence 5?

3. Which of the following sequences of sentences makes this paragraph most logical?

   A. NO CHANGE
   B. 1, 2, 5, 3, 4
   C. 1, 3, 2, 4, 5
   D. 2, 3, 1, 4, 5

Addition

(2-3 per test)

Addition questions ask you to judge the role and importance of a sentence and the potential effects of adding or not adding the sentence.

❑ Added sentences must be relevant to the focus of the passage and should support and strengthen the passage's ideas. It does not matter if the addition is interesting or well-stated; it must make sense where it would be added in the passage.

The baseball league has been criticized for ignoring the integrity of its players. It is unfortunate that there have been more reasons to encourage steroid usage than to prevent it. During the infamous "steroid era," the sport benefited from a great surge in popularity. The officials did finally announce stricter measures to prevent performance-enhancing drugs, but it was too little too late. These responses seem to be more about maintaining a public image of integrity than actually enforcing fair play. From the player's standpoint, there is hardly any reason to avoid steroids. ⟨?⟩ The risks of getting caught are not as strong as the potential benefits: wealth, fame, and glory.

The writer wants to include an example that makes clear to readers who do not know much about the sport of baseball why a player would choose to use steroids. Which of the following, if added here, would best accomplish this goal?

A. Steroids can help players increase their on-base and slugging percentage.
B. In the same way that a novelist may drink coffee to write more productively, baseball players take steroids to increase their ability to get work done.
C. Baseball is a sport that requires many skills that must be built and refined over a player's lifetime.
D. Many players had admitted to taking steroids, and some have given great reasons for why they did so.

Which answer choices would NOT be suitable for a reader unfamiliar with the sport?

Which answer choices do NOT provide an explanation for why players would choose to use steroids?

❑ Only choose to add material if it introduces new, useful information to the passage.

PUT IT TOGETHER

The office cubicle has been demonized as the cage of the modern professional. Made up of a desk surrounded by small, portable walls, the cubicle space is square and barely large enough to allow workers to swivel around in their chairs. ☐1 It has become the norm for office spaces designed to inexpensively fit a large number of employees.

The cubicle was not supposed to be so confining, or even square. It originated from a beautiful vision of a more creative, active workspace. Robert Propst, a designer and inventor, developed a model for work places called Action Office. ☐2 Whereas most office spaces were monotonous and static, Action Office was supposed to encourage movement and creativity. Rather than use permanent walls, Propst's design called for small, mobile partitions so that each employee could create unique work stations. Propst encouraged desks where workers could stand, rather than sit all day, as well as varied wall angles, rather than the standard ninety-degree angles. Overall, Action Office was a call toward a more personalized and dynamic office design.

☐3 Office managers were attracted to one aspect of the design: the mobile partitions. Ironically, these movable walls, which Propst designed for space and creativity, would make it possible to build small, inexpensive office spaces, while also reducing privacy so that employers could regularly monitor employees. The result was the cubicle: an infamous office design that has come to represent all of the problems that Propst's original vision was supposed to fix.

1. Which of the following statements, if added here, would most effectively continue the writer's negative portrayal of cubicles?

   A. I have only seen a few cubicle spaces that seemed comfortable and unique.
   B. The cubicle is known for being cheap, confining, and impersonal.
   C. Of course, some cubicles are designed to be more luxurious than others.
   D. Cubicle designs have had to change to accommodate new office technologies.

2. At this point, the writer is considering adding the following true statement:

   Propst worked alongside designer George Nelson, who later scorned the cubicle for creating a "dehumanizing" workplace.

   Should the writer make this addition here?

   F. Yes, because it provides information about Propst's own working conditions.
   G. Yes, because it adds a relevant example of how cubicles are useful for office space design.
   H. No, because it disproves the writer's point that Action Office was intended to promote creative, personal office space.
   J. No, because it would distract the reader from the paragraph's focus on Propst's intended effect on office space design.

3. Given that all are true, which of the following sentences, if added here, would best reinforce the main point made in this paragraph and most effectively transition from the previous paragraph?

   A. Unfortunately, Propst's vision was largely rejected because it gave so much space and control to employees.
   B. Eventually, Propst's design became very profitable.
   C. Office designs should prioritize low cost for employers rather than being pleasant for employees.
   D. Should Action Office be considered a total failure?

Deletion

(3-4 per test)

Deletion questions ask you to judge the role and importance of a sentence and the potential effects of deleting, or choosing not to delete, the sentence. Deletion questions often require an understanding of a sentence's function or purpose.

❑ Sentences should be deleted if they are not relevant to the focus of the passage or do not support and strengthen the passage's ideas.

If baseball players have had a history of performance-enhancing chemical use, why has this only been a controversy in recent times? The main issue may be fans' nostalgia. Before the "steroid era," Roger Maris had held a home-run record since 1961. Before him, the record was held by the legendary Babe Ruth. In those days, players used to hit fewer home runs than they do today. [?] In 1965, for example, Tony Conigliaro of the Red Sox led the American league with only 32 home runs. Since the 1990s, players have regularly reached over 50 in a season. In the eyes of some fans, this sudden increase due to steroids is an insult to the great players of the past.

The writer is considering deleting the following sentence. What would the writer lose from the essay if this information were removed?

A. Irrelevant material that distracts from the essay's main focus
B. Specific data about home-run rates during the "steroid era"
C. A concrete, well-known example of a player who has benefited greatly from using steroids
D. Factual data in support of the claim that home-run rates are higher than they used to be

What purpose does the underlined sentence serve in the paragraph? How does it relate to the sentences around it?

PUT IT TOGETHER

The study of ancient Egyptian art and sculpture has enabled present day researchers to envision the ways in which the Egyptians looked at the world. ☐1 With thousands of years separating the ancient Egyptians from modern scholars, the surviving art of the Egyptians is our best view into their beliefs and their lives.

The primary purpose of most ancient Egyptian art was to immortalize kings, queens, priests, and other respected figures. Many Egyptian tombs contained paintings and sculptures of slaves and supplies, because it was believed that these representations would become real provisions for the deceased in the afterlife. ☐2 In order to keep artistic images timeless, symbolism was strictly followed; in thousands of years of Egyptian art, the style of paintings and statues remained nearly unchanged. Even the physical media of Egyptian arts were designed to last forever. Paintings were coated in protective resins, sculptures were carved from hard stone, and tombs were carefully sealed. The fact that so much ancient Egyptian art remains today is a testament to the Egyptians' efforts to preserve artistic works forever. ☐3

With their art, the ancient Egyptians attempted to make their lives eternal, and in a sense they have succeeded. Due to the efforts of archeological researchers who study the preserved works of Egyptian art, succeeding generations can step back into this ancient world.

1. The writer is considering deleting the following sentence from the essay. The sentence should NOT be deleted because it:

   A. describes the techniques and methods used in various Egyptian arts.
   B. provides an explanation for why researchers study ancient Egyptians' art.
   C. explains how standards in Egyptian art have developed and changed over many years.
   D. indicates that all records of ancient Egyptian life have been lost, which is why it remains such a mystery.

2. If the writer were to delete the last part of the following sentence (ending the sentence with a period after the word *followed*), the paragraph would primarily lose:

   F. an explanation for why Egyptian artists followed certain styles.
   G. an indication of how well Egyptian artistic styles were preserved.
   H. a description of the artistic styles and conventions used by ancient Egyptians.
   J. nothing, because this information is stated elsewhere in the essay.

3. The writer is considering deleting the preceding sentence. Should the sentence be kept or deleted?

   A. Kept, because it suggests that Egyptians learned skills that are too complex for modern researchers to understand.
   B. Kept, because it connects the preceding details to the essay's main focus.
   C. Deleted, because it provides info that shifts the focus away from the specific description of Egyptian art media.
   D. Deleted, because it is irrelevant to the essay's central argument.

Transitions

Transition questions will ask you to choose the most appropriate and logical way to shift from one idea to another. These questions may ask you to choose the most appropriate transition between two sentences or clauses. More complicated questions ask you to choose a sentence to transition between paragraphs. In either case, you must first understand the ideas presented in both the preceding and following portions of the text.

❑ Transitions can be used to show the relationship between sentences or between clauses in a sentence.

There are three main types of transitions: contrasting, supporting, and cause/effect. Contrasting transitions are used to link opposing ideas. Supporting transitions are used to link supporting, related ideas. Cause/Effect transitions are used to link ideas that result from other ideas.

The following lists show the most common transitions:

Contrasting	Supporting	Cause/Effect
but	and	because
yet	thus	consequently
instead	as well as	if
despite	also	therefore
although	; (semicolon)	since

❑ Check for logical errors in underlined questions that involve transitions.

She really enjoyed the movie, (*and/but*) she thought the acting was great.

❑ Transition questions sometimes require you to correct run-on or fragment errors. When looking at the links between clauses, make sure sentences are complete and ideas connect logically.

❑ When you are asked to consider a transitional sentence at the beginning or end of a paragraph, first find the topic of each paragraph. Transitional sentences should logically connect the two topics and flow smoothly with the rest of the paragraph.

...players used to hit fewer home runs than they do today. In 1965, for example, Tony Conigliaro of the Red Sox led the American league with only 32 home runs. Since the 1990s, players have regularly reached over 50 in a season. In the eyes of some fans, this sudden increase due to steroids is an insult to the great players of the past.

⌊?⌋ Most sports media have suggested that steroids have been the only cause of these increasing home run totals. Though the rise of steroids has changed the game of baseball, there are other factors that have brought about the age of "power hitters." While the introduction of steroids certainly increased the number of home runs, several other factors have contributed...

The writer is considering adding a transitional topic sentence at the beginning of this paragraph. If all of the following choices are true, which would best accomplish this purpose?

A. Recent home run totals have reached levels that would have been unimaginable during Conigliaro's era.
B. Modern equipment would have protected Conigliaro from his batting injury in 1967.
C. Conigliaro never used any steroids, but there is a chance that he would have if he were playing today.
D. Of course, baseball is a sport that should not be changing so drastically.

What is the topic of the first paragraph?

What is the topic of the second paragraph?

Which answer choices are not relevant to the focus of either paragraph?

PUT IT TOGETHER

Throughout recorded history, there are accounts of people looking up at the night sky and marveling at the bright glow of Venus. Often mistaken for a star, Venus is, in <u>addition,</u> the
₁
planet closest to Earth and, in our solar system, the most similar in size. However, despite these resemblances, Venus and Earth are dramatically different in many ways. Because Venus is so nearby, we used to have grand hopes for human colonization of the planet. <u>Thus, these</u> hopes faded once we
₂
gained the technology for space flight to Venus.

Numerous unmanned probes have been sent to analyze Venus and have discovered a hostile planet surface. Venus is a dry world, with the only rain taking the form of sulphuric acid. Terrible storms with wind speeds up to 400 kilometers per hour are accompanied by intense lightning storms. The atmosphere is incredibly dense, with enough pressure to crush many of the probes sent to the Venusian surface. <u>Furthermore,</u>
₃
the temperature at the surface is nearly 500° C (nearly 900° F), the hottest of all the planets in the solar system. Scientists have been surprised and confused by many of these findings, which show Venus to be very unlike Earth.

Perhaps <u>Venus's greatest mystery has been its odd</u>
₄
<u>atmosphere.</u> It is believed that Venus was once very similar to
₄
Earth, with entire oceans of water and a much milder

1. **A.** NO CHANGE
    B. summary,
    C. fact,
    D. total,

2. **F.** NO CHANGE
    G. Therefore, these
    H. Furthermore, these
    J. These

> Read the sentence before and after a transition and determine how the ideas in the sentences relate.

3. **A.** NO CHANGE
    B. In other words,
    C. For example,
    D. Of course,

4. Which of the following sentences would most effectively introduce the subject of this paragraph and act as a transition from the preceding paragraph?

    F. NO CHANGE
    G. As astronomers discover more about the universe, they often have more new questions than answers.
    H. Research indicates that a planet's formation is influenced by its star.
    J. The Venera program, led by the Soviet Union, has sent over a dozen probes to Venus.

climate. <u>And so,</u> some catastrophic conditions must have
5
caused the drastic shift from Venus's Earth-like past to its
current, hostile state. Theories to explain this change include
greenhouse effects and collisions with asteroids. Now, the
climate on Venus is so extreme that some scientists speculate
it has reversed the rotation of the entire planet. Venus is odd in
that it rotates in the opposite direction of its orbit around the
sun, and also because its rotation is very slow: a "day" on
Venus is about as long as 8 months on Earth. It is possible that
Venus used to have a rotation similar to Earth's but its intense
atmosphere gradually pulled the planet into a backwards spin.

Another secret of Venus's atmosphere lies in its chemical
composition. Analysis has revealed the presence of certain
molecules, such as carbonyl sulfide, which are typically
created by organisms. Also, some patches of the Venusian
atmosphere seem to be absorbing solar energy, resembling
how ocean algae uses sunlight to power chemical reactions.
These occurrences could be explained by microbial organisms
living in the Venusian clouds. <u>In other words,</u> some scientists
6
believe Venus should be explored for extraterrestrial life.

Many scientists hope to uncover more about "Earth's
twin," but its dangerous environment makes exploration risky
and challenging. Despite the numerous efforts to study Venus,
the planet is still largely a mystery. Though we no longer
dream of living on Venus, we continue to study the planet
because so much about it is still not understood.

5. Which of the following alternatives to the underlines portion would NOT be acceptable?

   A. Therefore
   B. Thus
   C. Accordingly
   D. Besides

6. F. NO CHANGE
   G. For this reason,
   H. On the other hand,
   J. Even so,

Style

Style questions ask you to make sure that portions of the passage are precise, effective, and appropriate. Most of these questions require you to choose the most suitable of several related words. Others will ask you to choose between several phrases that range in levels of formality or complexity. More challenging questions will ask you to revise a sentence or consider the effects of a revision.

❑ Make sure the language of passages is consistent in tone and expresses appropriate ideas.

It is unacceptable to use slang or colloquialisms in the type of writing that appears on the English Test, even if the colloquial or slang word conveys the proper meaning.

Most sports media have suggested that steroids have been the only cause of increasing home-run totals. Though the rise of steroids has changed the game of baseball, there are other factors that have brought about the age of "power hitters." While the introduction of steroids certainly increased the number of home runs, several other factors have contributed. It's totally a fact that new baseball parks are built smaller than they used to be. This makes it easier to hit a home run, because less distance is needed to clear the far walls. Also, the balls themselves have changed, with the development of brighter cores and construction, so they fly farther. Additionally, more restrictions on pitchers have made it easier for batters to get hittable pitches. However, these represent the evolution of the sport and are changes that affect all players, whereas steroids represent unfair advantages.

A. NO CHANGE
B. For example,
C. Ponder the notion that
D. By way of illustration,

F. NO CHANGE
G. lighter
H. sunnier
J. OMIT the underlined portion

PUT IT TOGETHER

If you have <u>problems</u> with sleep, blame Humphry Davy.
                        1
Before Davy, human sleep patterns were dictated by natural

light. We woke and slept with the rising and setting of the sun.

But in the 1800s, brilliant inventors such as Davy began

experimenting with artificial light. Davy was the first to invent

electric light, which was later <u>improved</u> by Sir Joseph Swan.
                                          2
This artificial light allowed people to stay up later, which

created new problems with sleep.

1. Which of the following alternatives to the underlined portion would NOT be acceptable?

    A. difficulties
    B. issues
    C. questions
    D. complications

2. **F.** NO CHANGE
    G. increased
    H. enlarged
    J. enriched

Wordiness

On the ACT English Test, shorter and simpler is usually better. Questions on wordiness require you to eliminate redundancies and irrelevant information.

Simpler questions will have synonyms placed next to each other. More complicated questions will have ideas that are described multiple times or that are unrelated to the main focus of the passage.

❑ Remove unnecessary and repeated ideas.

> New regulations have <u>reduced and decreased</u> the prevalence of steroid abuse in professional baseball, as well as other sports. However, these rules cannot prevent all unfair advantages that players might use. This view may be seen as <u>pessimistic, which can be depressing,</u> but the pressures of professional sports have often driven players to seek any way to distinguish themselves and earn fame.

A. NO CHANGE
B. reduced and lessened
C. dropped and decreased
D. reduced

F. NO CHANGE
G. a perspective that is pessimistic,
H. one that can be seen as pessimistic,
J. pessimistic,

❑ The shortest answer is correct approximately 50% of the time.

The choice to OMIT a portion of a passage is correct almost 50% of the time.

PUT IT TOGETHER

Humans have evolved with natural sleep cycles based on "circadian rhythms," which are based on the twenty-four-hour day-night cycle. This is more than just a habit based on patterns; there is a biological reaction to lighting. During periods of darkness <u>when there is little light</u>, the brain's pineal
1
gland releases melatonin, a chemical that promotes sleep. If lighting becomes irregular, the naturally ordinary rhythm of sleep is disturbed and the body struggles to adjust. 2
Without natural light cycles, melatonin production changes and one may lose sleep. Therefore, treatment for sleeplessness may be simple: turn off the lights, and don't stare at a bright electronic screen. For those who need more help sleeping, there are melatonin supplements that can be taken. By recognizing the biological processes supporting sleep, we <u>in fact can indeed help</u> our bodies adapt.
3

1. **A.** NO CHANGE
    B. and gloomy times
    C. or reduced brightness
    D. OMIT the underlined portion

2. Which of the following words from the preceding sentence is NOT necessary and should therefore be deleted?

    F. irregular
    G. naturally
    H. ordinary
    J. struggles

3. **A.** NO CHANGE
    B. somehow, in some way, help
    C. could have helped
    D. can help

English – Rhetorical Skills Summary

Main Idea

❑ Every part of a passage should contribute to the passage's main idea.

Intent

❑ When asked to judge a passage based on the author's goals, pay careful attention to the wording of the question and answer choices.

Organization

❑ When organized properly, an essay's ideas should build upon each other and transition naturally.

Addition

❑ Only choose to add material if it introduces new, useful information to the passage.

Deletion

❑ Sentences should be deleted if they are not relevant to the focus of the passage or do not support and strengthen the passage's ideas.

Transitions

❑ Transitions can be used to show the relationship between sentences or between clauses in a sentence.

Style

❑ Make sure the language of passages is consistent in tone and expresses appropriate ideas.

❑ It is unacceptable to use slang or colloquialisms in the type of writing that appears on the English Test, even if the colloquial or slang word conveys the proper meaning.

Wordiness

❑ Shorter and simpler is usually better. Questions on wordiness require you to eliminate redundancies and irrelevant information.

English Practice

PASSAGE I

Do You Believe in Magic?

Everyone knows that magic tricks <u>aren't</u> real. Even so,
1
when I was younger, I thought that the magician could

actually make things disappear. Because he wouldn't tell me

how he did it, I thought that he had access to a special realm of

magic that was only <u>available, to a chosen few.</u> I wanted to
2

become one of those chosen few. ☐3

One of my kindergarten friends told me that if you

thought hard enough, <u>you could</u> move objects with your mind,
4

and even make them appear and disappear. Needless to say,

even after I thought really hard for an hour, the action figure

that I had been trying to make disappear was <u>still right there in</u>
5

<u>the exact same place where it started.</u> I determined that the
5

magician must have a better, more effective method. I needed

to find out.

---

1. **A.** NO CHANGE
    B. are'nt
    C. arent
    D. are

2. **F.** NO CHANGE
    G. available to a chosen few.
    H. available: to a chosen few.
    J. chosen to a few available.

3. The writer wishes to add a sentence that would both conclude this paragraph and also make a smooth and logical transition into the next paragraph. Given that all are true, which of the following sentences most specifically achieves this purpose?

    A. I had seen another magic show when I was younger, but I was too young to really understand what was going on.
    B. I started reading a lot of books about magical realms and mythical sorcerers who could vanquish fire-breathing dragons.
    C. The first step toward reaching this goal was to ask people I knew how I could start training to become an expert magician.
    D. I didn't trust my friends' advice about magic, so I went to my parents first because they were older and probably knew the secret behind it.

4. **F.** NO CHANGE
    G. one can
    H. one could
    J. you can

5. **A.** NO CHANGE
    B. still there.
    C. still right in the same exact place.
    D. OMIT the underlined portion.

I took out a book on magic from the library. The book, thereby, seemed to suggest that magic tricks were only illusions, and that things could not actually disappear.
₆

I concluded that the work of an amateur must be a book who had never himself figured out how to do real magic.
₇

Of course, I could have just asked my parents but I wanted to surprise them with my newfound magic skills. I imagined their surprise at my making household items move and be disappearing without a trace. I pictured the
₉

expression on my mom's face as I make her serving of green beans vanish into thin air.
₁₀

[1] It had at last come to the point where I had to ask my parents. [2] Finally one day, the same friend who said that people could move objects with their minds told me that he
₁₁

had heard that from an older boy, who had been lying to him. [3] The older boy had agreed with the library book: magic is an illusion. [4] I was stunned and in shocked disbelief. [5] There was no other option left open to me. [13]
₁₂

---

6. F. NO CHANGE
    G. as a result,
    H. furthermore,
    J. however,

7. A. NO CHANGE
    B. I concluded that real magic must not be about books written by amateurs who could not do it themselves.
    C. I concluded that the book must have been written by amateurs who could not do real magic themselves.
    D. Real magic, not done by amateurs, is not written about in books where people can't do it themselves.

8. F. NO CHANGE
    G. my parents but,
    H. my parents', but
    J. my parents, but

9. A. NO CHANGE
    B. move and disappearing without a trace.
    C. move; disappearing without a trace.
    D. move and even disappear.

10. F. NO CHANGE
    G. making
    H. had made
    J. will have made

11. A. NO CHANGE
    B. Finally, one day,
    C. Finally: one day
    D. finally, one day;

12. F. NO CHANGE
    G. I was stunned.
    H. I was stunned and shocked.
    J. I was stunningly shocked.

13. For the sake of logic and coherence, Sentence 1 of this paragraph should be placed:

    A. where it is now.
    B. after Sentence 2.
    C. after Sentence 3.
    D. after Sentence 5.

They gave me the dreaded news: magic is, after all, only

an illusion. Everyone knows that. Well, for a while I didn't

know, and I <u>think</u> my life was more exciting when I believed
14

magic was real.

14. **F.** NO CHANGE
    G. am thinking
    H. had thought
    J. think about the fact that

> Question 15 asks about the preceding passage as a whole.

15. The writer wants to add a concluding sentence that reveals his occasional wish to give magic another try. Given that all are true, which of the following sentences would accomplish the writer's goal?

    A. Magic is mostly for children, and believing in it is a phase that should be outgrown at an early age.

    B. I constantly read books about magic and have never been able to get over my initial fascination with it.

    C. I've grown up since then, but now and again, when I am alone, I still try to move small objects just a little a bit with my mind.

    D. I often wish that I were a kid again.

PASSAGE II

A Brief History of Baseball Cards

[1] Baseball cards were first produced in 1887. [2] Today, they are one of America's major collecting hobbies. [3] Card collecting has a draw for baseball fans of all ages and income levels. [4] Some cards cost only five or ten <u>cents; while</u> others cost upwards of one-
₁

hundred thousand dollars. [5] <u>There are not any baseball cards,</u>
₂
<u>however, that cost more than two million dollars.</u> [6] Baseball cards
₂
allow fans to both collect mementos of their favorite players and also make potential investments for the future.

The first cards were made on a cloth-like material, and were all about the same size: one-and-a-half by two inches. These cards are high <u>in value, because of their age and rarity.</u>
₃
An average card from this period would likely cost around $800 today.

Collectors refer to the period beginning in 1902 as the "Golden Age of Baseball," when cards began to be packaged with chewing gum, tobacco, and snacks. Cards also <u>begin</u>
₄

to be produced in <u>different and various</u> sizes and formats:
₅

1. **A.** NO CHANGE
    B. cents: while
    C. cents while
    D. cents, while

2. Which of the following sentences would make the most effective transition between sentences 4 and 6?

    F. NO CHANGE
    G. Either way, you should be able to get cards of players you like for an affordable price – most cards fall much closer to the five to ten cent range.
    H. Good cards are more expensive than bad cards, as would be expected.
    J. I have a lot of baseball cards myself, but they are not in very good condition, which lowers their value.

3. **A.** NO CHANGE
    B. in value because of their age, and rarity.
    C. in value because of their age and rarity.
    D. in value because of: their age and rarity.

4. **F.** NO CHANGE
    G. begun
    H. are beginning
    J. began

5. **A.** NO CHANGE
    B. inconsistent
    C. variously different
    D. different

tobacco cards were about the same size as original baseball

<u>cards but</u> some companies also produced rectangular sheets of
6

three cards that showed a play unfolding in three frames. As

baseball became more popular during this time period, so did

card collecting. ☐7

6. F. NO CHANGE
   G. cards; but
   H. cards. But
   J. cards, but

7. Which of the following sentences, if added
   here, would provide the most logical
   conclusion to the idea that the increase in
   card collecting was linked to the new and
   different ways in which cards were being
   marketed?

   A. Now that people could be exposed to
       baseball cards through the purchase of a
       number of different popular products,
       more and more people took an interest
       in them.
   B. The increase in card collecting was due
       more to the improved quality of the
       game than to any marketing strategies
       used by the card makers.
   C. It is difficult to find a definitive link
       between the growth of card collecting
       and the changing presentation of the
       cards.
   D. Most people did not keep their cards,
       and that is why the older ones have
       become rare and higher in value.

The 1950s saw the <u>uplifting</u> of modern card collecting.
8

This was when the first Topps cards were introduced. Topps

remains the bestselling brand of baseball cards. Topps, instead

of offering cards with tobacco, sold packs of cards with gum

in them. <u>Some of these cards are hard to find and are valuable</u>
9

<u>today, because they are in a good sort of condition.</u> In the
9

1950s no one knew that baseball cards would ever be valuable,

so kids mostly just used them to play games. Sometimes, kids

just put the cards in their bicycle spokes to make noise. Star

cards from this era can easily reach prices above $1,000.

8. F. NO CHANGE
   G. descent
   H. climbing
   J. rise

9. A. NO CHANGE
   B. Some of these cards, hard to find and
       valuable, are in good condition, but
       some are not.
   C. Some of these cards, in good condition,
       are both hard to find and valuable.
   D. Some of these cards can be valuable
       because they are hard to find in good
       condition.

[10] [1] Only Topps and a few other card companies like Donruss and Fleer produced cards. [2] This was the case through the 1970s and 1980s. [3] Many cards from this period aren't that valuable, because many were produced and they were all the same. [4] Today, however, there are hundreds of different brands covering all the major sports. [5] Each different pack offers their own benefits. [6] One pack may give
11
you the chance to get a piece of a game- used jersey from

Hank Aaron, while another, might offer you a chance to get an
12

old, authentic autograph from Ted Williams. [13]

10. Given that all are true, which of the following would provide the best opening phrase to the following sentence?

   F. NO CHANGE
   G. For many of the next years to come,
   H. For many years,
   J. Years later,

11. A. NO CHANGE
    B. it's
    C. its
    D. there

12. F. NO CHANGE
    G. while, another might offer
    H. while, another might, offer
    J. while another might offer

13. For the purpose of pointing out that there are some valuable cards from every year, even though some years don't have a lot of valuable cards, the writer composes the following sentence:

    Of course, there are still some cards made during this time period that are valuable, just not nearly as many as from other periods.

    If added, this sentence would logically be placed:

    A. at the beginning of the paragraph.
    B. after Sentence 1.
    C. after Sentence 3.
    D. after Sentence 4.

Baseball cards will continue to change to match the changing desires of collectors. As long as people like baseball, people will like baseball cards. <u>When collecting cards, the feeling most people have is one of taking</u> a small part in the game itself. The history of baseball cards has likely only just begun. 15

14. **F.** NO CHANGE
  G. When collecting cards, most people feel as if they are taking
  H. Most people, collecting cards, feel like they are taking
  J. Collecting cards, most people feel like taking

15. The writer wants to add a concluding sentence that encourages people who do not collect baseball cards to take a closer look at the hobby. Given that all are true, which of the following would best achieve this purpose?

  A. If you haven't tried card collecting, there are many minute details that are hard to master and that escape the eye of the amateur collector.
  B. Card collecting is a lot of fun, but it is a hobby mostly for little kids, who should be encouraged to try it out if they like baseball or other sports.
  C. Even if you might not be so sure at first, card collecting is a great deal of fun and really acquaints you with the game of baseball.
  D. I'm not as interested in card collecting as I used to be, but it still offers a good source of entertainment from time to time.

PASSAGE III

Greenhouse Gases and Their Effect on the Atmosphere

<u>Despite</u> many environmentally-friendly technological
1

advances, our society produces much more smoke and fumes

than it used to. With an increasing population <u>have</u> come an
2

increasing need for energy production. A great deal of this

energy comes from burning coal, oil, and natural gas. Burning

these fuels on a large scale, as we have done for years,

produces an overabundance of carbon dioxide that is harmful

to our environment – <u>particularly harmful, in fact.</u> This
3

overabundance causes <u>a known phenomenon, this being the</u>
4

<u>greenhouse effect.</u>
4

    [1] A certain amount of carbon dioxide <u>is</u> necessary to
5

maintain the Earth's atmosphere. [2] Gases like carbon

dioxide, methane, and nitrous oxide gather in the atmosphere

and trap energy from the Sun. [3] If they did not do this, then

the <u>average, overall</u> temperature of Earth would drop
6

approximately 60 degrees Fahrenheit. [4] The gases function

like the glass in a greenhouse, which makes it easy for the

Sun's rays to get in, but difficult for them to escape.

1. **A.** NO CHANGE
   B. In regards to
   C. Because of
   D. As relates to the

2. **F.** NO CHANGE
   G. has
   H. had
   J. would have

3. At this point in the essay, the writer is looking to replace the underlined portion with more specific information about the harm that is caused by carbon dioxide from burning fuel. Given that all of the choices are true, which of the following best accomplishes this task?

   A. carbon dioxide has toxic properties when present in great amounts.
    B. the environment continues to worsen in a few specific respects.
   C. we can no longer ignore this problem.
   D. particularly the Earth's atmosphere.

4. **F.** NO CHANGE
   G. a phenomenon, known as the greenhouse effect.
   H. a greenhouse effect phenomenon.
   J. a phenomenon known as the greenhouse effect.

5. **A.** NO CHANGE
   B. was
   C. could be
   D. should be

6. **F.** NO CHANGE
   G. average and overall
   H. wholesale
   J. average

[5] These gases are called greenhouse gases. | 7 |

Some carbon dioxide is processed by plants through photosynthesis, but when too much carbon dioxide is produced, the excess carbon dioxide rises into the atmosphere. As the amount of gas increases, the amount of warmth from the Sun that is trapped within the Earth's atmosphere also increases. The Earth's global temperature rises as a result.

Some scientists believe that in the course of the next decade, the amount of greenhouse gases in the atmosphere could be as much as doubling. If this occurred, the Earth's
        8
average temperature would rise anywhere from 1.5 to 6 degrees Celsius. Since this may not sound like a lot, it would
            9
in fact be enough to melt parts of the polar ice caps, creating flooding that would devastate major coastal cities such as St. Petersburg, New York, and Amsterdam. This would be overly
                                               10
disastrous.
   10

This is rather extreme, but the fact remains that we must
 11
address the greenhouse effect as a serious concern. We must find alternate sources of energy that are not as harmful to the environment, and do not have such dire long-term
     12

7. The writer is considering adding the following true statement to this paragraph:

> The atmosphere regulates the global temperature by using the sun's warmth for heat energy.

Should the sentence be added, and if so, where should it be placed?

A. after Sentence 1
B. before Sentence 4
C. after Sentence 4
D. Do not add the given sentence.

8. F. NO CHANGE
   G. could be doubling.
   H. could double.
   J. could as much as, double.

9. A. NO CHANGE
   B. Because
   C. While
   D. As

10. F. NO CHANGE
    G. This would be a disastrous state of affairs.
    H. This would be a big disaster.
    J. OMIT the underlined sentence.

11. A. NO CHANGE
    B. This current state of things
    C. This outlook
    D. This indubitable prediction

12. F. NO CHANGE
    G. environment. And do not
    H. environment and, do not
    J. environment and do not

consequences for the future of our race. [13] Further research

must be going on to determine how we can best fit our energy
14

needs to the needs of our atmosphere. [15]

13. The writer wants to add a sentence that specifies types of power that would be desirable alternate sources of energy. Given that all are true, which of the following sentences is best suited to this purpose?

   A. Wind and solar power are two major sources of energy production that, as yet, have not been maximized.

   B. Sources of energy that do not create so much carbon dioxide need to be the first alternate sources that we explore.

   C. These sources of energy must be both safe for the environment and significant enough to sustain a large amount of the United States' power.

   D. It is not feasible that we will be able to transition from fossil fuels to other forms of environmentally safe energy in the next several years.

14. F. NO CHANGE
     G. must be in action
     H. must be done
     J. must be accomplished

15. Which of the following sentences would form the most effective conclusion to this paragraph and the essay as a whole?

   A. This research should focus on alternate forms of energy like wind and solar power.

   B. Otherwise, grave environmental consequences could cause serious harm to us and to future generations.

   C. Fossil fuels will probably remain the primary source of energy for some time to come.

   D. If we just switch a little of our energy demand to wind and solar power, the problem of global warming will likely be completely prevented.

PASSAGE IV

A Canoe trip with Dad

My dad and I went canoeing once when I was 8. Neither of us had ever been canoeing <u>before but my dad</u> decided that
₁
we should rent a canoe and try it out. There was a nice river

that <u>was winding through the woods</u> in the town near us.
₂

<u>There was a sporting goods store near the river that rented</u>
₃
<u>canoes.</u> My dad chose this place to start our adventure.
₃

[1] <u>Another time,</u> we were floating down a stagnant,
₄
murky river through a pine forest. [2] We had not made it very

far. [3] The man at the store had shown my dad how to row so

that the canoe would go <u>straight, but my dad</u> apparently didn't
₅
catch on, because we weaved back and forth across the river

for 45 minutes before he finally got going straight. [4] Now we

were making some progress, <u>since</u> it didn't appear particularly
₆
scenic in the direction we were going. ☐ 7

1. A. NO CHANGE
    B. before but, my dad
    C. before, but my dad,
    D. before, but my dad

2. F. NO CHANGE
    G. winded through the woods
    H. wound through the woods
    J. had wound through the woods

3. A. NO CHANGE
    B. There was a sporting goods store near the river at which canoes were rented.
    C. Near the river, there was a sporting goods store that rented canoes.
    D. At a sporting goods store near the river, you could rent canoes there.

4. F. NO CHANGE
    G. Some indefinite time later,
    H. An hour or so later,
    J. At a later time,

5. A. NO CHANGE
    B. straight but, my dad
    C. straight, my dad
    D. straight, but my dad,

6. F. NO CHANGE
    G. and
    H. but
    J. while

7. The writer wants to add the following sentence to this paragraph to further illustrate the river's unappealing surroundings:

    > Mostly all I could see up ahead were thick, tangled reeds, dead tree branches, and the occasional crow.

    For the sake of logic and coherence, this sentence should be placed:

    A. before Sentence 1.
    B. after Sentence 2.
    C. at the end of the paragraph.
    D. at the beginning of the next paragraph.

There was something exciting that was keeping us going, however. The man at the shop told my dad to look for a Great Blue Heron that lived out in the woods, so my dad brought a pair of binoculars for bird watching. The only birds I saw <u>was</u> <u>a couple of crows</u> traveling from tree to tree. My dad was still
8

excited, though; he <u>says</u> that he thought there was a nice
9

stretch of <u>river in a few minutes upcoming.</u>
10

Then the unbelievable happened: <u>the thing we had been</u>
11
<u>waiting for.</u> My dad leapt up and grabbed my shoulder,
11
shaking me and saying "There it is, there it is!" He took his

binoculars and gaped at it. Unfortunately, in <u>his haste</u> to get
12

up, he had thrown the canoe off balance – <u>he had fallen off a</u>
13
<u>canoe only once before</u>. He rocked back and forth a couple of
13

8. F. NO CHANGE
   G. were a couple of crows
   H. were crows – a couple of them –
   J. were nothing but a couple of crows

9. A. NO CHANGE
   B. said
   C. had said
   D. was saying

10. F. NO CHANGE
    G. river, in a few minutes, coming.
    H. river coming up in a few minutes.
    J. river, this being upcoming in a few minutes.

11. The writer wants to be more specific about what it was that happened that was unbelievable. Which of the following phrases would succeed at making the first sentence more specific?

    A. NO CHANGE
    B. we finally saw the heron that we had been waiting to see.
    C. we finally saw the heron.
    D. the heron was suddenly viewed by us.

12. Which of the following phrases would NOT be an acceptable substitute for the underlined portion?

    F. his rush
    G. his attempt
    H. his hurry
    J. his scramble

13. A. NO CHANGE
    B. this was not the first time this had happened
    C. his fall was very humorous
    D. OMIT the underlined portion, and end the sentence with a period.

times and then pitched into the water, <u>tipping over the canoe</u> <u>and taking me with him.</u> The water was muddy and tepid, and
14

I felt weeds at my feet.

My dad's binoculars were ruined, and we never went canoeing again after that. My mom laughed at us when we came home, especially when I told her the story about Dad's tipping over the canoe. Dad wasn't too happy about that one, and after Mom left he told me never to bring it up again. 15

14. The writer is considering deleting the underlined portion. If he or she were to do so, the essay would primarily lose:

  F. an explanation of how the narrator was thrown into the water.
  G. the writer's opinion of his dad's decision to get up quickly and look at the heron.
  H. a criticism of the father's inability to properly handle the canoe.
  J. an illustration of the father's obsession with bird watching.

15. The writer wants to add a concluding sentence that is consistent with the humorous, nostalgic tone of the essay as a whole. Which of the following sentences most effectively accomplishes this?

  A. My mom did not appreciate the humor in the story after she heard about the ruined binoculars.
  B. I respected my dad's wishes and did not talk about the canoe trip again, except for once with a couple of my friends.
  C. Surprisingly, I got really into canoeing on my own and even entered a competition recently.
  D. I still bring up the old story sometimes, though, but only when dad is out or asleep.

PASSAGE V

Gatsby and the Powerlessness of Money

The Great Gatsby is about the failure of the American dream in the 1920s. <u>It is about a man Jay Gatsby,</u> who is very
¹

rich and <u>constant</u> throws grand parties. Although Gatsby
²
appears to be rich and happy, he actually has a lot of dark secrets. His money is not nearly enough to make him happy, and he has no real close friends. Even his lover, Daisy Buchanan, is married to another man, whom in the end she decides she will not leave to be with Gatsby. The moral is <u>the crucial, unforgettable fact</u> that money often just hides a lot
³
of problems and makes others forget about the rich person's real identity.

Gatsby turns out to have quite a dark side. Through the story, the narrator, Nick Carraway, learns that Gatsby made all his money by illegally selling alcohol. <u>Despite this,</u> Gatsby
⁴
associates with a number of criminals, including one man who was rumored to have fixed the World Series. <u>Gatsby's</u>
⁵
<u>criminal background is an important part of his character.</u>
⁵

1. **A.** NO CHANGE
   B. It is about, a man Jay Gatsby,
   C. It is about a man, Jay Gatsby
   D. It is about a man, Jay Gatsby,

2. **F.** NO CHANGE
   G. constantly
   H. more constantly
   J. is constant in

3. **A.** NO CHANGE
   B. the crucial fact
   C. the fact of greatest importance
   D. OMIT the underlined portion

4. **F.** NO CHANGE
   G. Conversely,
   H. Furthermore,
   J. Essentially,

5. Which of the following sentences makes the best transition between Gatsby's criminal background and the fact that his guests do not know about it?

   A. NO CHANGE
   B. Gatsby's criminal background gives him an air of mystery that draws people to him.
   C. Gatsby is very public about his misdeeds, and spends a great deal of effort trying to make up for them.
   D. Most guests at Gatsby's parties, however, do not learn these things about Gatsby because they do not really care.

These people are only using Gatsby for personal interest in
him, and what he provides is not to them an important
concern.
₆

[1] Gatsby also fails to get his lover. [2] Even though Daisy is married, she dislikes her husband and his brusque, arrogant personality and, actually considers leaving her husband and going with Gatsby for a while. [3] However, Daisy stays with her husband even though she loves Gatsby most of the two.

[4] Gatsby is killed, and no one except for the narrator

comes to his funeral. 10

Many people believe that being rich will immediately

make him happy. If you can have anything you want, go anywhere you want to go, and have any number of wealthy, influential people to grand parties at your house, how could

6. **F.** NO CHANGE
   G. These people are only using Gatsby for what he can provide, and take no personal interest in him.
   H. Gatsby is used by these people for the reason that they want the things with which he can provide them.
   J. These people, using Gatsby for what he provides, are not personally concerned with his real life.

7. **A.** NO CHANGE
   B. personality; she actually
   C. personality and, actually,
   D. personality, actually

8. **F.** NO CHANGE
   G. more.
   H. the most.
   J. mostly.

9. Which introductory phrase would best logically connect this sentence with the preceding one?

   A. NO CHANGE
   B. However,
   C. Additionally,
   D. As a result,

10. The writer reviews the paragraph and realizes that a piece of information has been left out. He composes the following sentence containing this information:

    There is a point when it genuinely appears that Gatsby will win Daisy away and achieve his lifelong goal.

    For the sake of logic and coherence, this sentence should be placed:

    F. after Sentence 1.
    G. after Sentence 2.
    H. after Sentence 3.
    J. at the beginning of the next paragraph.

11. **A.** NO CHANGE
    B. us
    C. them
    D. other people

you not be happy? 12 The story of Gatsby shows that there

are a lot of ways that a rich person can be unhappy. The

money replaces his identity and becomes the only thing about

which other people care – it cannot solve any of his problems.
13

Without love or morals, and without him ability to alter his
14

situation for the better, Gatsby had no substance to fall back

on. When the parties were over, everyone forgot about him.

12. The writer wants to add a supporting
sentence that revisits the specific ways that
Gatsby was unhappy. Given that all are
true, which of the following sentences most
logically address this issue?

F. Gatsby had serious character flaws that
lead to his tragic, inevitable demise.

G. Gatsby's goals were not feasible, and
thus he was doomed to fail from the
start, even though he was fabulously
wealthy.

H. Gatsby's inner corruption and
unfulfilled longing for a married woman
far outweighed the benefits of his great
wealth.

J. The reasons for Gatsby's unhappiness
have already been made, and it is left to
the reader to recall them.

13. A. NO CHANGE
B. care, it cannot
C. care, it cannot,
D. care it cannot

14. F. NO CHANGE
G. his
H. his'
J. Gatsbys'

Question 15 asks about the preceding
passage as a whole.

15. Suppose the writer had been assigned an
essay to examine the role of the narrator,
Nick Carraway, in the Great Gatsby. Does
this essay effectively address this topic?

A. Yes, because Nick Carraway is
mentioned in the topic sentence of
Paragraph 2.

B. Yes, because the narrator is the one who
finds out all of Gatsby's dark secrets.

C. No, because the essay is primarily about
Gatsby, and Nick Carraway is only
mentioned briefly and then forgotten.

D. No, because the essay does not give us
any background information about Nick
Carraway, like his hometown or
childhood history.

PASSAGE VI

An Investigation of Black Holes

Black holes are some of the most amazing phenomena in the universe. Scattered throughout the galaxy, <u>so much gravity is generated by black holes</u>
1
that, when anything comes close enough to one of them, it will be sucked in forever. Even light cannot escape from a black hole. That is why black holes are called "black:" no one can see what occurs inside of them because no light can be detected. ☐2

[1] A black hole <u>were created</u> by the death of a star.
3

[2] A star is kept burning by <u>its</u> immense supply of gas, but
4
when this gas eventually runs out, the star explodes in what is called a supernova. [3] The remnants of this <u>explosion,</u>
5
<u>collapse</u> together into an extremely dense point called a
5
neutron star. [4] A singularity is a point of nearly infinite density. [5] All of the mass of the star collapses into a tiny, almost non-existent point, which is the beginning of the black

1. **A.** NO CHANGE
    B. so much gravity generated by black holes
    C. black holes generate so much gravity
    D. black holes generate such a largely enormous degree of gravity

2. The writer is considering deleting the following clause from the essay (placing a period after the word "black"):

    > no one can see what occurs inside of them because no light can be detected.

    Should the writer make this deletion?

    F. Yes, because the clause repeats information that has already been presented in the paragraph.
    G. Yes, because the information doesn't fit in with the scientific, factual tone of the rest of the essay.
    H. No, because the clause clarifies how black holes got their name and how the name is related to light.
    J. No, because the information is interesting and engages the reader's attention.

3. **A.** NO CHANGE
    B. is created
    C. are created
    D. created

4. **F.** NO CHANGE
    G. it's
    H. its'
    J. the

5. **A.** NO CHANGE
    B. explosion collapse,
    C. explosion: collapse
    D. explosion collapse

hole. 6

There is a direct correlation between an objects' mass and
7
how much gravitational force it exerts on other objects: the

more the mass, the more the pull of gravity. An object with

less mass, all the while, tends to be pulled towards objects
8
with more mass. A black hole, although infinitely tiny, has an

enormous mass. 9 This dense mass generates an enormous

amount of gravitational force, so much so that no object, once

coming within a certain distance of the black hole, has enough

energy to pull away from it or be escaping it.
10

6. Upon reviewing the second paragraph, the
    writer realizes that some information has
    been left out. She composes the information
    into the following sentence:

    > If the supernova is large enough,
    > however, then the particles will collapse
    > into a singularity.

    For the sake of logic and coherence, the new
    sentence should be placed:

    F. at the end of the paragraph.
    G. after Sentence 2.
    H. after Sentence 3.
    J. after Sentence 4.

7. A. NO CHANGE
    B. objects
    C. object's
    D. object and its

8. F. NO CHANGE
    G. apparently
    H. conversely
    J. in fact

9. The writer wants to add a sentence that
    further illustrates the contrast between the
    black hole's tiny size and its gigantic mass.
    Which of the following sentences would
    best achieve this purpose?

    A. In this sense, the black hole is like a
        ping-pong ball that weighs billions of
        pounds.
    B. The black hole manages to have an
        almost infinite mass despite its almost
        infinitely tiny size.
    C. This information has been essential in
        scientists' research about the future
        threat black holes may play in our
        galaxy.
    D. Therefore, the black hole is like another
        large planet, but with a smaller mass.

10. F. NO CHANGE
    G. to be pulling away from it or be
        escaping it
    H. to pull away from it or to have escaped
        it
    J. to pull away from it or to escape it

That certain distance or the edge of the black hole is called the
                                                           11

event horizon., This is because no events can be seen past this
                 12
point.

The existence of black holes raises many questions.

13 What happens inside one of them? There are many

theories, ranging from the idea that everything is crushed into

virtual non-existence and be completely wiped out to the idea
                     14
that one could survive a black hole and would be brought by it

to another place in the universe, perhaps even another time.

Either way, until we find a way to move more quickly than the
                                                         15
speed of light, we will not be able to return from across the
     15
event horizon and report on the view inside a black hole.

11. **A.** NO CHANGE
    B. That certain distance, or the edge of the black hole,
    C. That certain distance; or the edge of the black hole
    D. That certain distance – or the edge of the black hole,

12. **F.** NO CHANGE
    G. event horizon due to no
    H. event horizon because no
    J. event horizon – this is because no

13. Which introductory phrase would best begin the following sentence to make the most logical transition from the preceding sentence?

    A. Instead,
    B. Moreover,
    C. In terms of their interiors,
    D. First of all,

14. **F.** NO CHANGE
    G. and be wiped out
    H. and be lost to humanity
    J. OMIT the underlined portion.

15. **A.** NO CHANGE
    B. than the extremely fast speed of light
    C. than light's tremendous speed
    D. OMIT the underlined portion

PASSAGE VII

Computers and the Change in High School

Computers have completely <u>changed: the essence of high</u>
<u>school.</u> Once, when there were only typewriters, one could not
1
simply go back and delete mistakes. One would either have to

white the mistakes out, which usually <u>look</u> shoddy and
2
unprofessional, or scrap the draft and rewrite the paper

entirely. Computers allow students to save time for real

academic pursuits, as opposed to spending hours <u>doing</u>
3
<u>repetitive things.</u>
3

[1] <u>For</u> few as twenty years ago, it was rare to see
4
computers in classrooms. [2] Today, a computer is a necessity

for academic success. [3] It is not only vital for writing reports,

but is also <u>tremendous useful</u> for doing research. [4] Before, if
5
one were assigned an essay, one would have to trek to the

library and search through the stacks <u>for the relevant few</u>
6
<u>books to one's purpose.</u> [5] The internet allows students
6

1. A. NO CHANGE
   B. changed, the essence of high school.
   C. changed the essence of: high school.
   D. changed the essence of high school.

2. F. NO CHANGE
   G. should look
   H. looks
   J. can be

3. Which of the following phrases would most
   specifically illustrate what the writer means
   by "doing repetitive things?"

   A. doing things that go on and on without
      any real purpose.
   B. retyping a long, important draft because
      it has several small punctuation errors.
   C. trying to sharpen one's understanding
      with comparisons and contrasts.
   D. repeating similar processes that do not
      provoke thoughts.

4. F. NO CHANGE
   G. As
   H. With
   J. Since

5. A. NO CHANGE
   B. more tremendously useful
   C. more useful
   D. tremendously useful

6. F. NO CHANGE
   G. for those relevant few books that were
      one's purpose.
   H. for the few books that were relevant to
      one's purpose.
   J. OMIT the underlined portion.

instantaneous access to all the desired facts. [6] One must only
                                                    7
go to a site, type in a few words, and one will likely have more
                              7
than enough information to write an excellent report. [8]
                    7

Computers do however, have their drawbacks – in terms
                              9
of academic performance. Computer games and social
        9
websites often distract students' attention from their academic

and personal responsibilities that it is their duty to perform. A
                                              10
student can become so immersed in an application that his

or her life can change. Computer games also allow the student
              11
to escape from reality and real problems and instead go into a

world where nothing has any consequences and one does not

---

7. If the writer were to delete this sentence, the essay would primarily lose:

    A. an explanation of how the internet is capable of directing students to the information they need.
    B. a description of the sole purpose of the internet.
    C. an unnecessary digression into the operational methods of internet service providers.
    D. a personal opinion that distracts the reader's focus from the logical progression of ideas in the essay.

8. The writer reviews the second paragraph and decides to insert the following sentence about computers not always being so common:

    A few families had them, but most schools did not require students to have them at home.

    For the sake of logic and coherence, this sentence would best be placed:

    F. at the beginning of the paragraph.
    G. after Sentence 1.
    H. before Sentence 4.
    J. after Sentence 4.

9. A. NO CHANGE
    B. Computers: however, they do have their drawbacks academically.
    C. Computers do, however, have their drawbacks in terms of academic performance, as well.
    D. Computers, do however, have their drawbacks in terms of performing academically.

10. F. NO CHANGE
    G. that they must perform dutifully.
    H. that they have to perform.
    J. OMIT the underlined portion and end the sentence with a period.

11. Given that all are true, which of the choices provides information most related to the main idea of the passage?

    A. NO CHANGE
    B. time can become occupied.
    C. problems can accumulate.
    D. grades can suffer.

SUMMIT
EDUCATIONAL
GROUP

have to prove <u>your</u> character meaningfully. Games are not
12

entirely a bad thing. They can be fun and can allow one time

to relax. They do, however, tend to tempt students away from

academics.

On the whole, computers have had a positive impact on

the learning process. They <u>eliminate</u> mundane aspects of
13

writing and research, and have allowed thoughts to be

communicated at a <u>more</u> faster rate than was possible before.
14

There are drawbacks, but this has always been the case with

any new form of technology. ☐15

12. **F.** NO CHANGE
    G. one's
    H. ones
    J. you're

13. **A.** NO CHANGE
    B. will have eliminated
    C. have eliminated
    D. are eliminating

14. **F.** NO CHANGE
    G. most
    H. much
    J. far and away

15. Given that all are true, which of the
    following sentences would provide the best
    conclusion to the writer's argument that
    computers are, on the whole, positive?

    A. NO CHANGE
    B. Computers will continue to present
        serious paradoxes to the human mind in
        the upcoming years of our lives.
    C. The gains in terms of transmission and
        presentation of knowledge far outweigh
        any distractions the computer might
        create.
    D. Academic performance will continue to
        be enhanced by computers for a time,
        but then computers will stop being as
        important as they once were.

PASSAGE VIII

Learning to Play Chess

[1]

Chess is not a difficult game to learn to play, but the decision that it takes a lifetime to master is very true. That is
1

what makes the game so enduring, it is a game that one can
2

never completely master.

[2]

[1] I started out playing a few games against my little

brother. [2] After he taught me, he was easy to beat. [3] My
3

father, however, proved much more of a challenge. [4] Since I
4

thought I had him cornered, it usually turned out that he had

baited me into a trap. [5] I soon became anxious and hesitant.

[6] He overwhelmed me.
5

1. **A.** NO CHANGE
   B. statement
   C. question
   D. issuance

2. **F.** NO CHANGE
   G. enduring: it is
   H. enduring it is
   J. enduring? It is

3. **A.** NO CHANGE
   B. After he taught me – he was easy to beat.
   C. After, he taught me he was easy to beat.
   D. After the teaching, he was easiest to beat.

4. **F.** NO CHANGE
   G. At those times when it seemed
   H. For
   J. When

5. The writer wants to add a sentence that explains how losing to his father caused the writer to doubt whether he wanted to continue playing chess. Given that all are true, which of the following sentences would best convey this intended meaning?

   A. NO CHANGE
   B. He outmaneuvered me so consistently that I wondered if I could ever become good enough to present him a real challenge.
   C. I had a lot of other responsibilities at the time and there were some days where I didn't think about chess as much.
   D. My dad offered to teach me a few different series of opening moves that might help improve my overall game.

[3]

[1] Still, I was fascinated with <u>the strategy in all of chess,</u>
₆
and kept playing. [2] I bought a computer-based chess game

<u>and played for at least two hours a day.</u> [3] The game gave me
₇

a <u>rating based on how good I was</u> at a few chess problems that
₈

it gave me. [4] I got a very bad rating at first. [5] <u>As I played
₉
more games, my rating began to rise, however, and develop
₉
better strategies.</u> [6] I started to think how situations might
₉
unfold two or three moves in advance, and my games with my

dad became a little tighter.

[4]

One day, I finally beat him. He made a mistake about ten

moves into the game and could never come back. When I

moved my queen into the checkmate position, I whooped for

joy. [10]

[5]

[1] I entered a tournament at school soon after my victory.

[2] I hadn't paid much attention before, but my school had a

6. F. NO CHANGE
    G. the whole strategy element that played
        into chess
    H. the chess strategy, all of it,
    J. all of the strategy of chess

7. If the writer deleted this phrase, the essay
    would primarily lose:

    A. a mathematical fact about the writer's
        improvement over time.
    B. an illustration of how much time the
        writer began to devote to chess once he
        was able to play on the computer.
    C. a rough estimate that is out of place in
        an essay that is about a specific topic
        such as chess.
    D. an example of how chess begins to
        distort the writer's perception of time.

8. F. NO CHANGE
    G. rating, and based on how good I was
    H. rating, and based on how good I were
    J. rating and based, on how good I was,

9. A. NO CHANGE
    B. As I played more games, however, I
        developed better strategies, and my
        rating began to rise.
    C. My rating began to rise, developing
        better strategies, as I played more
        games.
    D. As I played more games, my rating,
        which was in the process of rising, was
        affected by more games.

10. Given that all are true, which of the
    following choices would best conclude the
    given paragraph and make a smooth
    transition into the next paragraph about the
    writer's participation in the school
    tournament?

    F. I told a lot of people about it.
    G. I could tell my dad's pride was stung,
        but he was gracious in defeat, and he
        encouraged me to seek out some better
        competition.
    H. I entered myself in the school chess
        tournament soon after I beat my dad.
    J. Playing in a tournament still seemed to
        be far beyond my skill level, though.

thriving chess club that <u>is holding</u> tournaments each month.
                                11

[3] I made it through to the second round, but then I got

clobbered. [4] There were some really good chess players at

my school. [5] One of the kids was in my chemistry class. [6] I

<u>had never hardly known</u> what he did with his free time until
                   12

then.

[6]

I still play a lot of chess. It is a great workout for my

mind, especially my ability to plan ahead. I haven't won a

tournament yet, but I've been doing better <u>in it;</u> I even made it
                                          13

to the semi-finals <u>recently in time.</u> I can beat my dad a lot of
                        14

the time, but he still beats me a fair amount. I still have a lot of

room to improve.

11. **A.** NO CHANGE
    B. has held
    C. held
    D. holded

12. **F.** NO CHANGE
    G. had never known
    H. had hardly ever known
    J. had known, but hardly ever,

13. **A.** NO CHANGE
    B. while at them;
    C. with them;
    D. in them;

14. **F.** NO CHANGE
    G. during a recent time period.
    H. at a time that is very close to the present time.
    J. recently.

> Question 15 asks about the preceding passage as a whole.

15. The writer reviews the essay and decides that he wants to insert the following sentence:

> A few times, I even used on him the strategies that he first taught me, and he didn't even see them coming.

For the sake of logic and coherence, this sentence would best be placed:

A. at the beginning of Paragraph 2.
B. after Sentence 2 in Paragraph 2.
C. after Sentence 5 in Paragraph 3.
D. after Sentence 3 in Paragraph 5.

PASSAGE IX

A Counterargument to Editing Teen Shows for Content

I don't think that teen shows should be edited for content any more than <u>it is.</u> Adolescents need to learn to make
[1]
responsible decisions, but they also need to learn the

difference <u>between, what happens on television, and what is</u>
[2]
<u>acceptable in real life.</u> If an adolescent cannot do this, then
[2]

there is likely a larger problem at hand. It is the <u>parents</u>
[3]
responsibility to explain to children how behavior on television, while entertaining, is not an accurate reflection of normal behavior.

A lot of people criticize television for being too violent and sending teens a bad message. Heroes in television shows and movies often carry guns and defeat villains in grand, stylish fashion. Critics say that this leads teens to think of heroes as risk-taking, invincible, <u>gun-toting rebels; rather than</u>
[4]
as real role models who do real things. I do not think that this

1. A. NO CHANGE
    B. they ought to be.
    C. they are.
    D. it could be.

2. F. NO CHANGE
    G. between that which happens on television, and that which happens in real life.
    H. between what happens on television and what is acceptable in real life.
    J. between the television's happenings and those of real life acceptability.

3. A. NO CHANGE
    B. parent
    C. parents'
    D. parents' own personal

4. F. NO CHANGE
    G. gun-toting rebels rather, than
    H. gun-toting rebels, rather than
    J. gun-toting rebels rather than,

is the case. <u>Most kids I know are well aware of the line</u>
₅

<u>between entertainment and reality, and do not act out any</u>
₅

<u>violent behaviors found on television</u>. The very point of
₅

television shows <u>are</u> to have an escape from reality, such that
₆

one can think about different situations and give one's mind a

well-deserved break.

    It is true that many characters on television tell lies,

deceive, betray, and do not have <u>the morals that are good.</u>
₇

Usually, <u>meanwhile,</u> things do not work out well for these
₈

characters. Viewers get the positive message that, while one

can deceive for a time, it is always a bad move <u>when all the</u>
₉

<u>chips are counted.</u> Furthermore, these characters are usually
₉

not happy people. ⬚10

5. Which of the following sentences would
provide the best supporting evidence for the
author's claim that television is not
responsible for kids' violent actions?

  A. NO CHANGE
  B. I have a lot of evidence along this line.
  C. My best friend is the only one with
whom I talk about television violence,
and he agrees it is harmless.
  D. There has been a great deal of debate
over the role of television violence in
the lives of adolescents.

6. **F.** NO CHANGE
  G. was
  H. is
  J. being

7. **A.** NO CHANGE
  B. the good morality.
  C. good morals.
  D. morals, values, and principles.

8. **F.** NO CHANGE
  G. moreover
  H. yet
  J. however

9. **A.** NO CHANGE
  B. when everyone has written their scores.
  C. in the end.
  D. when things get started.

10. Which of the following sentences would
provide the smoothest transition from this
paragraph to the next paragraph?

  F. Therefore, the people who criticize
television violence are wrong on many
different levels.
  G. I have seen instances, however, where
the evil character does win in the end.
  H. Most discussions about television
violence do not involve real issues, but
only ones made up by detractors.
  J. Teen shows do not support the actions
of these characters, and people who
criticize these shows need to be aware
of this.

People who blame television <u>with</u> problems with teen
¹¹
attitudes need to take a look in the mirror. It is important to

have good values, <u>but</u> it is even more important to be able to
¹²

evaluate whether actions are <u>good – or bad,</u> real or unreal, in
¹³
an open-minded way.

[14] One should view these things as what they are and

take home the message that one should not engage in these

behaviors oneself because the outcomes are usually bad. I

favor self-responsibility, not censorship.

11. **A.** NO CHANGE
    B. on
    C. for
    D. to

12. **F.** NO CHANGE
    G. while
    H. as
    J. because

13. **A.** NO CHANGE
    B. good, or bad,
    C. good or bad,
    D. good or bad

14. Which of the following statements, if
    inserted here, would state the author's
    opinion on how people should approach
    television violence?

    F. Television is a good source of values
    and opinions, and people should accept
    it without reservations.

    G. One should not shut oneself from
    television because unseemly things
    happen in the shows.

    H. People who do not like television
    should never watch it or change their
    opinion about it.

    J. People who are not open-minded about
    television need to be more open-minded
    about it.

> Question 15 asks about the preceding
> passage as a whole.

15. Suppose the writer had been asked to write
    an essay on the <u>validity of arguments</u> about
    the bad effect of television violence on
    adolescents. Does this essay successfully
    address this topic?

    A. Yes, because the author examines and
    refutes several key points made by
    critics of television violence.

    B. Yes, because violence on television is
    mentioned at numerous junctions
    throughout the essay.

    C. No, because the author spends too much
    time addressing the opposing position,
    and does not adequately define his own.

    D. No, because the essay also discusses the
    parents' role in evaluating and
    discussing violence on television.

PASSAGE X

Tigers: Misunderstood Cats

The tiger is the <u>larger</u> of the cat family. Tigers have large,
                    1
muscular bodies, large paws, and very sharp claws.

Furthermore, like cats, <u>tigers stalk their prey, creeping through</u>
                                      2
<u>cover to within ten or so meters</u> and then jumping on prey in a
          2
sudden attack. Thus, the tiger has a reputation for being a

fierce, clever predator, ready to <u>jump on</u> an unsuspecting
                                        3
animal or human at any moment. <u>The tiger, however, is</u>
                                              4
<u>somewhat misunderstood: tigers rarely attack humans, and the</u>
          4
<u>ones that do are usually wounded or weak with old age.</u>
                                4

During the day, the tiger tends to rest either in the shade

or in a quiet pool of water – surprisingly to most people, tigers

are excellent swimmers. The tiger keeps a number of dens

throughout its "territory," such that <u>they have</u> numerous
                                              5
resting places. <u>Dens, in caves or other cavities, are usually</u>
                        6
<u>constructed beneath fallen trees or rocks or thickets.</u>
                        6

1. **A.** NO CHANGE
    B. most large
    C. largest
    D. most larger

2. **F.** NO CHANGE
    G. tigers stalk their prey; creeping through
        cover to within ten meters or so
    H. tigers are creeping through cover as
        they stalk their prey for ten meters or so
    J. tigers, while stalking their prey, are
        creeping through cover to within ten or
        so meters

3. Which of the following would NOT be an
    acceptable alternative to the underlined
    portion?

    A. pounce on
    B. leap on
    C. fixate on
    D. ambush

4. The writer is considering deleting this
    sentence. If the writer were to do this, the
    essay would primarily lose:

    F. an explanation of how tigers are often
        misunderstood.
    G. a dramatic detail that arouses fear in the
        reader.
    H. a description of why it is that tigers are
        not dangerous at all.
    J. a digression away from the main topic –
        tigers – to tigers' relationship with
        humans, who are not the subject of the
        essay.

5. **A.** NO CHANGE
    B. there should be
    C. it has
    D. it will be able to have

6. **F.** NO CHANGE
    G. Dens are usually constructed beneath
        fallen trees or rocks, in thickets, or in
        caves or other cavities.
    H. Dens in caves or other cavities are
        usually constructed beneath fallen trees,
        rocks, or thickets.
    J. In caves and other cavities is where the
        dens beneath fallen trees, rocks, and
        thickets are usually constructed.

After she gives birth, the female tiger stays in the den with her young until the babies are mature enough to follow her on hunting trips, <u>happening</u> at the age of two months.
₇
Young tigers initially hunt with their mothers, but by the time the young tigers are a year old they can <u>successfully: hunt on their own.</u> By two or three years of age, they will always hunt
₈
on their own.

[1] <u>They</u> prey on wild cattle, wild goats, and domestic
₉
animals. [2] They will also eat berries and birds' eggs if food is scarce. ☐10☐ [3] Tigers sneak up on their prey, stalking them

through cover such as thickets or tall grass and then <u>pounces.</u> [4]
₁₁
The tiger can leap from six to ten meters in a single jump, but sometimes the tiger will creep as close as two or four meters. [5]

<u>After</u> making the kill, the tiger often drags its prey near water,
₁₂

7. A. NO CHANGE
    B. which happens
    C. that happens
    D. which are happening

8. F. NO CHANGE
    G. successfully be hunting on their own.
    H. successfully hunt, on their own.
    J. successfully hunt on their own.

9. Which of the following provides the most specific transition to the next paragraph?

    A. The tigers' prey
    B. The youngest tigers
    C. Tigers
    D. Mother tigers

10. Which of the following sentences would provide the most specific transition to the discussion of the tiger's hunting strategy?

    F. Tigers prefer berries to live prey, but sometimes they like to hunt just for sport.
    G. The tiger is renowned for its ability to hunt its prey.
    H. Their superior hunting skill, however, usually allows them to find and capture food without too much trouble.
    J. The tiger is a feared predator that has inspired many legendary tales throughout human history.

11. A. NO CHANGE
    B. they pounce.
    C. pouncing.
    D. it pounces.

12. F. NO CHANGE
    G. Before
    H. In light of
    J. In regards to

such that it can eat and drink at the same time. [13]

13. The writer is considering adding the following sentence to the preceding paragraph:

> The same strategy can be seen when domestic cats hunt mice.

For the sake of logic and coherence, this sentence should be placed:

A. after Sentence 1.
B. after Sentence 2.
C. before Sentence 5.
D. at the end of the paragraph.

<u>Tigers can be only found in Asia.</u> They prefer to live in
14
dense jungles, or else the dense reeds and brush of riverbanks

<u>are good places for the tiger to reside.</u> Tigers do not, like some
15
people think, live in the African deserts.

Perhaps it is the many misconceptions about tigers that

make them such enchanting and haunting beasts.

14. F. NO CHANGE
G. Tigers' can only be found in Asia.
H. Tigers can only be found in Asia.
J. In Asia, that is where the only tigers can be found.

15. A. NO CHANGE
B. are the tigers preferred living locations.
C. are where the tiger is most comfortable living.
D. OMIT the underlined portion and end the sentence with a period.

SUMMIT
EDUCATIONAL
GROUP

Reading Overview

- ❏ The Reading Test

- ❏ Format

- ❏ Attractors

- ❏ Setting Your Goal

- ❏ Working Through the Reading Test

- ❏ General Tips

The Reading Test

❑ The ACT Reading Test measures your skills in reading, comprehending, and analyzing short passages. You've likely been practicing most of these skills on school assignments for years.

Format	40 questions Multiple-choice 4 answer choices
Content	Prose Fiction / Literary Narrative Social Science Humanities Natural Science

Scoring	Reading Test Score: 1-36
	Subscores:
	     Social Studies / Sciences: 1-18
	     Arts / Literature: 1-18

Time	35 minutes

❑ 4 single or paired passages with 10 questions each. You have roughly 8½ minutes to spend on each passage – about 4 minutes to read the passage and 30 seconds to answer each question.

Format

❏ The 4 Reading passages are always ordered by content type. Every ACT includes a Prose Fiction or Literary Narrative passage, a Social Science passage, a Humanities passage, and a Natural Science passage, in that order.

Each passage type requires different strategies.

❏ The instructions are the same on every ACT. Familiarize yourself with instructions before you take the test. At test time, you can skip the instructions and focus on the problems.

DIRECTIONS: There are four passages in this test. Each passage is followed by several questions. After reading a passage, choose the best answer to each question and fill in the corresponding oval on your answer document. You may refer to the passages as often as necessary.

Attractors

❑ Spot and avoid attractor answer choices.

The test writers predict potential mistakes by students and include those mistakes as answer choices. In other words, they set traps for the unsuspecting student. We call these answer choices "attractors." Attractors show up most often on medium and difficult problems.

Try to spot the attractor answer choices in the following problems.
Consider how a student might mistakenly choose each attractor answer.

NATURAL SCIENCE: This passage is adapted from "The Awful Power Beneath Us," an article by Joe Chandler.

As the world's first national park, Yellowstone has long been admired for its natural beauty and unique geology. In Yellowstone, the ground rumbles and geysers
5 erupt with such regularity that visitors have been lulled into seeing these seismic events as harmless spectacles. Unknown to many is that the same phenomenon that creates the Hawaiian Islands also powers this
10 geothermal activity. For millions of years, a "hotspot" in the Earth's molten core has pushed magma up under the land of Yellowstone. Beneath the park lies a thousand cubic miles of magma, more than a
15 quadrillion (1 with 15 zeroes) gallons of molten rock. This immense magma chamber is known as a caldera, and it can be thought of as an engine of heat which powers the many hot springs and other wonders, such as
20 the famous Old Faithful. A thin layer of earth lays over the caldera, sealing the incredible heat and creating an immense pressure. Eventually, this engine will generate too much energy to be contained by the earth
25 above it, and the entire area will erupt.

It will go like this: The massive explosion will obliterate anything within 100 miles and will be supersonic, so the boom won't be heard until after the destruction.
30 Lava will be flung out, starting countless fires. The states of Oregon, Idaho, Wyoming, Utah, Nevada, and Montana will be forfeit. Ash plumes will rise miles high, as twelve trillion cubic tons of dust rise from
35 Yellowstone and spread across the western half of America. A new cold will come, because the sun won't have the strength to penetrate the ashen clouds. Across the entire planet, average temperatures will drop by 20
40 degrees Fahrenheit. As the Yellowstone caldera is emptied, the land will break and collapse, creating violent earthquakes. Sound farfetched? This has happened before. 74,000 years ago, the eruption of the Toba caldera in
45 Indonesia created a global winter that nearly brought the extinction of all mankind.

We often take for granted that our planet has been, of recent, relatively peaceful. The terrible potential that lies is Yellowstone's
50 future is testament to the awe-inspiring power that has always rested beneath our feet.

1. As it is used in line 32, the word *forfeit* most
    nearly means:

    A. disappointed
    B. resigned
    C. folded
    D. ruined

2. The main function of the first paragraph is to:

    F. contrast the geography of Yellowstone with
        that of Hawaii.
    G. describe the historical eruptions that have
        occurred in Yellowstone.
    H. explain the geological features that will lead
        to a future eruption in Yellowstone.
    J. illustrate the destructive effects of a caldera
        eruption.

Setting Your Goal

❑ You receive 1 raw point for a correct answer. You lose nothing for incorrect answers. Your **raw score** is calculated by adding up raw points. Your raw score is then converted to a **scaled score** from 1-36.

❑ You don't have to get every question right to score well.

To score a 22 on the Reading Test – which is above the national average – you need to answer only 23 of the 40 questions correctly. That's only 58%, or just over half of the questions! On your regular school tests, 58% is a failing grade, but on the ACT, it's above average!

❑ Use the table below to set a target for the number of questions you need to answer correctly to hit your goal score for the Reading Test.

Reading Scaled Score	Reading Raw Score	Percent Correct
36	39-40	98%
35	38	95%
34	37	93%
33	36	90%
32	35	88%
31	34	85%
30	33	83%
29	32	80%
28	31	78%
27	30	75%
26	29	73%
25	27-28	68%
24	26	65%
23	25	63%
22	23-24	58%
21	22	55%
20	20-21	50%
19	19	48%
18	18	45%
17	17	43%
16	16	40%
15	15	38%
14	13-14	33%
13	12	30%
12	10-11	25%

❑ For most students, attempting every problem on the ACT will prevent them from scoring to their potential. Solving every question means you'll have to rush, which means you're more likely to make careless mistakes.

Having a realistic goal makes the test more manageable. With less pressure to answer every question, you can spend more time on easy and medium problems and less time on the difficult ones.

Remember, you get one raw point for each question, whether it's the simplest question or the hardest question. Whether it takes you ten seconds or three minutes, it's still one point.

❑ Create a Plan of Attack for the Reading Test.

Using your goal score and the score table, complete the Plan of Attack below. This will help you determine your best pace while working through the test.

Most of your time and energy should be spent on the questions needed to achieve your goal score. Assume that you will likely miss some of the questions you attempt, and use educated guessing on the rest.

Reading Test Plan of Attack

My overall ACT Goal: _____

My Reading Test Goal: _____

How many questions do I need to answer correctly (raw score)? _____

How many questions should I attempt? _____

> Questions you "attempt" are those that you give time and energy to solve. You should still use educated guessing to quickly answer the rest of the questions.

Working Through the Reading Test

❑ Focus on one passage at a time. Answer all of the questions to a passage before you move onto the next.

❑ Don't read the questions before you read the passage.

In order to move quickly through the Reading Test, you must efficiently solve the questions, which takes up most of your time. You will only be able to solve these questions with speed and confidence if you have thoroughly read the passage first. Resist the urge to rush ahead; the time spent reading the passages will pay off in the end!

❑ Don't skim the passage.

The Reading questions on the ACT require a strong understanding of the passage. A brief look at the passage won't be enough to solve the questions with accuracy and speed.

General Tips

❑ You will learn to move more quickly through the Reading passages by improving your approach to reading and learning how to attack the questions. Plenty of practice will help you read faster on the test without sacrificing comprehension. Work on improving your reading speed before the test.

❑ Don't worry if you're unfamiliar with the subject of a passage.

All the information you need about a subject will be contained within the passage. Questions are based strictly on the information provided in the reading, so don't allow prior knowledge to affect the way you answer them.

❑ Simplify complex or dense passages by paraphrasing.

SUMMIT
EDUCATIONAL
GROUP

Reading

- ❏ Active Reading

- ❏ Paired Passages

- ❏ Passage Types

  - o Literary Narrative or Prose Fiction
  - o Social Science
  - o Humanities
  - o Natural Science

- ❏ Answering Questions

- ❏ Anticipating the Answer

- ❏ Question Types

  - o Detail
  - o Generalization and Main Idea
  - o Comparative Relationships
  - o Cause-Effect
  - o Voice and Method
  - o Contextual Meaning
  - o Inference

Active Reading

❑ We do not recommend speed-reading, nor do we recommend reading the questions first. It is difficult enough to understand an ACT passage without trying to keep all the questions in your head at the same time!

❑ **Stay engaged**. Do not read passively, waiting for the passage to reveal information to you. Instead, interact directly with the passage and think about what the author saying and trying to accomplish.

   Never expect a passage to interest or entertain you. It's your job to get involved.

❑ **Map the Passage**. Use your Active Reading skills to develop an organized understanding of a Reading passage by finding the main idea of each paragraph.

   Each paragraph generally develops a thought, example, detail, or point. By finding the main idea in each paragraph, you can create an organized map of how the passage works and how the overall main idea is developed.

   In addition to helping you organize the information of the passage, Mapping also ensures that you do not lose focus or read through the whole passage without understanding it.

❑ Read with your pencil. Make notes that help you understand the reading. You can underline important words and phrases, mark where there are contrasting ideas, note where you have questions or confusion, and jot down ideas.

   Use a question mark to identify any part of the passage you don't understand. Often, when you read further, you will find additional information that clarifies the parts that had confused you before.

❑ Ask questions while you read:

   • What is the main point of each paragraph? Underline it, or make a note in the margin.

   • How does each paragraph fit into the development of the passage? What does each paragraph accomplish?

   • What is the main idea of the passage as a whole?

   • What is the author's purpose in writing this passage?

   • What is the author's tone/attitude? Look for strong verbs and adjectives.

TRY IT OUT

Map the passage and answer the following questions.

NATURAL SCIENCES: This passage is adapted from "A Sense of Scale" by Erin Bracken.

Despite what you may see in the movies, the natural world contains no giant gorillas or miniscule people. This is because the real world depends upon several guiding rules, one of which is the limit of
5 scaling, or the size of an organism. In all living things, there is a balance between surface area and volume which governs the maximum and minimum size of organisms.

A popular theme in monster movies is to pick a
10 creature (lizard, human, spider, etc.) and make it absurdly large. However, this trend in Hollywood shows a blatant ignorance of organic biology. The issue can be easily explained in terms of geometry: as size increases, area is squared and volume is cubed.
15 This leads to several issues with scaling. For example, if the dimensions of an organism are made 10 times larger, it gains 100 times more surface area for its lungs, but its body mass increases by 1000 times. Therefore, the organism won't be able to absorb
20 enough oxygen. Creatures such as King Kong would be too short of breath to put up much of a fight. Another consideration is that of muscle and bone. These materials gain strength based on thickness, or "lateral area," which also scales at a much lower rate
25 than volume. So, these giant creatures would be so weak they would be unable to move, and would likely break their bones from the pressure of their own weight.

On the other side of the scaling issue are animals
30 such as hummingbirds, which simply cannot get any smaller. Since volume scales more than surface area, smaller animals will have relatively large surface area compared to their size. As surface area is the amount of an organism that is exposed to the outside, these
35 small animals are more susceptible to the effects of environmental temperatures. For tiny animals, the line between health and starvation is a thin one— hummingbirds must eat more than their weight in food each day in order to maintain enough energy and
40 warmth to survive. For Hollywood, the world of shrunken organisms is also problematic. In films such as *Fantastic Voyage* and *Honey, I Shrunk the Kids*, people are miniaturized, more than a hundred times smaller. At one-hundredth normal size, a person loses
45 heat at a rate 10,000 times less, because of their decreased surface area. However, the mass of the body, which generates heat, has decreased by

1,000,000 times. Because of this, it would be a struggle to stay warm enough to stay alive.

50 As a biologist, I sometimes ignore these facts. It will only ruin movies for me, and others, to note that Godzilla's skin would burst from the pressure of his immense size, or that a shrunken human would require condensed molecules (making the person as dense as
55 the core of the sun). Sometimes, for the sake of entertainment, we must ignore the limits of reality to fully enjoy the wonders of imagination.

1. What is the main idea of the first paragraph?

2. What is the main idea of the second paragraph?

3. What is the main idea of the third paragraph?

4. What is the main idea of the last paragraph?

5. What is the main idea of the whole passage?

Simplify dense or complex passages by paraphrasing. Can you summarize lines 29-40 in your own words?

Paired Passages

❑ Sections of the Reading Test may contain two short passages that address the same or related topics.

The first few questions following the passages will relate to the first passage. Next will be several questions relating to the second passage. Finally, there will be several questions that address both passages.

❑ Paired passages are not longer than single passages, but they may be more complex than single passages because they require you to compare and contrast two viewpoints.

As you actively read the second passage, look for where the authors agree and disagree. This will prepare you for the later questions.

❑ Treat the paired passages as two separate passages.

1. Read the first passage and answer the questions for it.

2. Read the second passage and answer the questions for it.

3. Answer the questions that concern both passages.

PUT IT TOGETHER

SOCIAL SCIENCES: Passage A is adapted from the article "Both Sides of the Cowboy" by Mitchell Byrd. Passage B is adapted from the article "The End of A Western Romance" by Scott Rothberg.

Passage A by Mitchell Byrd

When I'm in New York but feeling nostalgic for Wyoming, I look for the Marlboro ads in the subway. What I'm craving to see are horseflesh, the glint of a spur, a line of distant mountains, brimming creeks—a
5　reminder of the ranchers and cowboys I rode with for eight years. But the men I behold in those posters, with their stern, humorless countenances, remind me of no one I knew there.

In our earnestness to romanticize the cowboy, we
10　overlook his true character. On a ranch, toughness has nothing to do with exhibitions of power. More often than not, circumstances—like the colt he's riding or an unexpected blizzard—subjugate him. It's not toughness but "toughing it out" that counts. In other
15　words, this macho cultural artifact is simply a man who possesses resilience, forbearance, and an instinct for survival.

The myth encompassing the cowboy is founded on an American fable about men: that a man's worth
20　is calibrated in relation to his physical courage. But the Westerner's courage is selfless, a form of compassion. What is required of him is an odd mix of physical vigor and maternalism. His function in the beef-raising industry is to birth and nurture calves and attend to
25　their mothers; his courage has less to do with facing danger than it does with acting on behalf of these creatures.

A rancher or cowboy is often thought of as a "man's man"—laconic, hard-drinking, inscrutable.
30　But in truth, he possesses many qualities which our society commonly considers feminine. There is almost no other type of personality in which the balancing act between male and female, masculinity and femininity, is more natural. A cowboy may be gruff and physically
35　fit, but he's an essentially androgynous being. Ranchers are midwives, nurturers, and conservationists all at once. What we've interpreted as toughness—weathered skin, callused hands, a squint in the eye, and a growl in the voice—only cloaks the
40　benevolence within. "Now don't go telling me these lambs are cute," one rancher warned me the first day I walked into his lambing sheds. The next thing I knew he was holding a lamb. "Ain't this little rat good-looking?"

Passage B by Scott Rothberg

45　When I first came West in 1948, I imagined, as did most simple-minded Easterners, that a cowboy was a type of hero. Like other such migrants, I could think of nothing more glorious than buying my own working cattle outfit and transforming myself into a
50　cowboy. It took me a long time to comprehend that there was something wrong with our most popular national fable—the cowboy and his cow.

I've been thinking about cows for many years, and I've grown more and more disgruntled with the whole
55　cattle business. There are too many cows. Almost everywhere you go in the American West, you find hordes of these ugly, stupid, stinking, fly-covered, disease-spreading brutes. They pollute our streams and rivers. They devastate our canyons, valleys, meadows,
60　and forests. They eat and destroy the native bluestems and bunch grasses, leaving behind jungles of thorns and weeds. They cause acres and acres of erosion, destabilizing the terrain. The damage cattle have done to Western lands is commonly called "overgrazing,"
65　but this label is too anemic. Most of the public lands in the West are what I call "cowburnt."

Western range beef is a miniscule item in the national beef economy. Most of our beef comes from Eastern and Midwestern states, where cattle need less
70　land and cattle herds do less ecological damage. But it is not a simple matter to argue that we should dispose of Western ranching. The cowboy myth obstructs us.

The beef industry's destruction of our Western lands is based on the old mythology of cowboys as
75　natural noblemen. I'd like to conclude with a few remarks about this most fanciful of American fairy tales. In truth, the cowboy is nothing more than a farm boy in funny boots and a comical hat. He is a herdsman who gets on a horse to do part of his work. He is a man
80　who strings barbed wire all over the range, drills wells and bulldozes out stock ponds, drives off elk and antelope and bighorn sheep, poisons coyotes and prairie dogs, and shoots eagles and bears and cougars. Then he leans back and grins at the TV cameras and
85　talks about how much he loves the American West.

Is a cowboy's work socially beneficial? No. Any public school teacher does more arduous, more perilous, and far more worthwhile work. The same thing applies to registered nurses and nurses' aides,
90　garbage collectors, and traffic cops. I have no dispute with cowboys as fellow humans. All I want to do is get their cows off federal lands. Let cattle ranchers find some harder way to make a living, as the rest of us have to do.

1. The narrator of Passage A describes the Westerner's courage as "selfless" (line 21) because:

    A. the cowboy puts the well-being of his herd first.
    B. the cowboy does not have enough strength to defend himself.
    C. although he feels pity for other creatures, the cowboy cannot express his own emotions.
    D. the cowboy is a loner, with no real ego, and cannot relate well to others.

2. The narrator of Passage A uses the word "androgynous" in line 35 to refer to how cowboys exhibit:

    F. endurance and physical courage.
    G. ruggedness and gentleness.
    H. interest in economic and political issues.
    J. patience and resilience.

3. The narrator uses the quotes in lines 40-44 to illustrate that:

    A. the cowboy's work is dirty and unglamorous.
    B. the cowboy distances himself emotionally from animals that will be slaughtered.
    C. the cowboy has to take on other jobs in the off-season.
    D. the cowboy's hardened manner belies his empathy for nature and its creatures.

4. The narrator of Passage A seems to believe that the popular misconception of the cowboy is based on a misunderstanding of:

    F. cattle ranching.
    G. mythology.
    H. masculinity.
    J. ecology.

5. In discussing the figure of the cowboy, the narrator of Passage A takes which of the following into account?

    A. The cowboy's historical function as the primary unit of labor in the economic development of the old West
    B. The cowboy's place as a mythological hero fulfilling the nation's dream of self-reliance and independence
    C. The cowboy's depiction as a rough-hewn, taciturn, unflinching exemplar
    D. The cowboy's stature as a brave adventurer who regularly risks his life for great profits

6. As it is used in line 48, the word "glorious" most nearly means:

    F. radiant.
    G. beautiful.
    H. famous.
    J. wonderful.

7. Which of the following would make the strongest point against the narrator's argument in lines 55-72?

    A. The problem of overgrazing calls for a hard look at the regulations governing federal land management.
    B. The reduced demand for beef in the national diet will probably lead to smaller herds of cattle.
    C. Western range beef has been decreasing in sales and employment for the past 10 years, and the general public does not seem to care.
    D. If more beef is grown with less damage in the Midwest and East, cattle are not the problem.

8. The phrase "leans back and grins" (line 84) conveys the author's opinion that cowboys are:

    F. uncivilized.
    G. hypocritical.
    H. ignorant.
    J. lighthearted.

9. Which of the following is true of both passages?

    A. Each uses details from the cowboy's everyday existence to reveal his human shortcomings.
    B. Each attempts to dispel the myth of the cowboy.
    C. Each contrasts the cowboy's treatment of cattle to his treatment of other animals.
    D. Each judges the cowboy on the basis of the social utility of his occupation.

10. Which of the following is a viewpoint from Passage A that the narrator of Passage B would be most likely to reject?

    F. Cowboys have an instinct for survival.
    G. Cowboys are both nurturers and conservationists.
    H. Cowboys are stern and humorless.
    J. Cowboys now play a trivial role in the beef industry.

Literary Narrative or Prose Fiction Passages

❏ The first passage in the Reading Test will be a Literary Narrative or Prose Fiction passage. This is typically an excerpt from a novel, short story, memoir, or personal essay.

❏ Pay attention to characters' relationships and feelings.

> For the few months we were friends, I thought Bill was the smartest man I'd ever known. He was nearly twice as old as me and had given me a job in his souvenir shop, though there were barely enough customers to keep him in business. The time I'd spent working with Bill wasn't extraordinary in any way, but we formed a bond. I spent most of my time watching the register or restocking. I helped build new shelves for the store, and Bill showed me how to use the power saws. His son, he told me, was a skilled carpenter. They weren't close, and Bill hadn't heard from him in years.
> Once, on a quiet day at the shop, I said to him, "Bill, if you had been my dad, I might have turned out alright."
> "Don't tell me that," he said, dragging his fingers through his balding hair. "Just let me sign your paychecks, and we'll leave it at that."

How does the narrator feel about Bill? _____

How does Bill feel about the narrator? _____

❏ Pay attention to figurative language.

Metaphors are common in dialogue. Characters often say something different from what they really mean. When you see quoted dialogue, consider whether the character implied a deeper meaning.

> My mother's parents are Pickfords, and they are as unlike my grandparents Hiddle as a donkey is unlike a pickle. Grandmother and Grandfather Pickford stand straight up, as if sturdy, steel poles ran down their backs. They wear starched, ironed clothing, and when they are shocked or surprised (which is often), they say, "Really? Is that so?" and their eyes open wide and their mouths turn down at the corners.

What is the general personality of the Pickfords? _____

What can you assume about the Hiddles' personalities? _____

_____

❏ Sometimes, these passages can't be divided into paragraphs as easily as other passage types, because ideas may shift quickly and dialogue can create many paragraph breaks. To use the Mapping the Passage strategy on a Literary Narrative or Prose Fiction passage, organize by scenes or shifts in idea.

Social Science Passages

❏ The second passage in the Reading Test will be a Social Science passage. This is typically a research-based essay analyzing a civilization, society, or culture.

Social Science topics include history, economics, archaeology, anthropology, sociology, political science, and education.

❏ Pay attention to comparisons, cause-effect relationships, and sequences of events.

❏ Find the main idea. Identify the topic and determine what point the author is making about that topic.

For most Social Science passage questions, it is not necessary to understand every word or even every sentence. As long as you can find the main idea of each paragraph, you should be able to answer most questions confidently.

In the late eighteenth century, new ideas in philosophy challenged the long-held concepts of human dignity in the Western world. Before this time, most people viewed themselves as powerless pieces dependent on larger governing machines. The influential writings of Prussian philosopher Immanuel Kant encouraged people to consider new, radical views on freedom and moral rights. In bold defense of individual liberty, Kant declared, "Man has his own inclinations and a natural will which, in his actions, by means of his free choice, he follows and directs. There can be nothing more dreadful than that the actions of one man should be subject to the will of another." With these ideas came a newfound desire for autonomy, and a growing wariness of the oppressive tyranny of monarchs emerged. The eighteenth-century revolutions of France and America indicate how the idea of individual self-governance moved the intellectual communities of the time.

Summarize the passage in your own words: _____

_____

_____

Humanities Passages

❏ The third passage in the Reading Test will be a Humanities passage. This is typically an essay discussing elements of art or literature.

Humanities topics include music, theater, architecture, film, and literary criticism. Many Humanities passages deal with the relationship between ideas, certain historical people, or events. Some Humanities passages are taken from personal essays or memoirs, so they may resemble Prose Fiction passages.

❏ Find the main idea and themes. Pay attention to the author's judgment or point of view on the topic.

Humanities passages are often challenging because they deal with abstract ideas. These passages may consider how the works of an artist can reveal his or her character, how culture and experience can shape a personality, how a piece of art can embody an entire social movement, etc. As long as you understand the central points of the passage, you should be able to answer most questions confidently.

> Among the mysterious roots of blues music, Robert Johnson is a man of legend. In a time when photographs and recordings were rare, Johnson left little behind. Most of what remains of Robert Johnson, aside from his few recorded songs, is a collection of stories. Accounts of Johnson describe him as shy and secretive. During his recording sessions, he was known to face a wall, with his back to the recording engineers. He was the archetypical blues man, secretive and somber, singing about life's difficulties and tragedies.
>
> At the core of Johnson's legendary persona is the odd development of his talents. For years, he had toured around the South without gaining fame. Little more than a poor vagrant, he would travel from town to town, carrying his guitar and trying to scrape together enough cash to stay alive. But then Johnson disappeared for a year, and he returned a changed man. His guitar-playing was suddenly so skillful and his singing was so soulful, people remarked he seemed possessed. A scandalous story began spreading, explaining his newfound talents. As the story goes, Johnson had been traveling and was waiting at a crossroad when the Devil walked up to him and offered him a deal: Johnson's soul in exchange for incredible musical talent. The story gained credence when Johnson died shortly after his rise to fame. Officially, he died from drinking a bottle of poisoned whiskey, supposedly from the jealous husband of a woman Johnson was seeing. However, some believe that he met his end when the Devil returned to collect his debt. His enduring fame can be attributed to his secrets as much as to his talent.

What is the main idea of the first paragraph? _____

_____

How does the lack of knowledge about Johnson contribute to his fame? _____

_____

Natural Science Passages

❑ The last passage in the Reading Test will be a Natural Science passage. This is typically an essay discussing scientific topics including biology, astronomy, geology, or physics.

❑ Pay attention to comparisons, cause-effect relationships, and sequences of events.

❑ The Natural Science passage is the most detail-oriented passage of the Reading Test, so note the key information that supports the passage's central points.

Natural Science passages commonly include technical language related to the topic. Don't worry if some of the vocabulary is unfamiliar. Often, important terms will be defined within the passage. Also, you only need to understand these technical words if they are referenced in a question. Generally, as long as you understand the main idea and the significance of major details, you should be able to answer most questions confidently.

> In 1911, researchers exploring ancient tombs in Egypt were shocked by the discovery of several iron beads. The beads themselves were not unusual, but they were dated 5,000 years old. This is 2,000 years before the onset of the Iron Age, when humans began mastering the art of ferrous metallurgy. Extracting iron from oxidized ore would require an oven that could reach incredibly high temperatures, and there is no evidence of the Egyptians having this technology. The beads presented a mystery: how did the Egyptians manage to utilize iron so early?
> Scientists analyzed the beads and discovered that they contained a nickel-rich iron alloy. This is not typical in smelted iron, but it is characteristic of another source of iron: meteorites. It seems that ancient Egyptian craftsmen used meteorites for metalsmithing. At the time, it would have been unlikely that the Egyptians understood the origins of these iron nuggets, which would have been easily spotted in the Egyptian sands. However, as later research of ancient societies has shown, meteoric iron was a treasured commodity. Before the advent of iron smelting, this metal was rarer than gold, making it very valuable. Now, we know that iron is one of the most common elements on the planet, and we have the necessary technology to extract it in mass quantities.

What is the main idea of the passage? _____

_____

What are the key details in the passage? _____

_____

Checkpoint Review

Time yourself as you work through the following passage. Try to complete the reading and answer the questions within 9 minutes.

SOCIAL SCIENCE: This passage is adapted from the essay "A History of Disease" by Jamie Flock.

In 2010, the world celebrated the 30th anniversary of smallpox eradication. Named for its telltale red spots, this virus was passed mainly through respiration; as an infected person coughed, sneezed, or talked, he
5 or she transmitted the illness to others in the vicinity. When introduced to those with no immunity, smallpox could decimate entire populations and leave survivors' bodies marked with deep, pitted scars.

It took mankind more than a millennium to rid the
10 world of this ailment. In that time, smallpox played a crucial role in human history. In particular, the virus had a large effect on European colonialism, as it was spread from explorers to native populations, such as the Aztecs, Incas, and Aborigines. It is even surmised
15 that, due to the pockmarks on his mummy, King Ramesses V of Egypt may have died of this illness in 1142 B.C. Even before there existed an established scientific method, people around the world noticed that those who survived this illness, while often marked by
20 vicious scars, never caught it again. In 430 B.C., Athenian historian Thucydides wrote of an outbreak in Greece: "The sick and the dying were tended by the pitying care of those who had recovered, because they knew the course of the disease and were themselves
25 free from apprehensions. For no one was ever attacked a second time, or not with a fatal result." This observation led to centuries of experimentation, with one main goal: to induce a less dangerous form of smallpox in order to induce immunity.

30 Early attempts to immunize were risky, as the virus samples used were often at full strength. In ancient China, physicians used a method called insufflation; a powder made from the scabs of healing smallpox was inhaled by healthy people. In India,
35 healthy people wore the clothes of infected persons in order to "protect themselves." In 17th century Europe, it was common practice for parents to purposefully expose their children to smallpox; sometimes, they would require healthy boys and girls to sleep next to an
40 infected person. Also, children would be sent to "buy the smallpox," a practice of visiting the home of a recovering patient to purchase crusts of bread, in the hope that the children would contract a mild case of the illness. Unfortunately, these methods could lead to full
45 infections, which were often fatal.

In the early 1700s, when smallpox was the leading cause of death in Europe, there were finally significant breakthroughs in smallpox prevention. People found that subcutaneous inoculation, achieved by inserting a
50 needle with viral material into a healthy patient's vein, was even less likely to cause a full-blown case of the sickness than other methods; most who underwent this treatment had a reaction at the infection site, but it did not spread to the entire body.

55 The most important discovery of that century, however, is attributed to English physician Edward Jenner. In 1796, Jenner treated a milkmaid who had contracted a virus on her hands. Called "cowpox," this affliction caused those who touched sores on an
60 infected cow to get smallpox-like marks on their hands. The milkmaid noted that peasants who caught cowpox never seemed to catch the more serious smallpox. Jenner, who had survived a traumatic immunization as a child, used this information to create the first
65 smallpox vaccination; he conducted his first trial by infecting his gardener's son with cowpox, then following with smallpox. Fortunately, the boy remained healthy even after several deliberate infections. While Jenner's vaccine was not perfect, the
70 cowpox virus was close enough to smallpox to offer a degree of immunity. He chose not to patent his discovery, in order to make it accessible to all. Vaccinations with cowpox became common practice around the world for hundreds of years and saved
75 millions of lives. The term "vaccination," including the Latin root *vacca*, or "cow," pays homage to the role that Jenner's discovery played in medical history.

In 1967, while the smallpox virus had been eliminated from the United States, it still existed in less
80 developed nations around the world, and so the World Health Organization (WHO) enacted a plan to rid the world of this affliction. Through selected vaccination and containment, the goal was reached in little more than a decade. In 1980, the WHO declared "the world
85 and its people" free from naturally-occurring smallpox. Today, the smallpox vaccination stands as a symbol of the crucial role of scientific research. The government of the United States does retain a stockpile of the virus, just in case; if smallpox were to somehow resurface,
90 naturally or through a bioterrorism attack, researchers would be able to make vaccinations to keep it at bay.

1. The main purpose of this passage is to:

    A. discuss the progression of smallpox infection in order to compare it to other diseases.
    B. highlight the efforts made by one scientist in order to demonstrate the process of the scientific method.
    C. describe one method of vaccination in order to help readers understand the challenges of treating illnesses.
    D. chronicle the impact of a disease and the development of a treatment in order to express the importance of medical research.

2. The author cites all of the following as methods used for smallpox immunization EXCEPT:

    F. inhalation of infected tissue.
    G. exposure to infected people.
    H. consumption of infected foods.
    J. infection with a similar disease.

3. As it is used in line 43, the word *contract* most nearly means:

    A. bargain.
    B. shrink.
    C. incur.
    D. spread.

4. The main purpose of the last paragraph is to:

    F. present a summary of the life of Edward Jenner.
    G. describe a typical example of how modern diseases are treated.
    H. show the lasting impact of smallpox vaccination.
    J. acknowledge that the complete elimination of any disease is impossible.

5. The function of the second paragraph (lines 9-29) in relation to the passage as a whole is to:

    A. use common examples to explain the technical language of vaccination research.
    B. explain why it took so long for an effective vaccine for smallpox to be developed.
    C. establish the historical impact of smallpox and the development of vaccination methods.
    D. emphasize the importance of using multiple methods when developing treatments.

6. The reference to the outbreak in Greece (lines 21-26) is used to illustrate the point made in the passage that:

    F. royalty and political figures were most susceptible to smallpox infection.
    G. diseases were poorly understood in ancient Greece.
    H. Europe had the greatest need for a treatment for smallpox.
    J. immunization was recognized long before an effective vaccine was developed.

7. The author characterizes the relationship between cowpox and smallpox as one that:

    A. represents the reliance of medical researchers on common traditions and myths.
    B. led to a new understanding of viruses and a breakthrough in vaccination research.
    C. demonstrates the danger of how viruses can evolve and render vaccines ineffective.
    D. is neither important to historians nor relevant to modern medical practices.

8. The passage indicates that, before the 1700s, attempts to develop immunity to smallpox were:

    F. potentially fatal because they might cause a dangerous infection with the disease.
    G. not organized well enough to be widely effective.
    H. major sources of revenue in large cities.
    J. highly effective, but unknown to medical researchers.

9. Which of the following questions is NOT answered by information given in the passage?

    A. Why was cowpox used to prevent smallpox?
    B. What makes smallpox infection potentially fatal?
    C. How can smallpox infection be prevented?
    D. How is smallpox infection spread?

10. The passage indicates that, compared to smallpox, cowpox is:

    F. more expensive to treat.
    G. more easily spread by infected people.
    H. more physically disfiguring to its victims.
    J. more survivable for infected people.

Answering the Questions

❑ Questions do not follow the order of the passage, nor do they progress from easy to difficult. In order to work strategically through the questions, you will have to use your knowledge of question types and your sense of which questions are more challenging.

❑ Tackle each passage's questions using the following three steps:

1. Attack the easy and medium questions first.

   After you've finished actively reading the passage, work through the set of questions, doing all of the questions that seem to be easy and medium in difficulty.

   Remember, you get one raw point for each question, whether it is simple or challenging, whether it takes you 10 seconds or 3 minutes.

2. Make a second pass through the questions to work on the problems you skipped and marked, focusing on the ones you think you are most likely to answer correctly.

   Do as many of these as you can. For some, you might be able to find the right answer. For others, you might be able to eliminate answer choices and make an educated guess.

   As you answer the other questions for the passage, you'll gather information that will often help you to answer the difficult questions you've skipped.

3. Guess on the remaining questions.

   Before you move on to the next passage, guess on any remaining questions. Even if you feel like you really don't know the answer, it will be easier to guess while you're still thinking about the passage.

❑ When a question refers to specific line numbers, read a few lines before and after the given lines to get the full context.

Line numbers point you to the general area where the correct answer is found. You will almost always need the context around those lines to get the correct answer.

Anticipating the Answer

❏ Understand the question before you look at the answer choices. Jumping too quickly into the answer choices is like relying on an inaccurate map to give you directions.

With practice, you'll learn to trust yourself and not be misled by wrong answers.

If necessary, practice by covering up the answer choices with your hand and answering the question without looking at the answer choices.

❏ Many of the questions on the ACT Reading Test have answer choices that seem correct but don't properly answer the question. If you try to solve Reading questions by testing which answer choices could be true, you will likely get stuck on several answer choices that all seem to work. This is not only frustrating, but also time-consuming. You will be able to work with more speed and confidence if you anticipate the answer before looking at the answer choices.

> We all, from time to time, accidentally push on the wrong side of a door while trying to open it or use a car's windshield wipers instead of the turn signal. As frustrating as this is, the problem in these cases often lies not with the user, but the design. A well-designed object's characteristics make its use self-evident. The function of a thing should be instinctive. For example, if a door has identical handles on the inside and the outside, it's impossible to tell at a glance whether to push or pull. Designers call flaws such as these "Human Factors" problems. The study of product usability is known as ergonomics, and it has been a crucial field of research throughout the last century.

The author uses the description of the door handles to make the point that:

Before you look at the answer choices, try to come up with your own answer for the question, based on the information in the passage.

Answer: _____

Look at the answer choices provided. Which is most similar to your own answer? _____

    A. humans are prone to errors because they do not follow instructions.
    B. many products look too similar, which makes it difficult for consumers to make choices.
    C. some problems are the fault of poor design rather than improper use.
    D. designers should look for unique ways to improve on traditional designs.

TRY IT OUT

Actively read the following passage. Answer the questions that follow using your own words.

NATURAL SCIENCE: This passage is adapted from the article "To Cavendish, and Back Again" by Jamey Q. Wels.

Many people enjoy finding a variety of apples in a market because they can find the exact variety that fits their desired taste and texture. However, this diversity is important for more than just consumer
5 choice; for most fruits, planters grow different crops in order to protect against disease. If one variety of apple is infected, farmers can reduce the effect and save their orchards by having plenty of other varieties that may be resistant to the disease. In this way, farmers can take
10 advantage of the genetic diversity of different varieties of a fruit. And yet, though we often see several varieties of most fruits, there is usually just one type of banana: the Cavendish. This banana variety, which we are so familiar with, is under threat of extinction,
15 and farmers are trying to determine how to save it.

The Cavendish is a man-made hybrid of other banana varieties. By cross-breeding different banana plants, agriculturists were able to create a banana that had the combined traits of other varieties. Though the
20 Cavendish, relative to other banana varieties, has little flavor and is easily bruised, it is desirable to farmers because of its resistance to certain diseases. Unfortunately, the half-breed Cavendish is also sterile. In order to grow more Cavendish trees, planters must
25 cut a shoot off the banana plant and place it in the correct soil. This means that all Cavendish are actually clones of each other, which is why these bananas always look so similar. This can be beneficial because it allows the banana industry to create predictable,
30 standardized shipments of the fruit, but it also creates a potentially enormous problem: any disease that can kill one banana can kill all of these bananas. While that may sound extreme, it has happened before.

Until the mid-1900s, the predominant banana in
35 America was the Gros Michel, nicknamed "Big Mike." This variety was soft, creamy, and fragrant. The flavor is described as being similar to the artificial banana flavoring found in some candies and puddings, which is much stronger and sweeter than the relatively
40 bland Cavendish. For many years, the Gros Michel was the predominant banana seen in all American markets, until the crop was almost entirely devastated. A fungus known as "Panama disease" infected the Gros Michel plants, and the banana-growers of the
45 world scrambled to find a variety of the banana that would be immune to this destructive disease. Thus, the Cavendish was chosen as the next main banana crop: not for its flavor or consistency, but for its hardiness.

Today, the Gros Michel is nearly extinct, and the
50 Cavendish faces a similar fate.

In recent years, a new strain of the Panama disease has surfaced, and it is threatening the banana industry. This new strain, unlike previous ones, can infect Cavendish plants. Farmers are now left with two
55 options: switch to a new variety of banana, or try to use genetic modification to create disease-resistant varieties. The banana industry has switched varieties before, and this may help avoid the new strain of the Panama disease, but it will likely be only a matter of
60 time until a new strain threatens crops again. Also, some banana-producers fear that consumers will not be interested in another banana variety. Unlike apples, which people often enjoy for their diversity, bananas are so similar that people expect them to always be the
65 same and may not be so willing to experiment with other varieties of banana. The best solution to preserve banana crops may be the use of modern science to engineer bananas that are genetically immune to all strains of the Panama disease.

70 Scientists are attempting to develop bananas that are both resistant to Panama disease and desirable to consumers. Researchers have experimented with putting the genes of other banana varieties into the Cavendish. There has been some success in creating
75 new disease-resistant varieties, but these transgenic specimens are far from perfect. By altering the genes, many attributes of the fruit change, and scientists have yet to create a variety of banana that is immune to Panama disease and also has qualities that make it
80 marketable: the right taste, pleasant consistency, thick skin to prevent bruises, and ideal ripening. There is no banana in nature that has all of these qualities, and it may take several years for geneticists to engineer one. There are also some worries that consumers will not
85 want bananas that they know have been genetically modified, but scientists believe that bananas are excellent candidates for genetic modification because, due to their sterility, bananas cannot spread any potential mutations.

90 While much of the banana industry fears the fall of the Cavendish, some agriculturists see greater opportunities through the potential benefits of genetic engineering. Rather than save the Cavendish, the Gros Michel could be revived. Since the only thing that was
95 keeping "Big Mike" off our supermarket shelves was its susceptibility to disease, we may now have the ability to genetically engineer a hardier variety that can replace the Cavendish.

1. In the context of the passage, it is most reasonable to infer that the phrase "not for its flavor or consistency" (line 48) means that:

    _____

    _____

    _____

2. The passage suggests that some banana farmers would rather strengthen the Gros Michel banana than the Cavendish because the Gros Michel is:

    _____

    _____

    _____

3. What does the passage offer as evidence that it is preferable to cultivate multiple varieties of a fruit?

    _____

    _____

    _____

4. As it is used in line 25, the term *shoot* most nearly means:

    _____

    _____

    _____

5. The main purpose of the second paragraph (lines 16-33) is to point out:

    _____

    _____

    _____

6. According to the passage, the qualities of the Gros Michel and the Cavendish bananas can be best described by which of the following statements?

    _____

    _____

    _____

7. It can be reasonably inferred from the passage that "consumers will not want bananas that they know have been genetically modified" (lines 84-86) because:

    _____

    _____

    _____

8. Which of the following questions does the passage NOT directly answer?

    _____

    _____

    _____

    Can you anticipate the answer to this question? What is the best way to solve this type of question?

PUT IT TOGETHER

For each question, find the answer choice that best matches your answer on the previous page.

NATURAL SCIENCE: This passage is adapted from the article "To Cavendish, and Back Again" by Jamey Q. Wels.

Many people enjoy finding a variety of apples in a market because they can find the exact variety that fits their desired taste and texture. However, this diversity is important for more than just consumer
5   choice; for most fruits, planters grow different crops in order to protect against disease. If one variety of apple is infected, farmers can reduce the effect and save their orchards by having plenty of other varieties that may be resistant to the disease. In this way, farmers can take
10   advantage of the genetic diversity of different varieties of a fruit. And yet, though we often see several varieties of most fruits, there is usually just one type of banana: the Cavendish. This banana variety, which we are so familiar with, is under threat of extinction,
15   and farmers are trying to determine how to save it.

The Cavendish is a man-made hybrid of other banana varieties. By cross-breeding different banana plants, agriculturists were able to create a banana that had the combined traits of other varieties. Though the
20   Cavendish, relative to other banana varieties, has little flavor and is easily bruised, it is desirable to farmers because of its resistance to certain diseases. Unfortunately, the half-breed Cavendish is also sterile. In order to grow more Cavendish trees, planters must
25   cut a shoot off the banana plant and place it in the correct soil. This means that all Cavendish are actually clones of each other, which is why these bananas always look so similar. This can be beneficial because it allows the banana industry to create predictable,
30   standardized shipments of the fruit, but it also creates a potentially enormous problem: any disease that can kill one banana can kill all of these bananas. While that may sound extreme, it has happened before.

Until the mid-1900s, the predominant banana in
35   America was the Gros Michel, nicknamed "Big Mike." This variety was soft, creamy, and fragrant. The flavor is described as being similar to the artificial banana flavoring found in some candies and puddings, which is much stronger and sweeter than the relatively
40   bland Cavendish. For many years, the Gros Michel was the predominant banana seen in all American markets, until the crop was almost entirely devastated. A fungus known as "Panama disease" infected the Gros Michel plants, and the banana-growers of the
45   world scrambled to find a variety of the banana that would be immune to this destructive disease. Thus, the Cavendish was chosen as the next main banana crop: not for its flavor or consistency, but for its hardiness.

Today, the Gros Michel is nearly extinct, and the
50   Cavendish faces a similar fate.

In recent years, a new strain of the Panama disease has surfaced, and it is threatening the banana industry. This new strain, unlike previous ones, can infect Cavendish plants. Farmers are now left with two
55   options: switch to a new variety of banana, or try to use genetic modification to create disease-resistant varieties. The banana industry has switched varieties before, and this may help avoid the new strain of the Panama disease, but it will likely be only a matter of
60   time until a new strain threatens crops again. Also, some banana-producers fear that consumers will not be interested in another banana variety. Unlike apples, which people often enjoy for their diversity, bananas are so similar that people expect them to always be the
65   same and may not be so willing to experiment with other varieties of banana. The best solution to preserve banana crops may be the use of modern science to engineer bananas that are genetically immune to all strains of the Panama disease.

70   Scientists are attempting to develop bananas that are both resistant to Panama disease and desirable to consumers. Researchers have experimented with putting the genes of other banana varieties into the Cavendish. There has been some success in creating
75   new disease-resistant varieties, but these transgenic specimens are far from perfect. By altering the genes, many attributes of the fruit change, and scientists have yet to create a variety of banana that is immune to Panama disease and also has qualities that make it
80   marketable: the right taste, pleasant consistency, thick skin to prevent bruises, and ideal ripening. There is no banana in nature that has all of these qualities, and it may take several years for geneticists to engineer one. There are also some worries that consumers will not
85   want bananas that they know have been genetically modified, but scientists believe that bananas are excellent candidates for genetic modification because, due to their sterility, bananas cannot spread any potential mutations.

90   While much of the banana industry fears the fall of the Cavendish, some agriculturists see greater opportunities through the potential benefits of genetic engineering. Rather than save the Cavendish, the Gros Michel could be revived. Since the only thing that was
95   keeping "Big Mike" off our supermarket shelves was its susceptibility to disease, we may now have the ability to genetically engineer a hardier variety that can replace the Cavendish.

1. In the context of the passage, it is most reasonable to infer that the phrase "not for its flavor or consistency" (line 48) means that:

   A. the Cavendish variety is inferior to other varieties in several ways.
   B. the Gros Michel was the most flavorful of all banana varieties.
   C. Cavendish trees are sterile and cannot reproduce without assistance from planters.
   D. scientists cannot genetically improve the flavor or consistency of the Cavendish banana.

2. The passage suggests that some banana farmers would rather strengthen the Gros Michel banana than the Cavendish because the Gros Michel is:

   F. hardier.
   G. more flavorful.
   H. not sterile, and therefore easier to reproduce.
   J. a cross-bred variety.

3. What evidence does the passage offer that it is preferable to cultivate multiple varieties of a fruit?

   A. Producers appreciate the reliability from standardization.
   B. Consumers do not want to bother with having to choose from many options.
   C. Different varieties of fruit have different susceptibilities to diseases.
   D. Some cultures prefer bananas that are relatively firm and sour.

4. As it is used in line 25, the term *shoot* most nearly means:

   F. fire.
   G. sprout.
   H. gutter.
   J. stream.

5. The main purpose of the second paragraph (lines 16-33) is to point out:

   A. the strengths and potential weaknesses of the Cavendish banana.
   B. the ethical dilemmas of biological cloning.
   C. the benefits of cultivating only a single variety of a fruit.
   D. the methods used to create the Cavendish banana.

6. According to the passage, the qualities of the Gros Michel and the Cavendish bananas can be best described by which of the following statements?

   F. The Cavendish is more flavorful but is more susceptible to disease than the Gros Michel.
   G. The Cavendish is blander but is more susceptible to disease than the Gros Michel.
   H. The Gros Michel is blander but is more susceptible to disease than the Cavendish.
   J. The Gros Michel is more flavorful but is more susceptible to disease than the Cavendish.

7. It can be reasonably inferred from the passage that "consumers will not want bananas that they know have been genetically modified" (lines 84-86) because:

   A. they are not interested in unfamiliar varieties of banana.
   B. it will likely be only a matter of time until a new strain of the Panama disease threatens crops again.
   C. they prefer banana varieties that are sterile.
   D. genetic modification can result in undesirable defects that can be passed down to later generations.

8. Which of the following questions does the passage NOT directly answer?

   F. How much of the Cavendish crop has been lost to the new strain of Panama disease?
   G. Why is the Gros Michel banana no longer seen in most American markets?
   H. What is the benefit of cultivating multiple varieties of a crop?
   J. What is the risk from genetically modifying plants such as bananas?

Process of Elimination

❑ Correct answers to Reading questions might not jump out at you. Often, you will have to eliminate answer choices. Wrong answers range from clearly wrong to almost right.

❑ Make sure that you've found the **best** answer, not just a good one. Reading questions, especially difficult ones, will usually contain at least one or two choices that are "almost right."

❑ Eliminate answer choices that:

- aren't relevant or true.

- might be true but don't answer the question asked.

- might be true but are too broad.

- might be true but are too narrow.

- are exactly the opposite of what is correct.

- address the wrong part of the passage.

- use words and phrases from the passage but do not answer the question correctly.

- are too extreme.

❑ Look for opposites.

If two answer choices are exact opposites, one of them is likely the correct answer.

❑ Be careful of answer choices that are only mostly correct.

Some answer choices will be almost perfect, but will have one detail or word that does not work. Do not choose an answer choice just because parts of it sound good.

❑ Be careful of incorrect names and facts.

Some answer choices will be almost correct—the right answer, but with the wrong name plugged in, or with the names swapped.

❑ Be on the lookout for answer choices that are designed to attract your attention away from the correct answer.

> In World War I, engineers realized that advancements in airplanes had neglected the safety and efficiency of pilots. Though planes had become faster, stronger, and more maneuverable, they were harder to fly. Therefore, throughout the war (and the next World War to follow), teams of researchers refined aircraft to be easier and safer to use. Controls were redesigned, displays were simplified, and cockpits were reorganized. This sparked a new mode of thought, considering man's interaction with tools and technology. Engineers began viewing the man-machine interface as a sort of conversation, in which the user inputs signals (such as moving a joystick or flipping a switch), and the machine offers a response (such as illuminating a light or activating a rotor).
>
> In the modern world, as technology becomes increasingly powerful and prevalent, there is an effort to ensure that tools are streamlined and simple to use. This may not seem overly important with something such as a vending machine, which only requires that the user provide payment and input the desired product. However, with a machine as robust as a smartphone, the user interface is carefully crafted so that the vast array of possible inputs does not overwhelm or confuse the user.

What does the statement about smartphones most strongly suggest about the "conversation" described in the first paragraph?

A. Over time, users have become much better at adapting to complicated controls.
B. If users become overwhelmed by their interaction with a tool, they should instead focus on using simpler tools.
C. All modern technologies are based on lessons learned from the failures of World War I.
D. The relationship between technology and user has become a critical consideration for modern devices.

Try to isolate the correct answer by eliminating the other answer choices. Explain how you can prove answers are incorrect.

A. _____

B. _____

C. _____

D. _____

❑ Using Process of Elimination doesn't mean you should rush through the question and immediately start reading answer choices. With each question, your first step should be to understand the question and to try to answer it before reading the answer choices.

PUT IT TOGETHER

LITERARY NARRATIVE: This passage is adapted from the short story "A Wake Awake" by Cynthia C. Washer.

We gathered in my great-grandmother's room. The women of the family, some apart for many years, had gossip and family stories to relate. Ancient springs squealed as they perched on the edges of my great-
5   grandmother's bed. Their voices echoed off the walls of the small room. I was silent, because it seemed most appropriate. Their talking made me uncomfortable, as if we were being rude, but logically there was no reason to quiet down. In the center of this chamber was
10   my old ancestor, as calm in her rest as a pearl within an oyster. Her skin seemed waxy and gray. I finally recognized how old she had been.

My great-grandmother had never looked like this before; at least, not in front of me. She had always
15   refused to be seen until she had made herself ready. For her, this meant ruby lipstick, darkened eyebrows, and rouge. In later years, I discovered that it also meant inserting her dentures, and that her little pillbox hats had become less of a fashion statement and more a
20   means to conceal thinning hair. I only ever saw her after all of her primping and grooming, so it had seemed that she had never aged during my lifetime. As a child, I had suspected that her heavy makeup was a natural part of her face.

25   There in the room with her body, I slouched against the doorway as the other women of the family retold stories about her. They joked about when my great-grandmother began to call all of the women of the family "Mami;" then they guessed at when they
30   first knew her memory was beginning to fail. I fiddled with the locket of my necklace and remembered the final time that my great-grandmother uttered my own name aloud; we had been in that same house, and she had taken off her gold necklace and pressed it into my
35   hand. It was a gift, she explained. I had struggled to open the locket, but it remained firmly clasped, like a startled clam. I asked her what was inside the golden pendant, and she smiled back at me. "My legacy. Can you keep it safe?" she asked. I nodded and put the
40   necklace on. That had been several years earlier, and I had worn it every day since.

She was a careful, reserved woman. I remembered bracing myself for embarrassment whenever we went out to eat with her. I knew, at some point, she would
45   herd all of the little containers of marmalade and coffee creamer, along with the sugar packets and straws, into a little hill, and then dump them hastily into her bag. In her kitchen, there was always a used teabag, graying from multiple steepings, hanging to

50   dry over the dish rack, keeping company with the clear plastic bags she had washed for reuse. She was reluctant to let anything go to waste. In the same way, it seemed to me, she held tightly onto her few prides.

I fondly remembered her moving expertly around
55   her kitchen. Her tools and ingredients were plain, but her food was always incredible. Her pantry was stocked with all manner of canned goods; pears in sticky syrup, cannellini beans, and, most importantly, the staple of all Italian-American matriarchs: stewed
60   tomatoes. I used to help her open the large cans and then watch her pour the tomatoes into her large cooking pot. At first, they would peek out timidly above the tomato juice, plump red frogs in a crimson pond. Somehow, with that culinary sorcery inherent to
65   grandmothers, her creaky hands would transform the simple ingredients into a delicious sauce. The secrets of her magic were closely guarded; when others asked for the recipe, they would quickly discover that she had intentionally omitted some mysterious essentials.
70   By doing this, she had protected her respected position among the members of our family.

My mother, aunts, great-aunts, and cousins shared these stories and more. Even as the lively conversation made their cheeks flushed and breath short, it only
75   served to make my great-grandmother's skin seem more colorless and her chest more still. And then, abruptly as twittering blackbirds, the flock of women abandoned their bedside perches and swooped into the kitchen, where they began preparing for dinner.

80   I felt the need to address my great-grandmother in some way, but did not know where to begin. I moved toward the casket, but I was stopped by an exposed nail extending from the doorway. It caught the chain of my necklace, and after a strangled yelp and brief
85   struggle, I saw the locket fall through my grasping fingers to the floorboards. The pendant had burst open. My frustration quickly turned to wonder as I examined the golden remains. In place of the expected family portraits, the locket held something far more precious.
90   In precise script, my great-grandmother had outlined the recipe for her famed marinara sauce, leaving no ingredient out of the mix. I read it in disbelief—here was the very secret that, for my whole life, relatives had been trying to uncover. Holding the treasured
95   scrap in my hands, I finally knew how to honor her. After reading the words one last time, I carefully tore the paper into tiny fragments. Carefully, I placed all of the pieces back into the locket, and smiled. Her legacy was now secure.

1. The passage can best be described as primarily:

   A. a narration of several events that have restored the bonds of a broken family.
   B. an attempt by a young woman to understand the peculiarities of her great-grandmother.
   C. a young woman's remembrance of and tribute to her great-grandmother.
   D. a dialogue between members of two generations of a family.

   Give reasons for eliminating incorrect answers.

   A. _____

   B. _____

   C. _____

   D. _____

2. It is reasonable to conclude from the events in the passage that the narrator tears apart the paper found in the locket because she:

   F. felt jealous of her great-grandmother's cooking skills.
   G. was trying to get more attention from her other relatives.
   H. needed a way to express her grief physically.
   J. wanted to protect her great-grandmother's secret.

3. The descriptions in lines 42-53 are examples of:

   A. the great-grandmother's thrifty nature.
   B. reasons why the narrator never enjoyed spending time with her great-grandmother.
   C. secrets that the family was not aware of until the great-grandmother's death.
   D. traditional meals the family enjoyed together.

   Before jumping to the answers, make sure you understand the question, and try to answer it without looking at the answer choices. Doing so will make it easier to use POE and to find the correct answer.

4. The narrator uses all of the following to characterize her great-grandmother EXCEPT:

   F. physical details.
   G. descriptions of the narrator's memories.
   H. references to how other family members describe her great-grandmother.
   J. comparisons between the narrator and her great-grandmother as a young woman.

5. The descriptions in the second paragraph (lines 13-24) and fifth paragraph (lines 54-71) depict the great-grandmother as someone who:

   A. is unwilling to reveal information about herself.
   B. prefers to be alone rather than to share time with her family.
   C. makes great efforts to be respected.
   D. frugally keeps and reuses things in order to save money.

   Give reasons for eliminating incorrect answers.

   A. _____

   B. _____

   C. _____

   D. _____

SUMMIT
EDUCATIONAL
GROUP

Detail Questions

❑ Detail questions ask about information that is directly presented in the passage.

Each passage has several detail questions. They are most frequently found in Natural Science and Social Sciences passages.

❑ Detail questions typically appear in the following forms:

The passage states that...
The author makes it clear that...
The narrator asserts that...

❑ Watch for rewording.

The correct answers to detail questions may be hard to find because they have been reworded. Pay attention to how information can be stated differently.

❑ Detail questions sometimes ask you to spot one detail that does **not** fulfill a certain description. These questions are easily identified because they contain the words "EXCEPT" or "NOT." These questions can be confusing, because they need to be solved in reverse.

Often, the exception that satisfies one of these questions is a detail that does appear in the passage but does not answer the question asked.

Keep in mind that these questions take longer to solve than most Reading questions.

❑ EXCEPT or NOT questions typically appear in the following forms:

The author cites all of the following EXCEPT...
Which of the following questions is NOT answered in the passage?

PUT IT TOGETHER

SOCIAL SCIENCE: This passage is adapted from the article "Living Long & Living Well?" by Donald Cutler.

Impatience is one characteristic of advancing old age. As a writer I have been looking ahead to deadlines my entire career, but there is now another deadline looming, all too aptly named, the one that Time's
5 winged chariot is heading for. I can never get enough done. There is not enough time to do everything that matters to me, and at the end of every day I always think of one more page I should have written or one more person I should have seen.

10 Old age has had a mixed press but (as so often in literature and in life) the negative side is more strongly emphasized than the positive. Shakespeare judged that "when age is in, the wit is out." Even Goethe, whose wit was never out, remarked that, far from bringing us
15 wisdom, the passing years make it hard for us to preserve what wisdom we may have acquired. In a restaurant the other day, I listened to a young woman speculating about "how miserable it must be to be old." I am here to tell you that I am old and I am not
20 miserable. Writers tend not to retire, though they may fade slowly away. I am still working; I still have my family and friends. I have no complaints about old age that are any worse than the complaints I had about every other age I lived through – from childhood on
25 upwards. They have each been difficult in their own particular way and each rewarding like no other.

What has happened to social conventions about aging? This question cannot be answered without comparing how things are today with how things were
30 before industrialization, when society was really no more than the family on a large scale, and the family straddled all ages. There was very little specialization by age and indeed people might not even know how old they were unless they were able to use a well-
35 known public event, such as a war or a coronation, for a reference point. As society has progressed to our highly organized modern world, people have been turned into numbers. The time a person has been on this earth is used to slot each of us into the general
40 chronology of society. People's birthdays have become rites of passage, allowing one to go to school, buy alcohol, marry, vote, and much else besides. People born at a particular time are expected to behave in important respects like other people born with the
45 stamp of that same year upon them. Parents introduce their children to these standards when they compare them with other children of the same age, noticing they are growing faster, walking earlier, or talking more. The adult world is also propped up by notions of age

50 and attainment, with timetables defining when a person may be considered "too old" to marry or begin a career. This all adds up to what I call "the cult of age-measurement," and these social conventions, I would argue, foster anxiety in most of us and inhibit our
55 ability to make the most of the time that is given to us.

I guess what I resent the most is the constant comparison our society makes between one age and another. We have a habit of thinking of people in terms of numbers. We insist on estimating whether someone
60 is happy on the basis of their age, as if people were happiest as infants. There should be a more intrinsic, more personal approach to deciding whether someone is happy that has more to do with how they live their lives, the work they do and the people they know and
65 love.

---

1. The author considers all the following examples of how society constrains people on the basis of age EXCEPT:

    A. Certain jobs are supposed to be held by people of certain ages.
    B. Parents are entirely responsible for imposing age restrictions on children.
    C. People are expected to behave in the same way as other people the same age.
    D. A person's accomplishments are often judged in relation to his or her age.

Generalization Questions

❑ Generalization questions ask you to make broad observations or summaries of information in the passage. Generalization is strongly related to the skill of paraphrasing.

These questions often ask you to evaluate a character's overall traits, or to restate, in simple terms, a complex idea or argument.

❑ Generalization questions typically appear in the following forms:

According the passage, _____ can best be described as...

Which best describes the structure of the passage?

The best summary of the third paragraph is...

Based on the passage, _____ can best be characterized as...

Which of the following best paraphrases the statement in lines _____?

The passage primarily focuses on...

PUT IT TOGETHER

SOCIAL SCIENCE: This passage is adapted from the article "Living Long & Living Well?" by Donald Cutler.

Impatience is one characteristic of advancing old age. As a writer I have been looking ahead to deadlines my entire career, but there is now another deadline looming, all too aptly named, the one that Time's winged chariot is heading for. I can never get enough done. There is not enough time to do everything that matters to me, and at the end of every day I always think of one more page I should have written or one more person I should have seen.

Old age has had a mixed press but (as so often in literature and in life) the negative side is more strongly emphasized than the positive. Shakespeare judged that "when age is in, the wit is out." Even Goethe, whose wit was never out, remarked that, far from bringing us wisdom, the passing years make it hard for us to preserve what wisdom we may have acquired. In a restaurant the other day, I listened to a young woman speculating about "how miserable it must be to be old." I am here to tell you that I am old and I am not miserable. Writers tend not to retire, though they may fade slowly away. I am still working; I still have my family and friends. I have no complaints about old age that are any worse than the complaints I had about every other age I lived through – from childhood on upwards. They have each been difficult in their own particular way and each rewarding like no other.

What has happened to social conventions about aging? This question cannot be answered without comparing how things are today with how things were before industrialization, when society was really no more than the family on a large scale, and the family straddled all ages. There was very little specialization by age and indeed people might not even know how old they were unless they were able to use a well-known public event, such as a war or a coronation, for a reference point. As society has progressed to our highly organized modern world, people have been turned into numbers. The time a person has been on this earth is used to slot each of us into the general chronology of society. People's birthdays have become rites of passage, allowing one to go to school, buy alcohol, marry, vote, and much else besides. People born at a particular time are expected to behave in important respects like other people born with the stamp of that same year upon them. Parents introduce their children to these standards when they compare them with other children of the same age, noticing they are growing faster, walking earlier, or talking more. The adult world is also propped up by notions of age and attainment, with timetables defining when a person may be considered "too old" to marry or begin a career. This all adds up to what I call "the cult of age-measurement," and these social conventions, I would argue, foster anxiety in most of us and inhibit our ability to make the most of the time that is given to us.

I guess what I resent the most is the constant comparison our society makes between one age and another. We have a habit of thinking of people in terms of numbers. We insist on estimating whether someone is happy on the basis of their age, as if people were happiest as infants. There should be a more intrinsic, more personal approach to deciding whether someone is happy that has more to do with how they live their lives, the work they do and the people they know and love.

1. Which of the following statements best describes the approach the author takes to aging?

   A. He discusses it on the basis of his own experience and in relationship to social changes.
   B. He surveys the attitudes of specific people he knows.
   C. He examines its relationship to literary periods.
   D. He analyzes children's experiences in school.

2. In the passage, the author can best be characterized as someone who:

   F. wishes he could return to the simpler times of his youth.
   G. has grown too old to enjoy his many interests.
   H. is active and satisfied in his old age.
   J. regrets not making accomplishments at certain ages.

3. By his statement in lines 2-5, the author most nearly means:

   A. he is tired of the pressures of his career.
   B. he senses that he will not live much longer.
   C. he feels as if he is in a hopeless career.
   D. he has a history of procrastinating.

Main Idea Questions

❑ Main idea questions ask you to determine the author's focus or point in writing a particular paragraph or in the passage as a whole.

Through Mapping the Passage, you should already know or have found the main idea of each paragraph and the whole passage.

❑ Main idea questions typically appear in the following forms:

The main idea of the first paragraph is that...
Which of the following statements best expresses the main idea of the passage?
The passage primarily focuses on...
The main focus of the first two paragraphs is...

❑ Do not assume that the first paragraph will contain the main idea of the passage or that the first sentence will contain the main idea of a paragraph. Although you may have learned to write essays this way, not all authors will follow these guidelines.

❑ As you read through the possible answers for a main idea question, eliminate answer choices that:

• cover more than the passage does.

• talk about only a portion of the passage.

• have nothing to do with the topic.

• may sound plausible, but are not mentioned in the text.

Make sure that you focus on the correct part of the passage. Incorrect answers often seem correct when you consider a part of the passage that is different from the part referenced by the question.

PUT IT TOGETHER

SOCIAL SCIENCE: This passage is adapted from the article "Living Long & Living Well?" by Donald Cutler.

Impatience is one characteristic of advancing old age. As a writer I have been looking ahead to deadlines my entire career, but there is now another deadline looming, all too aptly named, the one that Time's
5 winged chariot is heading for. I can never get enough done. There is not enough time to do everything that matters to me, and at the end of every day I always think of one more page I should have written or one more person I should have seen.

10 Old age has had a mixed press but (as so often in literature and in life) the negative side is more strongly emphasized than the positive. Shakespeare judged that "when age is in, the wit is out." Even Goethe, whose wit was never out, remarked that, far from bringing us
15 wisdom, the passing years make it hard for us to preserve what wisdom we may have acquired. In a restaurant the other day, I listened to a young woman speculating about "how miserable it must be to be old." I am here to tell you that I am old and I am not
20 miserable. Writers tend not to retire, though they may fade slowly away. I am still working; I still have my family and friends. I have no complaints about old age that are any worse than the complaints I had about every other age I lived through – from childhood on
25 upwards. They have each been difficult in their own particular way and each rewarding like no other.

What has happened to social conventions about aging? This question cannot be answered without comparing how things are today with how things were
30 before industrialization, when society was really no more than the family on a large scale, and the family straddled all ages. There was very little specialization by age and indeed people might not even know how old they were unless they were able to use a well-
35 known public event, such as a war or a coronation, for a reference point. As society has progressed to our highly organized modern world, people have been turned into numbers. The time a person has been on this earth is used to slot each of us into the general
40 chronology of society. People's birthdays have become rites of passage, allowing one to go to school, buy alcohol, marry, vote, and much else besides. People born at a particular time are expected to behave in important respects like other people born with the
45 stamp of that same year upon them. Parents introduce their children to these standards when they compare them with other children of the same age, noticing they are growing faster, walking earlier, or talking more. The adult world is also propped up by notions of age

50 and attainment, with timetables defining when a person may be considered "too old" to marry or begin a career. This all adds up to what I call "the cult of age-measurement," and these social conventions, I would argue, foster anxiety in most of us and inhibit our
55 ability to make the most of the time that is given to us.

I guess what I resent the most is the constant comparison our society makes between one age and another. We have a habit of thinking of people in terms of numbers. We insist on estimating whether someone
60 is happy on the basis of their age, as if people were happiest as infants. There should be a more intrinsic, more personal approach to deciding whether someone is happy that has more to do with how they live their lives, the work they do and the people they know and
65 love.

1. Which of the following best expresses the main idea of the passage as a whole?

    A. A successful past is ultimately less satisfying than a hopeful future.
    B. Age is not as effective a measure of maturity as knowledge or compassion.
    C. Rather than judging people on how long they have lived, we should judge them on how well they live.
    D. As we grow older, we become wiser and therefore happier with life.

2. Which of the following best describes the main point of the second paragraph (lines 10-26)?

    F. Despite common criticisms, the author does not find old age to be particularly negative.
    G. The author has gone through many hardships in his life, but he tries to stay optimistic.
    H. The opinions of others are just as important as our own experiences.
    J. As we age, we have more opportunities for happiness because we have more rights.

Comparative Relationship Questions

❑ Comparative relationship questions ask you to judge the similarities or differences between subjects or ideas.

❑ Comparative relationship questions typically appear in the following forms:

The passage indicates that _____ differs from _____ in that...
In the second and third paragraphs, the author constructs a contrast between...
The author likens _____ to _____ because both...
Which of the following best describes the difference between _____ and _____?
In comparison to _____, the _____ seems...
Which of the following comparisons regarding _____ does the author make?

❑ In order to solve a comparative relationship question, you must first summarize or find the main ideas of portions of the passage.

Use your Mapping the Passage skills to identify the main idea of each of the paragraphs and note how they relate to each other.

❑ These questions typically appear in passages containing multiple characters, subjects, or points of view. As you read, note when you find opposing or conflicting ideas.

PUT IT TOGETHER

SOCIAL SCIENCE: This passage is adapted from the article "Living Long & Living Well?" by Donald Cutler.

Impatience is one characteristic of advancing old age. As a writer I have been looking ahead to deadlines my entire career, but there is now another deadline looming, all too aptly named, the one that Time's
5 winged chariot is heading for. I can never get enough done. There is not enough time to do everything that matters to me, and at the end of every day I always think of one more page I should have written or one more person I should have seen.

10 Old age has had a mixed press but (as so often in literature and in life) the negative side is more strongly emphasized than the positive. Shakespeare judged that "when age is in, the wit is out." Even Goethe, whose wit was never out, remarked that, far from bringing us
15 wisdom, the passing years make it hard for us to preserve what wisdom we may have acquired. In a restaurant the other day, I listened to a young woman speculating about "how miserable it must be to be old." I am here to tell you that I am old and I am not
20 miserable. Writers tend not to retire, though they may fade slowly away. I am still working; I still have my family and friends. I have no complaints about old age that are any worse than the complaints I had about every other age I lived through – from childhood on
25 upwards. They have each been difficult in their own particular way and each rewarding like no other.

What has happened to social conventions about aging? This question cannot be answered without comparing how things are today with how things were
30 before industrialization, when society was really no more than the family on a large scale, and the family straddled all ages. There was very little specialization by age and indeed people might not even know how old they were unless they were able to use a well-
35 known public event, such as a war or a coronation, for a reference point. As society has progressed to our highly organized modern world, people have been turned into numbers. The time a person has been on this earth is used to slot each of us into the general
40 chronology of society. People's birthdays have become rites of passage, allowing one to go to school, buy alcohol, marry, vote, and much else besides. People born at a particular time are expected to behave in important respects like other people born with the
45 stamp of that same year upon them. Parents introduce their children to these standards when they compare them with other children of the same age, noticing they are growing faster, walking earlier, or talking more. The adult world is also propped up by notions of age

50 and attainment, with timetables defining when a person may be considered "too old" to marry or begin a career. This all adds up to what I call "the cult of age-measurement," and these social conventions, I would argue, foster anxiety in most of us and inhibit our
55 ability to make the most of the time that is given to us.

I guess what I resent the most is the constant comparison our society makes between one age and another. We have a habit of thinking of people in terms of numbers. We insist on estimating whether someone
60 is happy on the basis of their age, as if people were happiest as infants. There should be a more intrinsic, more personal approach to deciding whether someone is happy that has more to do with how they live their lives, the work they do and the people they know and
65 love.

1. The distinction the author makes between modern society and pre-industrial society is that:

   A. modern society makes elderly people feel more impatient.
   B. modern society imposes more limits based on age.
   C. pre-industrial society was more organized.
   D. pre-industrial society made people feel more socially separated.

2. The narrator suggests that his life as a younger man, as compared to his current life, was:

   F. more satisfying and enjoyable.
   G. less satisfying and enjoyable.
   H. more socially complicated.
   J. not better or worse overall.

Cause-Effect Questions

❏ Cause-effect questions ask you to identify how one event leads to another.

These are most common in Prose Fiction and Natural Science passages, where you will be asked to identify the result of a character's actions or the outcome of a scientific process.

❏ Cause-effect questions typically appear in the following forms:

According to the passage, the cause of _____ is attributed to...
The author cites which of the following as a cause of _____?
The author mentions that _____ would be caused by each of the following EXCEPT...
According to the author, _____ is a response to...
The passage suggests that the results of _____ were...

❏ A simple cause-effect question will only require a basic understanding of events described in the passage. However, some cause-effect questions are more challenging because they require you to make assumptions based on limited explanations in the passage.

❏ Some cause-effect questions ask you to determine the order of a sequence of events.

These questions are more easily solved if you have effectively used the Mapping the Passage strategy.

PUT IT TOGETHER

SOCIAL SCIENCE: This passage is adapted from the article "Living Long & Living Well?" by Donald Cutler.

Impatience is one characteristic of advancing old age. As a writer I have been looking ahead to deadlines my entire career, but there is now another deadline looming, all too aptly named, the one that Time's
5 winged chariot is heading for. I can never get enough done. There is not enough time to do everything that matters to me, and at the end of every day I always think of one more page I should have written or one more person I should have seen.

10 Old age has had a mixed press but (as so often in literature and in life) the negative side is more strongly emphasized than the positive. Shakespeare judged that "when age is in, the wit is out." Even Goethe, whose wit was never out, remarked that, far from bringing us
15 wisdom, the passing years make it hard for us to preserve what wisdom we may have acquired. In a restaurant the other day, I listened to a young woman speculating about "how miserable it must be to be old." I am here to tell you that I am old and I am not
20 miserable. Writers tend not to retire, though they may fade slowly away. I am still working; I still have my family and friends. I have no complaints about old age that are any worse than the complaints I had about every other age I lived through – from childhood on
25 upwards. They have each been difficult in their own particular way and each rewarding like no other.

What has happened to social conventions about aging? This question cannot be answered without comparing how things are today with how things were
30 before industrialization, when society was really no more than the family on a large scale, and the family straddled all ages. There was very little specialization by age and indeed people might not even know how old they were unless they were able to use a well-
35 known public event, such as a war or a coronation, for a reference point. As society has progressed to our highly organized modern world, people have been turned into numbers. The time a person has been on this earth is used to slot each of us into the general
40 chronology of society. People's birthdays have become rites of passage, allowing one to go to school, buy alcohol, marry, vote, and much else besides. People born at a particular time are expected to behave in important respects like other people born with the
45 stamp of that same year upon them. Parents introduce their children to these standards when they compare them with other children of the same age, noticing they are growing faster, walking earlier, or talking more. The adult world is also propped up by notions of age

50 and attainment, with timetables defining when a person may be considered "too old" to marry or begin a career. This all adds up to what I call "the cult of age-measurement," and these social conventions, I would argue, foster anxiety in most of us and inhibit our
55 ability to make the most of the time that is given to us.

I guess what I resent the most is the constant comparison our society makes between one age and another. We have a habit of thinking of people in terms of numbers. We insist on estimating whether someone
60 is happy on the basis of their age, as if people were happiest as infants. There should be a more intrinsic, more personal approach to deciding whether someone is happy that has more to do with how they live their lives, the work they do and the people they know and
65 love.

1. According to the passage, Shakespeare and Goethe both believed that old age caused:

   A. a weakening of mental abilities.
   B. increased anxiety due to the fear of death.
   C. greater wisdom of the world and oneself.
   D. greater bonds between family members.

2. The passage suggests that the anxiety caused by "the cult of age-measurement" is a result of:

   F. the loss of traditional, family-based cultures.
   G. social pressures to be different from everyone around us.
   H. increased levels of organization in modern society.
   J. outdated opinions expressed by classic artists.

> Where does the author mention "the cult of age-measurement"?

Voice Questions

❑ Voice questions appear in two major types: those concerned with the tone of the passage and those concerned with the author's point of view.

❑ For voice questions that ask you to make broad observations about the mood, atmosphere, or attitude of a passage, pay attention to word usage. Strong adjectives and verbs are good clues for identifying tone.

These kinds of voice questions typically appear in the following forms:

The passage's tone is best described as one of...
The author's overall tone can best be described as...
Which of the following best characterizes the author's attitude toward _____?
In terms of mood, which of the following best describes lines _____?

These questions are similar to generalization questions because both require you to make a sweeping statement about a passage.

❑ For voice questions that ask you to consider the perspective of the author, it often helps to determine whether the author has a positive or negative attitude toward the subject. Some questions will require you to determine the author's level of familiarity or expertise with the subject.

These kinds of voice questions typically appear in the following forms:

The point of view from which the passage is told is best described as that of...
Which of the following statements would the author most likely agree with?

These questions are similar to main idea questions, because both require you to understand the overall point of the passage.

❑ Passages may have a neutral, informative tone if they are simply presenting information. Fact-based passages, such as Social Science and Natural Science, typically have neutral tones.

❑ Avoid extremes.

When reviewing your answer choices for voice questions, beware of answers that are too strongly worded. Ask yourself if the degree of intensity suggested by the answer corresponds with the degree of intensity of the passage.

PUT IT TOGETHER

HUMANITIES: This passage is adapted from Larzer Ziff's introduction to "Nature and Selected Essays," a collection of essays by writer and philosopher Ralph Waldo Emerson.

In his constant emphasis on the self, Emerson was reacting to the social tyranny of the American crowd. He did not for a moment believe that the counter to majority rule should be a return to some form of
5 monarchy. Rather, he pursued the ideal of disbanding the mob through bringing to each of its members a sense of identity as a separate person. Ideally, each of us can develop a sense of self that resists grouping if we follow our reason rather than our understanding.
10 The rightness of our own uniqueness takes precedence over the mere correctness of common sense. Where others gazed upon a church congregation or a political gathering and saw a mass unified by a purpose or a prejudice, Emerson saw individuals, each with his or
15 her own integrity, an integrity that was being destroyed by the preacher or party boss who encouraged them to think of themselves as a collectivity.

In May 1839, Emerson returned from attending
20 church to vent in his journal his displeasure with the minister he had heard: "Cease, thou unauthorized talker, to preach of consolation, and resignation, and spiritual joys, in neat and balanced sentences. I know these folk who sit below you, and on the hearing of
25 these words look up. Hush, quickly: for care and crisis are real things to them. There is Mr. Tolman, the shoemaker, whose daughter is gone mad, and he is looking up through his spectacles to hear what you can offer for his case. Here is my friend, whose clients are
30 all leaving him, and he knows not what to turn his hand to next. Here is my wife, who has come to church in the hope of being soothed and strengthened after being wounded by the sharp tongue of an intruder in her house. Here is the stage-driver who had the jaundice,
35 and cannot get well. Here is B. whose courage failed last week, and he is looking up. O speak real things, then, or hold thy tongue." These comments are an example of how Emerson saw one plus one plus one when he saw a group. For him this was not a trick of
40 perception; it was a moral necessity.

European reformers of the day struggled against the tyranny of one or another monarch and were enraged by the cruel division of their native land into parcels. They opposed their rulers by attempting to
45 rally their compatriots and create powerful mobs. But America was a land in which the tyrant was already a collectivity. In this different political environment, Emerson pursued a different tactic. He attempted to disperse the American mob and encouraged each
50 citizen to have their own, individual voice. He writes in his journal in April 1841: "Let there be one person, let there be love and truth and virtue in one individual, in two individuals, in ten individuals, then can there be community: then is community for the first time
55 possible. Now nothing can be gained by merely adding zeroes to a faceless sum."

The revolution which Emerson incites is moral. He urges us to realize that when we follow our individual reason, each of us is a majority of one already.
60 Emerson argues that if we each yield to a numerical majority, we simply add zeroes to ourselves, as our own voice is lost in the crowd's. In this sense, to join the majority is to participate in our own diminishment and in the degradation of democracy.

1. The point of view from which the passage is told is best described as that of:

   A. a distant relative of Emerson who wants to preserve his ancestor's honor.
   B. a fan of history who is confused by Emerson's philosophical views.
   C. a minister who wants to demonstrate the challenges of delivering a sermon.
   D. a writer and historian who wants to explain one of Emerson's beliefs.

2. Emerson's overall tone when describing the minister can best be described as:

   F. neutral.
   G. careful.
   H. dismissive.
   J. criticizing.

3. In lines 21-22, the phrase "unauthorized talker" characterizes the minister as someone who:

   A. has risen to speak before getting the audience's permission.
   B. needs no authorization to speak.
   C. speaks without first checking the texts from which he is quoting.
   D. has no right to talk down to his listeners.

Method Questions

❑ Method questions appear in two major types: those concerned with function and those concerned with purpose.

❑ For method questions that ask you to determine how a part of a passage functions, consider what would be lost if that part of the passage was missing. Consider how that part of the passage relates to the parts around it and what role it serves.

These kinds of method questions typically appear in the following forms:

If the fourth paragraph were deleted, the passage would lose...
Lines _____ primarily serve to...
The main function of the first paragraph is to...
Which of the following best describes what the third paragraph adds to the passage?
The main function of the first paragraph in relation to the passage as a whole is to...

❑ For method questions that ask you to consider a passage's purpose, consider why the passage is constructed as it is. Try to determine what reasons the author had for creating the passage.

These kinds of method questions typically appear in the following forms:

The main purpose of the passage is to...
One of the main purposes of the last paragraph is for the author to...
The author uses the details listed in lines _____ primarily to...

PUT IT TOGETHER

HUMANITIES: This passage is adapted from Larzer Ziff's introduction to "Nature and Selected Essays," a collection of essays by writer and philosopher Ralph Waldo Emerson.

In his constant emphasis on the self, Emerson was reacting to the social tyranny of the American crowd. He did not for a moment believe that the counter to majority rule should be a return to some form of
5 monarchy. Rather, he pursued the ideal of disbanding the mob through bringing to each of its members a sense of identity as a separate person. Ideally, each of us can develop a sense of self that resists grouping if we follow our reason rather than our understanding.
10 The rightness of our own uniqueness takes precedence over the mere correctness of common sense. Where others gazed upon a church congregation or a political gathering and saw a mass unified by a purpose or a prejudice, Emerson saw individuals, each with his or
15 her own integrity, an integrity that was being destroyed by the preacher or party boss who encouraged them to think of themselves as a collectivity.

In May 1839, Emerson returned from attending
20 church to vent in his journal his displeasure with the minister he had heard: "Cease, thou unauthorized talker, to preach of consolation, and resignation, and spiritual joys, in neat and balanced sentences. I know these folk who sit below you, and on the hearing of
25 these words look up. Hush, quickly: for care and crisis are real things to them. There is Mr. Tolman, the shoemaker, whose daughter is gone mad, and he is looking up through his spectacles to hear what you can offer for his case. Here is my friend, whose clients are
30 all leaving him, and he knows not what to turn his hand to next. Here is my wife, who has come to church in the hope of being soothed and strengthened after being wounded by the sharp tongue of an intruder in her house. Here is the stage-driver who had the jaundice,
35 and cannot get well. Here is B. whose courage failed last week, and he is looking up. O speak real things, then, or hold thy tongue." These comments are an example of how Emerson saw one plus one plus one when he saw a group. For him this was not a trick of
40 perception; it was a moral necessity.

European reformers of the day struggled against the tyranny of one or another monarch and were enraged by the cruel division of their native land into parcels. They opposed their rulers by attempting to
45 rally their compatriots and create powerful mobs. But America was a land in which the tyrant was already a collectivity. In this different political environment, Emerson pursued a different tactic. He attempted to disperse the American mob and encouraged each
50 citizen to have their own, individual voice. He writes in his journal in April 1841: "Let there be one person, let there be love and truth and virtue in one individual, in two individuals, in ten individuals, then can there be community: then is community for the first time
55 possible. Now nothing can be gained by merely adding zeroes to a faceless sum."

The revolution which Emerson incites is moral. He urges us to realize that when we follow our individual reason, each of us is a majority of one already.
60 Emerson argues that if we each yield to a numerical majority, we simply add zeroes to ourselves, as our own voice is lost in the crowd's. In this sense, to join the majority is to participate in our own diminishment and in the degradation of democracy.

1. The quote in lines 51-56 is meant to show that:

    A. Emerson did not support the collectivization by reformers in Europe.
    B. Emerson was more alarmed by the prospect of individual power than by mob anarchy.
    C. European reformers and Emerson responded differently to different kinds of despotism.
    D. Emerson advocated stronger laws to prevent mob violence.

2. Emerson discusses Mr. Tolman in lines 26-29 primarily as an example of:

    F. someone who focuses more on collective groups than individual people.
    G. an individual with unique problems, which were ignored by the minister.
    H. a petty nobleman in need of a job.
    J. a pitiable character who appears in one of his transcendentalist essays.

3. The primary purpose of the third paragraph (lines 41-56) is to:

    A. present a historical background to illustrate why Emerson is largely forgotten today.
    B. list other historical figures who shared Emerson's view on collectivism.
    C. discuss the mathematical arguments that challenged Emerson's moral arguments.
    D. explain why Emerson's view differed from common ideas of his time.

Contextual Meaning Questions

❑ Contextual meaning questions ask you what a word, phrase, or statement means in the context of the passage.

These questions do not test your vocabulary as much as they test your ability to understand how words can have different meanings in different situations.

❑ Contextual meaning questions typically appear in the following forms:

As it is used in line ___, the word _____ most nearly means that...
In the context of the passage, the statement in lines ___ most nearly means that...
The phrase _____ refers to the...
Which of the following words from the passage is used figuratively?
The author uses the term _____ to refer to...
In the context of the passage, the phrase _____ can most nearly be paraphrased as...
When the author says, "_____," she most nearly means...

❑ The correct answer to a contextual meaning question is often a secondary and obscure definition of the selected term. Incorrect answer choices usually include more common usages or definitions.

❑ Read the entire sentence to understand the context in which the word or phrase is used. If necessary, also read the sentences which appear before and after.

When you encounter a word you don't recognize or a sentence you don't understand, you can use the surrounding information to help you determine what it means. Even if you can't determine the exact meaning, you should be able to make an educated guess.

❑ If you are stuck, try plugging in. Reread the sentence with each of the answer choices and see which works best.

PUT IT TOGETHER

HUMANITIES: This passage is adapted from Larzer Ziff's introduction to "Nature and Selected Essays," a collection of essays by writer and philosopher Ralph Waldo Emerson.

In his constant emphasis on the self, Emerson was reacting to the social tyranny of the American crowd. He did not for a moment believe that the counter to majority rule should be a return to some form of
5 monarchy. Rather, he pursued the ideal of disbanding the mob through bringing to each of its members a sense of identity as a separate person. Ideally, each of us can develop a sense of self that resists grouping if we follow our reason rather than our understanding.
10 The rightness of our own uniqueness takes precedence over the mere correctness of common sense. Where others gazed upon a church congregation or a political gathering and saw a mass unified by a purpose or a prejudice, Emerson saw individuals, each with his or
15 her own integrity, an integrity that was being destroyed by the preacher or party boss who encouraged them to think of themselves as a collectivity.

In May 1839, Emerson returned from attending
20 church to vent in his journal his displeasure with the minister he had heard: "Cease, thou unauthorized talker, to preach of consolation, and resignation, and spiritual joys, in neat and balanced sentences. I know these folk who sit below you, and on the hearing of
25 these words look up. Hush, quickly: for care and crisis are real things to them. There is Mr. Tolman, the shoemaker, whose daughter is gone mad, and he is looking up through his spectacles to hear what you can offer for his case. Here is my friend, whose clients are
30 all leaving him, and he knows not what to turn his hand to next. Here is my wife, who has come to church in the hope of being soothed and strengthened after being wounded by the sharp tongue of an intruder in her house. Here is the stage-driver who had the jaundice,
35 and cannot get well. Here is B. whose courage failed last week, and he is looking up. O speak real things, then, or hold thy tongue." These comments are an example of how Emerson saw one plus one plus one when he saw a group. For him this was not a trick of
40 perception; it was a moral necessity.

European reformers of the day struggled against the tyranny of one or another monarch and were enraged by the cruel division of their native land into parcels. They opposed their rulers by attempting to
45 rally their compatriots and create powerful mobs. But America was a land in which the tyrant was already a collectivity. In this different political environment, Emerson pursued a different tactic. He attempted to disperse the American mob and encouraged each
50 citizen to have their own, individual voice. He writes

in his journal in April 1841: "Let there be one person, let there be love and truth and virtue in one individual, in two individuals, in ten individuals, then can there be community: then is community for the first time
55 possible. Now nothing can be gained by merely adding zeroes to a faceless sum."

The revolution which Emerson incites is moral. He urges us to realize that when we follow our individual reason, each of us is a majority of one already.
60 Emerson argues that if we each yield to a numerical majority, we simply add zeroes to ourselves, as our own voice is lost in the crowd's. In this sense, to join the majority is to participate in our own diminishment and in the degradation of democracy.

1. The word "counter" in line 3 most nearly means:

   A. addition.
   B. support.
   C. ledge.
   D. antidote.

2. By the expression "one plus one plus one" in line 38, the author emphasizes Emerson's:

   F. oversimplified view of human differences.
   G. reliance on mathematical logic to support his philosophy.
   H. belief in the importance of each individual person.
   J. conviction that people are as interchangeable as numbers.

3. In line 44, the word "parcels" most nearly means:

   A. segments.
   B. packages.
   C. camps.
   D. groups.

4. In line 61, the statement that "we simply add zeroes to ourselves" most nearly means that:

   F. the way to accumulate wealth for ourselves is to cooperate with others.
   G. the way to gain support for our cause is to adapt it to the wishes of the majority.
   H. we gain nothing by opposing public opinion.
   J. we gain nothing by aligning ourselves with the biggest constituency.

Inference Questions

❑ Inference questions ask you to draw a conclusion that is not directly stated.

❑ Inference questions typically appear in the following forms:

> It can be logically inferred from the passage that...
> It is implied in the fifth paragraph that...
> A reasonable conclusion from _____ is that...
> In the context of the passage as a whole, it is most reasonable to infer that...
> What does the author suggest when he states that _____?

❑ It is important to make sure that your inferences are based on the information in the passage and not on outside knowledge or vague possibilities. Remember, an inference is a logical conclusion based on evidence.

❑ Inference questions can be very challenging, because they require a deep level of understanding of the passage.

You may want to leave these questions for last. Answering the other questions may help you to understand the passage better, which will make it easier to answer difficult questions like these.

PUT IT TOGETHER

HUMANITIES: This passage is adapted from Larzer Ziff's introduction to "Nature and Selected Essays," a collection of essays by writer and philosopher Ralph Waldo Emerson.

In his constant emphasis on the self, Emerson was reacting to the social tyranny of the American crowd. He did not for a moment believe that the counter to majority rule should be a return to some form of
5 monarchy. Rather, he pursued the ideal of disbanding the mob through bringing to each of its members a sense of identity as a separate person. Ideally, each of us can develop a sense of self that resists grouping if we follow our reason rather than our understanding.
10 The rightness of our own uniqueness takes precedence over the mere correctness of common sense. Where others gazed upon a church congregation or a political gathering and saw a mass unified by a purpose or a prejudice, Emerson saw individuals, each with his or
15 her own integrity, an integrity that was being destroyed by the preacher or party boss who encouraged them to think of themselves as a collectivity.

In May 1839, Emerson returned from attending
20 church to vent in his journal his displeasure with the minister he had heard: "Cease, thou unauthorized talker, to preach of consolation, and resignation, and spiritual joys, in neat and balanced sentences. I know these folk who sit below you, and on the hearing of
25 these words look up. Hush, quickly: for care and crisis are real things to them. There is Mr. Tolman, the shoemaker, whose daughter is gone mad, and he is looking up through his spectacles to hear what you can offer for his case. Here is my friend, whose clients are
30 all leaving him, and he knows not what to turn his hand to next. Here is my wife, who has come to church in the hope of being soothed and strengthened after being wounded by the sharp tongue of an intruder in her house. Here is the stage-driver who had the jaundice,
35 and cannot get well. Here is B. whose courage failed last week, and he is looking up. O speak real things, then, or hold thy tongue." These comments are an example of how Emerson saw one plus one plus one when he saw a group. For him this was not a trick of
40 perception; it was a moral necessity.

European reformers of the day struggled against the tyranny of one or another monarch and were enraged by the cruel division of their native land into parcels. They opposed their rulers by attempting to rally their
45 compatriots and create powerful mobs. But America was a land in which the tyrant was already a collectivity. In this different political environment, Emerson pursued a different tactic. He attempted to disperse the American mob and encouraged each

50 citizen to have their own, individual voice. He writes in his journal in April 1841: "Let there be one person, let there be love and truth and virtue in one individual, in two individuals, in ten individuals, then can there be community: then is community for the first time
55 possible. Now nothing can be gained by merely adding zeroes to a faceless sum."

The revolution which Emerson incites is moral. He urges us to realize that when we follow our individual reason, each of us is a majority of one already.
60 Emerson argues that if we each yield to a numerical majority, we simply add zeroes to ourselves, as our own voice is lost in the crowd's. In this sense, to join the majority is to participate in our own diminishment and in the degradation of democracy.

1. Emerson's remarks in lines 21-37 most strongly suggest that:

    A. his community is struggling through a period of unusual hardship.
    B. the minster's broad statements are not helpful for people with unique problems.
    C. the minister is not well-spoken, but his logic is correct.
    D. church members are more interested in gossiping about others than solving their own problems.

2. It may be reasonably inferred from the passage that the "social tyranny of the American crowd" (line 2) was the result of:

    F. support for monarchy.
    G. support for individuality.
    H. opposition to majority rule.
    J. opposition to despotism.

> **Use Process of Elimination. Eliminate answer choices that are not in line with the beliefs of the "American crowd."**

Reading Summary

Reading the Passages

❑ Stay engaged. While reading, you should be thinking about the information, reflecting on what you have already read, anticipating what will come next, and analyzing how the passage is constructed.

❑ Map the passage. Find the main idea of each paragraph.

❑ Make notes that help you understand the reading.

❑ Treat paired passages as two separate passages.

 1. Read the first passage and answer the questions for it.

 2. Read the second passage and answer the questions for it.

 3. Answer the questions that concern both passages.

Answering the Questions

❑ Questions do not follow the order of the passage, nor do they progress from easy to difficult.

❑ Tackle each passage's questions using the following three steps:

 1. Attack the easy and medium questions first.

 2. Make a second pass through the questions to work on the problems you skipped and marked, focusing on the ones you think you are most likely to answer correctly.

 3. Guess on the remaining questions.

❑ When a question refers to specific line numbers, read a few lines before and after the given lines to get the full context.

❑ Understand the question before you look at the answer choices.

❑ Make sure that you've found the best answer, not just a good one. Reading questions, especially difficult ones, will usually contain at least one or two choices that are "almost right."

Reading Practice

Passage I

PROSE FICTION: The following is adapted from the short story "A Grand Sun" by Cristina Weiss.

Harrison couldn't remember if he had ever watched a sunrise before. Waves pushed and pulled against the shore like the ocean's breath. He had listened to the water all night. He could understand
5 now why people bought those machines with the artificial sounds of nature. Crashing waves, steady rain, rolling thunder, bubbling brooks. It was calming, in a way; there was a rhythm to it; you knew what to expect next, and if you let it, the sounds brought you into a
10 state of relaxation. He had stretched himself across the roof of his car, watching as the sky changed from gray to blue to orange, then pink to yellow. The world came into focus around him.

Despite the steady sound of waves, he sensed a
15 reverent silence. It reminded him of the hush in a church. He welcomed the soothing emptiness in his mind. There were so many things he didn't want to think about. He had a blanket in the backseat and the car was comfortable enough, but he didn't want to be
20 comfortable. The roof of the car was unforgiving; it began to grind into the bonier parts of his spine, but even this he enjoyed for its distraction.

As the sun crested the horizon, Harrison felt its growing heat. At first, he had been unsure that the sky
25 was turning color, until its blush grew into a blaze. Soon, he was squinting, and then it was too brilliant to look at. He laid with his eyes closed, felt his skin warming. In the back of his mind, he felt thoughts of his grandfather creeping into his head. There was a
30 lingering frustration and anger he tried to ignore.

It was easier to maintain a clear mind if he kept moving, so he hopped off the roof of the car. His back suddenly felt cold, and he shuddered in the ocean wind. Sand crunched beneath his steps. He tasted salt in his
35 breath. The beach was smooth, untouched by the vacationers and locals who would gather here later in the morning. At the edge of the tide, he let the waves lick at his shoes. Down the beach, a woman was picking shells from the sand. Harrison was surprised to
40 see anyone else out there. Had he actually believed that he was alone, the only person in the world? He sometimes got so lost in his own head that he couldn't see outside of it.

A man jogged past him, huffing heavily along the
45 tide's edge. Harrison imagined himself in camouflage fatigues and a pack of gear, jogging in unison along with a troop of fellow soldiers. It was a thought he had been avoiding, but now the image was stuck in his mind, bringing a mixture of excitement and anxiety.

50 Now his mental barricades were breaking down and the stresses of the past few days came rushing in. He could no longer ignore his troubles.

He thought of when he had walked into the Army recruiting office. The man at the desk had asked him
55 why he was interested in joining the service, and Harrison struggled to come up with a better reason than needing a change of pace. Was it possible to feel stuck at home and lost in the world at the same time? He had told the recruitment officer that he wanted to do
60 something that would honor his family, but that wasn't at all true. The best honor would be to stay at his grandfather's shop and inherit the family business. He wasn't interested in being a soldier, but any option seemed brighter than the dullness of the shop.

65 He thought of when he had told his grandfather. Harrison had expected him to be proud – the old veteran, the great war hero – but it quickly turned into an argument. What Harrison called an opportunity and a heritage, his grandfather called a fool's gamble and a
70 waste. They were both stubborn; it was one of many traits the Harrison has inherited, and so they had dug their trenches and refused to budge in the slightest. Before Harrison left the house, they had been shouting at each other. He now felt embarrassed for having
75 punched a dent in a wall and for slamming the door on the way out.

His grandfather owned an auto repair shop, where Harrison had spent most of his time growing up. The heavy smells of transmission fluid and motor oil were
80 a part of him, soaked too deeply into his skin to ever wash out. As a child, he had listened to the mechanics joking and cursing about things he didn't understand. He learned to call his grandfather Eddie at the shop and Pa at home. As a teenager, he had worked after school
85 at the front desk of the shop, answering phone calls and scheduling appointments. He had never been interested in understanding how cars worked, or how they could be made to work again. He didn't like the noise, the smell, the dirty rags and oil stains. He hated being
90 trapped inside, with the cars boxing him in. He usually just wanted to read his books or wander outside.

He knew he would have to go back home or back to the shop, but he procrastinated. He tossed shells into the water and scratched drawings into the sand until
95 people started gathering on the beach. Uncomfortable around the strangers tanning and laughing, he climbed back up the dune to his car. When he turned the key in the ignition, the only sound was a faint *click, click, click*. Was it a bad solenoid? He tried to remember the
100 diagnosis for this, all the car repair lessons he'd learned from his grandfather. He gritted his teeth and turned the key. He tried again and again.

1. One of the main purposes of the seventh and
    eighth paragraphs (lines 53-76) is to describe
    Harrison's recent memories in a way that:

    A. emphasizes his bond with his grandfather.
    B. compares the values of modern society to
       those when Eddie was Harrison's age.
    C. demonstrates his lack of knowledge about
       automotive repair.
    D. illustrates the complicated situation he is in.

2. As it is used in line 31, the word *clear* most nearly
    means:

    F. transparent.
    G. visible.
    H. open.
    J. unbothered.

3. Which of the following statements best expresses
    why Harrison feels both "excitement and anxiety"
    (line 49)?

    A. He recognized the man jogging on the beach.
    B. He is eager to try something new, but does
       not want to upset his grandfather.
    C. He plans to stay at the shop and eventually
       take on the responsibility of owning it.
    D. He recalls his grandfather's past experiences
       as a soldier.

4. The main purpose of the information in lines 81-
    91 is to further illustrate that Harrison believes his
    grandfather's shop:

    F. is not financially profitable.
    G. needs more open space to be comfortable.
    H. is not an ideal workplace for him.
    J. is charming but unappreciated.

5. The main conflict in the passage could best be
    described as:

    A. a grudge between family members who will
       not forgive each other.
    B. Harrison's struggle to choose between his
       own ambitions and his grandfather's hopes.
    C. the tension between a grandfather and
       grandson, who both want to control each
       other.
    D. Eddie's resentment of Harrison for being
       careless and unappreciative.

6. In the first four paragraphs (lines 1-43), the
    narrator describes all of the following elements of
    Harrison's surroundings EXCEPT the:

    F. ocean waves.
    G. setting sun.
    H. beach sand.
    J. salty air.

7. Which of the following best paraphrases the
    question "Had he actually believed that he was
    alone, the only person in the world" (lines 40-41)?

    A. Harrison was surprised that anyone else
       would ever come to the beach.
    B. Harrison was lost in thought and had stopped
       paying attention to his surroundings.
    C. Harrison wanted to be in a place where
       nobody would ever bother him.
    D. Harrison felt as uncomfortable in public
       spaces as he did at his grandfather's shop.

8. It can most reasonably be inferred that Harrison's
    inability to start his car or diagnose its problems is
    for him a source of:

    F. embarrassment because he knows his
       grandfather will mock him.
    G. regret because he spent too much money on a
       faulty car.
    H. frustration because it is the latest of several
       recent complications in his life.
    J. relief because he did not want to go home.

9. According to the second paragraph (lines 14-22),
    Harrison enjoyed being at the beach because:

    A. he was comfortable lying on the car.
    B. he needed rest after a long shift at work.
    C. the sounds of waves reminded him of a song.
    D. it was a distraction from his problems.

10. In this passage, the writer primarily shows
    Harrison's feelings through:

    F. Harrison's actions as remembered by his
       grandfather.
    G. Harrison's thoughts in relation to his
       surroundings.
    H. the conversations Harrison has with his
       grandfather.
    J. the description of the auto repair shop.

Passage II

PROSE FICTION: The following is an excerpt from "A Lonely Crowded Room" by Benjamin Steckel.

The museum was full of people. One could hardly see the paintings. But Vincent had seen the paintings every day for the past fifteen years. It was the people that he liked to watch. He thought that Monet and
5 Picasso were good and nice, but what he found beautiful was the curiosity of a child rummaging through the museum halls—it always brought a smile to his face.

He made his way through the people. He was on
10 his last rounds of the day. He had to make sure that no one touched any of the paintings. If he were to spot any suspicious behavior he would have to tell Carl, the Security Supervisor. Carl was almost twenty years younger than he.

15 "Winston, are you on your rounds? Or are you standing around dreaming again?" Vincent heard from the radio.

"No sir, doing my rounds, sir," he called back into the radio. Carl didn't answer back. Carl didn't like
20 Vincent. Vincent felt he did a good job, but Carl was always on his case for one thing or another.

Vincent saw a young couple, and he stopped to look at them.

"Excuse me sir, where is the bathroom?" Vincent
25 looked down and saw a young boy standing on the tips of his feet. Vincent smiled at him.

"Right this way, young sir. How are you enjoying your trip to the museum today?" Vincent started walking and the boy, who must've been around eight,
30 followed.

"What?" The noise of the crowd made it difficult to have a conversation in the museum.

"I said, how are you enjoying your trip to the museum?" Vincent said louder.

35 "It's OK. I come every week with my parents… they changed where the bathrooms are," the little boy said. Vincent smiled. The bathrooms were not on his route and although Carl was still mad at him for some reason, he decided he would show the boy. It would
40 take him five minutes to walk to the bathrooms and another five to get back to his route.

"How's everything else then, Tim? …how's school? Everything going good? Yes?" Vincent smiled shyly as he looked down at the boy through his big
45 heavy glasses.

"It's OK." Tim looked at Vincent in a confused manner.

"And Mom and Dad? How are they? They're good I hope," Vincent said worriedly. He scratched his head
50 through his short white hair. Vincent was embarrassed that he couldn't think of anything that he felt would interest Tim.

"Good, I guess. Busy with work. How did you know my name?" Vincent and Tim entered a quiet part
55 of the museum. It was a walkway reserved for security staff. Carl had told him previously not to let visitors through there, but Vincent had forgotten all about that.

"Well, they want the best for you… and Lisa, you know." Vincent said more quietly now that they were
60 no longer bothered by the sounds of the crowd.

"How did you know my name?"

"Wha—what's that?"

"My name, how'd you know it?"

"Oh, well, when you get to be working at a
65 museum for as long as I have, you pick up a few things here and there. I see you here every week. I just kind of picked up your name." Vincent smiled, but Tim still looked confused. Vincent nervously shifted his eyes and said, "Well you know, they train us to do that, so
70 that we can be friendlier to visitors of the museum, and all that."

"Makes sense," Tim said with a content confidence. Vincent opened another door and they now faced the bathrooms.

75 "Well, there you go, Tim. I'll see you next week, OK? If… if you ever need anything, you can tell me, by the way… It was good talking to you, I really enjoyed it."

"OK."

80 "…my name is Vincent by the way!"

"OK, bye Vincent."

"Wait, Tim! Will you find your way back alright?"

"Yeah, I think so."

"OK then… if you don't, you can ask for me
85 through any of the security staff."

"OK, thanks." Vincent smiled as his eyes filled with water. All he had in life was his family at the museum.

1. At the time of the events of the passage, Vincent is:

    A. the Security Supervisor at a museum.
    B. a small boy of about eight.
    C. a lower-level security guard.
    D. a solitary single father.

2. It can reasonably be inferred from the passage as a whole that Vincent views his specific guard route as:

    F. an essential part of his job, straying from which might have disastrous consequences.
    G. a guideline he should preferably keep to.
    H. confining, because it doesn't allow him to look at the paintings he wants to see.
    J. symbolic of the miserable monotony that characterizes his job.

3. It can reasonably be inferred that Carl's relationship with Vincent is:

    A. one of amicability, after years of pleasant comradeship.
    B. characterized by jealousy and tense dislike.
    C. professional, but the cause of irritation on Carl's part.
    D. characterized by the paternal affection Vincent feels for Carl.

4. The passage states that Vincent's job includes all of the following responsibilities EXCEPT:

    F. guarding the paintings.
    G. reporting any suspicious activity to the appropriate authority.
    H. communicating with his superiors.
    J. guiding wayward visitors to the restroom when need be.

5. The familiarity Vincent has with the particulars of Tim's family comes from:

    A. the years of enjoyment he has experienced as a treasured family friend.
    B. the fact that Vincent's own eight-year-old son knows Tim well from school.
    C. Tim and his family's frequent visits to the museum.
    D. Vincent's conversations with Tim on several other occasions.

6. Which of the following statements best describes the way the last paragraph (lines 86-88) functions in the passage as a whole?

    F. It provides the first indication that Vincent wishes he had a more important career.
    G. It shows that Vincent's knowledge of Tim is a reflection of his own loneliness.
    H. It sets up a contrast between Vincent's life and Carl's life.
    J. It repeats the argument made at the beginning of the passage.

7. It can reasonably be inferred that Vincent views his conversation with Tim with:

    A. embarrassment and self-consciousness.
    B. indifference and preoccupation.
    C. resentment and frustration.
    D. impatience and indictment.

8. The passage states that Vincent first enters into a conversation with Tim because:

    F. Vincent is lonely and wishes he had a child of his own.
    G. Tim asks Vincent for his help.
    H. Vincent doesn't know where the bathroom is located.
    J. Vincent needs to be friendlier to patrons.

9. According to the passage, in which order did the following events occur?

    I.   Vincent learns Tim's name.
    II.   Tim learns Vincent's name.
    III. Tim asks for directions to the bathroom.
    IV.   Carl checks on Vincent over the radio.

    A. I, II, III, IV
    B. IV, III, I, II
    C. IV, III, II, I
    D. I, IV, III, II

10. After Vincent explains how he knows Tim's name, Tim's first reaction is one of:

    F. terror.
    G. confusion.
    H. confidence.
    J. sadness.

Passage III

LITERARY NARRATIVE: This passage is adapted from the novel "Dry Peaks" by Jolene Rossi.

For years, I have loved a man so quiet and reserved he is barely known even in this small town. He is Benny Lawson, and I suppose I still hold onto an ounce of love for him.

5   Although Benny will never be remembered as the most industrious worker to ever work for the city of Bannerpole, he is known for his consistency. A man of routine and humility, he never sought to advance his station, preferring to stay with the familiarity of his 10 simple job, mowing the lawns and emptying the trash cans at the city's several parks. He had been offered several other positions, including the respected role of manager of Park Services (there had been a lack of desirable employees). But he declined every chance to 15 increase his wages, fearing it would bring more responsibilities. Perhaps he would be most satisfied if he wouldn't be remembered at all. His greatest joy is found in watching the lives of others while remaining unnoticed, a discreet observer as unremarkable as the 20 park benches or trees. To most of Bannerpole, he is just another feature of the parks that he cares for.

During the historic winter that brought six feet of snow, crippled the highways, and nearly led to the ruin of the city, Benny was a teenager stocking frozen 25 foods at the local grocery store. He had several other jobs before, including a position at the animal shelter where he spent more time walking the dogs than cleaning their kennels, but all of these occupations had been brief. He had never been fired from a job (all of 30 his employers had pitied him for his simple charm), but would stop arriving for work once he grew too bored or anxious or distracted. That winter, storms were severe enough that the ice clinging to the power lines caused them to snap. For days, the city went 35 without electricity. The enormous refrigeration units went dead, and Benny was charmed by the irony of frozen food spoiling because it was too cold outside. In an act of spontaneity and certainty that was unlike his typical character, Benny took all of the thawing 40 foods from their refrigerators and carried them outside, where he planted them into the drifts of snow. It wasn't long before people noticed and started sneaking bags of peas and pints of ice cream from the snowy mounds behind the store. His manager was too 45 surprised and amused to be angry, so Benny kept the job for as long as he continued to show up for his shifts. The following spring, when the ice and snow finally melted away, there were still packs of frozen chicken and whole pies left outside, long spoiled by

50 then. If Benny's name ever comes up in a local conversation, it's usually in remembrance of that.

Despite the opinions of several gossips, Benny has no weakness or defect of mind. His school teachers knew him to be an average student with the potential 55 to be surprisingly clever. "Unusual" and "shy" were traits commonly applied to him. I met him at the library, where he came weekly to stock up on dense novels. We quickly became friends – a bond forged by a shared appreciation for the Russian novelists. He had 60 considered applying for a job at the public library (a possibility I suggested to him, since he came to visit so often), but he rejected this idea when he realized he would be expected to converse with library patrons. We did date for several months, nearly a year, and I 65 assume he enjoyed my company simply because I was a librarian, which allowed us to have conversations about a wide range of books. As much as I grew to care for him, I always sensed a distance, like an invisible barrier he had erected between the two of us. I once 70 asked what it was like to view life through his eyes. He responded, "I often feel like the world is in a television set and I'm the only person watching." I told him that this seemed terribly lonely, but he said he didn't feel that way. I have spoken with other women 75 who have also loved him. Most had been surprised by his lack of interest in socializing or even speaking. Benny fell in love often. He showed the same great intensity with relationships as he did with books, passionately taking in all the information and then 80 quickly exhausting his interest. He didn't exactly grow bored with people, though several times he was accused of this. Rather, he would come to a point where there were no new details to hold his interest. Similarly, he never reread a novel, and even avoided 85 reading more than a single book from each author.

His job, the one he finally dedicated himself to, is simple. In summer, when the grass grows quickest, he has to trim the park lawns twice a week. In late fall and winter months, he can often ignore them altogether. 90 There are only three parks in the city, each big enough for a game of baseball or perhaps a pair of birthday parties. Most of his work time is spent watching people play sports or exercise their dogs.

As the years have passed, we have remained 95 something like friends. I have learned much about him and his life, but only through my own nosiness and perseverance. And as much as I desire to know him and be closer to him, I am sure he is content with watching the world from a distance.

1. The events in the passage are described primarily from the point of view of a narrator who presents the:

   A. inner thoughts and feelings of Benny exclusively.
   B. inner thoughts of Benny and his employer exclusively.
   C. inner thoughts of Benny and his employer, as well as her own feelings.
   D. inner thoughts and feeling of all the citizens of Bannerpole except for Benny.

2. That Benny observed life similar to how someone might observe television was:

   F. an inference the narrator made based on her observations of his behavior with strangers.
   G. a fact he mentioned to his boss as a way of explaining his mistakes.
   H. a detail that the narrator learned from a local gossip who was spreading rumors explaining Benny's behavior.
   J. a comment he made in a conversation with the narrator.

3. According to the passage, all of the following were places where Benny was employed EXCEPT:

   A. the grocery store.
   B. the public library.
   C. Bannerpole's parks.
   D. the animal shelter.

4. Which of the following questions is NOT answered by the passage?

   F. How did the narrator meet Benny?
   G. What is Benny's current age?
   H. What are Benny's responsibilities at his job?
   J. How does the narrator feel about Benny?

5. To develop the characterization of Benny, the narrator uses all of the following EXCEPT:

   A. a physical description of Benny.
   B. references to Benny's past jobs.
   C. description of how others respond to Benny.
   D. dialogue between Benny and the narrator.

6. Benny is characterized in the passage as:

   F. sensitive and slow-moving.
   G. unambitious and introverted.
   H. lazy and irrational.
   J. self-centered and funny.

7. One of the main ideas of the second paragraph (lines 5-21) is that:

   A. Benny prefers a life of modesty to one of wealth or esteem.
   B. Benny is much wealthier than he once was.
   C. the narrator has forgotten most of what she knew about Benny.
   D. Benny was considered odd by most people who knew him.

8. The primary focus of lines 32-51 is:

   F. the relationship between Benny and the narrator.
   G. Benny's personality, as shown by a story from his past.
   H. the history of Bannerpole and its residents.
   J. the narrator's feelings for Benny.

9. When the narrator says "there had been a lack of desirable employees" (lines 13-14), she most likely means that:

   A. Benny was not an ideal candidate, but there were no better options.
   B. Benny was the ideal candidate, but he did not want to be considered for the position.
   C. Benny was always respected by his fellow employees.
   D. Benny quit most of the jobs he had.

10. The passage suggests that, compared to his work at the grocery store, Benny found his work for the city's parks to be:

   F. more enjoyable.
   G. less enjoyable.
   H. more profitable financially.
   J. less profitable financially.

Passage IV

PROSE FICTION: This passage is adapted from the story "The Awakening" by Kate Chopin.

Edna walked down to the beach rather mechanically, not noticing anything special except that the sun was hot. She was not dwelling upon any particular train of thought. She had done all the
5 thinking which was necessary after Robert went away, when she lay awake on the sofa till morning.

She had said over and over to herself: "To-day it is Arobin; to-morrow it will be someone else. It makes no difference to me, it doesn't matter about Leonce
10 Pontellier—but Raoul and Etienne!" She understood now clearly what she had meant long ago when she said to Adele Ratignolle that she would give up the unessential, but she would never sacrifice herself for her children.

15 Despondency had come upon her there in the wakeful night, and had never lifted. There was no one thing in the world, which she desired. There was no human being whom she wanted near except Robert; and she even realized that the day would come when
20 he, too, and the thought of him, would melt out of her existence, leaving her alone. The children appeared before her like antagonists who had overcome her; who had overpowered her and sought to drag her into the soul's slavery for the rest of her days. But she knew
25 a way to elude them. She was not thinking of these things when she walked down to the beach.

The water of the Gulf stretched out before her gleaming with the million lights of the sun. The voice of the sea is seductive, never ceasing, whispering,
30 clamoring, murmuring, inviting the soul to wander in abysses of solitude. All along the white beach, up and down, there was no living thing in sight. A bird with a broken wing was beating the air above, reeling, fluttering, circling disabled down, down to the water.

35 Edna found her old bathing suit still hanging, faded, upon its accustomed peg.

She put it on, leaving her clothing in the bathhouse. When she was there, beside the sea, she stood in the open air, at the mercy of the sun, the
40 breeze that beat upon her, and the waves that invited her.

How strange and awful it seemed to stand under the sky! How delicious! She felt like some newborn creature, opening its eyes in a familiar world that it had
45 never known.

The foamy wavelets curled up to her feet, and coiled like serpents about her ankles. She walked out.

The water was chill, but she walked on. The water was deep, but she lifted her body and reached out with a
50 long sweeping stroke. The touch of the sea is sensuous, enfolding the body in its soft, close embrace.

She went on and on. She remembered the night she swam far out, and recalled the terror that seized her at the fear of being unable to regain the shore. She did
55 not look back now, but went on and on, thinking of the blue-grass meadow that she had traversed when a little child, believing that it had no beginning and no end.

Her arms and legs were growing tired.

She thought of Leonce and the children. They
60 were a part of her life. But they need not have thought that they could possess her, body and soul. How Mademoiselle Reisz would have laughed, perhaps sneered, if she knew! "And you call yourself an artist! What pretensions, Madame! The artist must possess
65 the courageous soul that dares and defies."

Exhaustion was pressing upon and overpowering her.

"Good-by—because I love you." He did not know; he did not understand. He would never understand.
70 Perhaps Doctor Mandelet would have understood if she had seen him—but it was too late; the shore was far behind her, and her strength was gone.

She looked into the distance, and the old terror flamed up for an instant, then sank again. Edna heard
75 her father's voice and her sister Margaret's. She heard the barking of an old dog that was chained to the sycamore tree. The spurs of the cavalry officer clanged as he walked across the porch. There was the hum of bees, and the musky odor of pinks filled the air.

1. When the passage states, "There was no one thing in the world, which she desired," (lines 16-17), the author implies that:

   A. Edna's wealthy husband, Robert, has provided her with all the material possessions she needs.
   B. Edna is so fulfilled that she feels as though there is nothing left for her to want.
   C. Edna feels like some newborn creature, opening its eyes in a familiar world that it has never known.
   D. Edna's despair is so absolute that she no longer cares for anything.

2. In the context of the passage, the bird mentioned in lines 32-34 could symbolize all of the following EXCEPT:

    F. Edna's desire to be free of the life that incarcerates her.
    G. Edna's descent into despair.
    H. Edna's sense that she is losing the ability to fight what she finds suffocating.
    J. Edna's appreciation of those close to her.

3. It can be reasonably inferred that Edna's relationship with her children is:

    A. comforting in her time of need.
    B. becoming increasingly intimate as she grows older.
    C. suffocating and soul-destroying.
    D. fading as they each marry and move away.

4. In the author's description of the beach, *foamy wavelets* are compared to:

    F. birds with beating wings.
    G. blue grass in meadows.
    H. abysses of solitude.
    J. coiled serpents.

5. According to the passage, the only person whom Edna wanted close to her was:

    A. Arobin.
    B. Robert.
    C. Adele Ratignolle.
    D. Leonce Pontellier.

6. In the context of the passage, the main point of the first paragraph (lines 1-6) is that:

    F. Edna has forgotten why she is at the beach.
    G. Edna missed Arobin last night and couldn't sleep.
    H. Edna does not go down to the beach with the intention of doing herself harm.
    J. the touch of the sea is sensuous and seductive.

7. As stated in the passage, the sea is described as which of the following:

    I. reeling
    II. sweeping
    III. clamoring

    A. II and III
    B. II and I
    C. III only
    D. I, II and III

8. According to the passage, the result of Edna's standing by the sea is that she:

    F. realizes how superficial her relationship with her children is.
    G. finds inspiration to forget Robert and move on with her life.
    H. is seduced by the water and moves towards it.
    J. misses her husband Robert.

9. As it is used in line 25, the word *elude* most nearly means:

    A. discharge or emit.
    B. evade or escape from.
    C. make an indirect reference to.
    D. make clear or plain.

10. As stated in the passage, the following events occur in what sequence?

    I. Edna puts on her bathing suit.
    II. Robert leaves.
    III. Edna steps into the water.
    IV. Edna walks down to the beach.

    F. I, III, IV, II.
    G. IV, I, III, II.
    H. II, IV, I, III.
    J. I, IV, III, II.

Passage V

SOCIAL SCIENCE: This passage is adapted from the article "What Markets Cannot Buy" by Kassandra C. Myren.

It's an old truth that there are some things money cannot buy: happiness and love have long been the standards of pricelessness. Yet in modern times it seems that less and less is beyond your reach if you
5 have enough cash. For example, the purchase of "carbon credits" gives companies the liberty to pollute. For a mere $10.50, you can lawfully spew a metric ton of carbon dioxide into our atmosphere. In such an economy, a company may choose to reduce
10 pollutants or may simply raise prices to compensate. Thus, the consumer takes on an added burden, and the problem of pollution remains unabated. In the recent past, this conduct would have been unacceptable. A few generations ago, private corporations wouldn't be
15 allowed to advertise their products within schools; society would have been appalled at the thought of buying a sickly stranger's life insurance policy so you can receive the benefits from their death; the idea of prisoners paying for fancier jail cells would have
20 seemed absurd. Today, these are all realities of our modern economy. So what has changed?

Economic systems rely on the management, or lack thereof, of greed. Some people may always want to have more than their neighbors, some just want as
25 much as their neighbors or enough for comfort, but we all *want*. This is a principle of humanity, unchanged in its nature throughout history, but we have found different ways to deal with it. In a true "market economy," this greed would have complete freedom to
30 satisfy itself by any means. As can be imagined, and as history has proven, this is likely to lead to exploitation, as those with more wealth are able to take more and more power from those without wealth. Humanity's track record of slavery, child labor, and
35 monopolization shows that we need some rules to limit our greedy impulses. Thus, no true market economy exists in the modern world, because restrictions are necessarily put in place to protect citizens from being unfairly deprived of opportunities and rights. In
40 economic policies, there is a balance between how much freedom citizens are given to satisfy their greed and how many restrictions are enforced in order to ensure citizens are protected from the greed of others. Traditionally, defining the terms of this balance has
45 been the responsibility of governments. Recently, however, the lines between what is or is not for sale have been subject to the values of society.

Since the 1980s, American economic policies have operated under the assumption that businesses
50 and industries will regulate themselves without government intervention. For decades, there was faith that competition among businesses and the need to satisfy customers would be enough to ensure that businesses would not exploit or endanger citizens.
55 However, this faith has been called into question by recent events, particularly the Global Financial Crisis of 2007-8. Through many risky investments and much manipulation of consumers, the markets earned widespread distrust. Some say that the problem at the
60 core of these issues is a change of modern values, a rise in greed at the cost of morals. But while it is true that greed is a problem, it is certainly not a new one. And so if we cannot point the blame at modern morals, where else can we find the source of our recent
65 problems?

Perhaps the most significant and insidious change in modern times is that greed has been given more opportunities to assert itself: If you don't want to wait in line for an event, several new companies offer
70 "standers" for hire; Some medical groups have begun allowing patients to pay "priority fees" in order to take appointment times from other patients. In a society where more and more is available for purchase, those with more capital have more opportunities to claim
75 power. If the only advantage that came from great wealth was that one could afford nicer cars or bigger homes, there would be less concern with the inequality of income. But as more of our lives are covered in price tags, more of our personal liberties are
80 surrendered to those with fatter wallets. Take the example of airplane seating, with first-class passengers getting shorter waits, priority seating, larger space, more service, finer foods, and so on, and extend that privilege through every realm and moment
85 of our lives: this is where our current path leads. Some may consider this a plutocracy, in which the wealthiest people become the governing power. In less absolute terms, it can be called a "market society," as the rules that dictate the economy spill over into our cultural
90 values and interactions. While there is no clear solution to our current economic woes, I see a certain obstacle before us: we must determine and limit the role that markets play in our personal lives and relations. The protection and reclamation of our rights
95 begins with deciding what money cannot buy. Our capitalist markets, in their nature, care primarily about money, but we have more important values to preserve.

1. The main point of the third paragraph (lines 48-65) is that:

   A. American economic policies have been unchanged and unquestioned for decades.
   B. the problems of the Global Financial Crisis could be avoided in a true market economy.
   C. there was less greed in American society before the 1980s.
   D. recent events showed that market restrictions are needed to prevent exploitation.

2. The main function of the last paragraph is to:

   F. demonstrate the effects of certain economic policies and declare a call to action.
   G. explain the necessity for business practices that offer special treatment for higher costs.
   H. justify the author's feelings of greed, which are a source of anxiety.
   J. outline the various policies that could be changed or enacted in order to solve modern economic problems.

3. In the context of the passage, the author's statement that "we all *want*" (lines 25-26) most nearly means that:

   A. there is not enough wealth for all people to satisfy their needs.
   B. people are too inclined to follow trends and buy whatever is most popular.
   C. people will always desire to get more things.
   D. it is a part of human nature that we all want to manage our own businesses.

4. As it is used in line 74, the term *capital* refers to:

   F. official.
   G. center.
   H. assets.
   J. importance.

5. The passage most strongly suggests that the Global Financial Crisis was caused by which of the following?

   A. The sale of "carbon credits" to industries that generate pollutants
   B. Consumer distrust in the economic markets
   C. Businesses taking advantage of their lack of regulation
   D. Changes in modern values regarding greed and investment

6. The passage suggests that all of the following arc examples of a market society EXCEPT:

   F. paying for the right to release harmful industrial byproducts.
   G. offering prisoners the chance to upgrade their lodging for a fee.
   H. having the option to buy several car types.
   J. the division of airline seating into different classes based on benefits and expenses.

7. If the first paragraph were deleted, what important information would be lost?

   A. An explanation of a major economic concern, as presented by the author
   B. A definition of a market economy, as presented by the author
   C. An important similarity between modern economic policies and those before the 1980s, as presented by the author
   D. A personal experience of the benefits and setback of a market economy, as presented by the author

8. The author uses the examples in lines 68-72 in order to illustrate:

   F. clever solutions to common problems.
   G. popular businesses created in the 1980s.
   H. how modern society grants privileges based on wealth.
   J. the specific causes of the Global Financial Crisis.

9. The last paragraph most strongly suggests that a "market society" is a society:

   A. with valuable resources and investments.
   B. based on strict rules and regulations.
   C. that has monetized many aspects of daily life.
   D. known for not preventing unlawful activities.

10. The author of the passage claims that the role of markets must be limited because these markets:

   F. create too many laws and restrictions that are imposed on citizens.
   G. require too much oversight to manage effectively.
   H. inspire positive values for society.
   J. promote inequality by providing more advantages to the wealthy.

Passage VI

SOCIAL SCIENCE: This passage is adapted from the essay "Ever Speaking" by Stephany Kush. The Maori are a group of South Pacific islanders that settled New Zealand, which was conquered by Europeans in the 1800s.

When PhD student Helen Hogan discovered a 150-year-old Maori language manuscript, it gave researchers new insight into the world-view and lives of historic native New Zealanders. That Hogan is an
5 80-year-old grandmother and earned her PhD in her retirement makes her story almost as noteworthy as those she uncovered. Her work translates and brings to light the accounts of Maori individuals and groups traveling around the Pacific and overseas to Europe,
10 one hundred and fifty years ago. Her most recent translation is called *Bravo, Neu Zeeland*, and chronicles the European travels of the author, Te Rerehau, and his companion, Wiremu Toetoe. Both Hogan's journey and that of Te Rerehau and Wiremu
15 illustrate the wonderful rewards that can come from exchange between distant and distinct cultures.

Many people unfamiliar with Maori history are amazed that there is a written Maori language, as it was generally assumed that New Zealand's native
20 inhabitants had no written alphabet associated with their largely oral culture. Even more astonishing, to some, is that the Maori allowed Hogan, a *pakeha*, to delve into their closely guarded past. Part of her success can be attributed to Hogan's cultural
25 sensitivity; she tracked down descendants of all the writers, gained their confidence, and only then asked permission to use their ancestors' manuscripts for her dissertation. Edie Neha, a fifth generation descendant of the manuscript's authors, was greatly impressed by
30 Hogan's *wairua*, admiring her wonderful presence and sincere approach to the translating, editing and publication of his people's cultural inheritance. Social acceptance by these Maori was essential for Hogan to obtain all the materials she required. In a way, the
35 travel experiences of Maori authors in the *pakeha* universe mirror her journey into the world of their descendants.

Working their passage to Trieste on the frigate *Novara*, in 1859, Te Rerehau and Wiremu Toetoe
40 traveled to Vienna, where they were apprenticed at the Imperial Printery. They exchanged tutoring in the German and Maori languages, possibly with a curator of the Vienna museum's new, extensive Maori collection. In their first official public appearance, they
45 were cheered by the Austrian spectators as they walked together along the streets of Vienna. In the procession, Wiremu, his face embellished with intricate *ta moko*, doubtless seemed the more exotic of the two.

Europeans had never seen such elaborate designs in
50 skin and ink. According to the diary, "that day was an outing on which we were on display, and those people greatly marveled at us, the people of New Zealand."

The Maori were profoundly touched by the hospitality and goodness of the people they met. "The
55 Austrians are a very fine people, the best we have encountered in European countries. There were many kindnesses in invitations to go to their houses and have meals prepared for us."

A climax of the travelers' visit was a private
60 meeting with Habsburg Emperor Franz Josef. "Everywhere we looked there were soldiers, and as we proceeded we paid tribute by bowing." As soon as the door of the inner chamber was opened, "the great leader courteously stood up to receive us." Wiremu
65 gave a speech in Maori, and the two men presented a two-sided, bilingual version of the speech to the king.

Ironically, when Wiremu and Te Rerehau returned to New Zealand in 1860 from their triumphant tour, the Europeans in New Zealand outnumbered the Maori,
70 and rumors of war between the two groups were spreading. A printing press given to them by the Austrians was used to publish a newspaper called *Te Hokioi e Rere Atu Na* (which translates to *The Mythical Bird that Flies up There*). Already, the Maori
75 understood that, in their political struggle, the written word would be their most potent weapon.

At the tearful, cathartic ceremony to inaugurate *Bravo*'s publication, to get the ancestors' blessings, and to honor Te Rerehau, Hogan was asked to hold the
80 traditional family walking stick of *Haki Neha*, carved with Te Rerehaus's life story. A copy of the book was covered with a *korowai*, or ceremonial cloth and blessed by a Maori minister. Hogan, the first woman to speak at the dedication, found it difficult to speak at
85 first, so overwhelming were the emotions of the people around her.

1. It can reasonably be inferred that the intention of this passage is to:

   A. theorize about the changes that took place in both Hogan and the Maori when they were placed in contact with each other.

   B. explain the thousands of Maori words that are still in use.

   C. decry the insularity of the native New Zealand society.

   D. demonstrate the benefits of cultural discovery and exchange.

2. The discussion of the Maori ancestors and the strong emotions they elicit demonstrates that the:

   F. spirit of the past is very much alive in the Maori culture.

   G. pain of losing loved ones never goes away.

   H. emotions are valued by the Maori people.

   J. Maori have ingrained superstitions surrounding death and dying.

3. As it is used in line 30 of the passage, *wairua* is likely a quality that:

   A. is typically despised in Maori culture.

   B. promotes trust between individuals of different cultural backgrounds.

   C. is common in Western intellectuals.

   D. is crucial to the development of a free press.

4. Hogan's cultural explorations are compared to those of Te Rerehau (lines 13-16) in that both:

   F. traveled to Vienna, where they were apprenticed at the Imperial Printery.

   G. received PhDs in retirement.

   H. initially feared the *pakeha*, but eventually learned to respect them.

   J. were challenged by cultural barriers, but ultimately had successful and enlightening journeys.

5. It can reasonably be inferred that when the author says Wiremu "paid tribute" (line 62), she means that they:

   A. gave gifts of native Maori artifacts.

   B. showed honor and respect.

   C. prevented a military confrontation.

   D. acknowledged the soldiers as their masters.

6. It can reasonably be inferred from the passage that social acceptance of a non-Maori by the Maori was:

   F. invaluable to Hogan's work.

   G. respectful, but not necessary.

   H. impossible to truly attain.

   J. easy for Hogan to acquire.

7. The dates referred to in the passage indicate that Hogan's journey and that of the Maori travelers occurred:

   A. almost simultaneously.

   B. with Hogan's occurring shortly after Te Rerehau and Wiremu Toetoe's journey.

   C. with Hogan's preceding that of Te Rerehau and Wiremu Toetoe by roughly 150 years.

   D. with Hogan's following that of Te Rerehau and Wiremu Toetoe by roughly 150 years.

8. It can most reasonably be inferred from the third paragraph (lines 38-52) that the Austrian people's reaction to the Maori travelers was one of:

   F. horror and disgust.

   G. surprise and admiration.

   H. anger and outrage.

   J. jealousy and irritation.

9. It can be inferred that the word *cathartic*, as it is used in line 77, primarily refers to the ceremony's:

   A. sleepy and lethargic atmosphere.

   B. resentful undertones.

   C. lack of wairua.

   D. emotional significance.

10. According to the passage, which of the following is a Maori ceremonial cloth?

   F. *korowai*

   G. *Haki Neha*

   H. *Hokioi*

   J. *pakeha*

Passage VII

SOCIAL SCIENCE: Passage A is adapted from the article "Community Signs: How Vineyarders Enabled Themselves" by Bridget Goffman. Passage B is adapted from "Seeing Voices: A Journey Into the World of the Deaf" by Oliver Sacks.

Passage A by Bridget Goffman

In the history of Martha's Vineyard, there was a time when a significant portion of the population was deaf. When Gale Huntington was a boy in the early 1900s, for instance, ten deaf people lived in the small
5 town of Chilmark alone. I asked him what the hearing people in town had thought of the deaf people.

"Oh," he said. "They didn't think anything about them; they were just like everyone else."

"But how did people communicate with them—by
10 writing things down?"

"No," said Gale, surprised. "You see, everyone here spoke Sign Language."

"You mean deaf people's families?" I inquired.

"Sure," Gale replied. "And everybody else in town
15 too—I used to speak it, my mother did, everybody."

What I learned from Gale was confirmed by other older people I spoke to: The entire community was once bilingual in English and Sign Language. The inability to hear simply did not affect a person's status
20 in island society. In 1895, a reporter observed of gatherings on Martha's Vineyard: "The spoken language and Sign Language are so mingled in conversation that people pass from one to the other, or use both at once, almost unconsciously. Deaf people
25 are not uncomfortable because the community has adjusted itself to the situation so perfectly."

There are no longer any deaf people in this community, but the most striking fact I learned from talking to the people who remembered them is this: the
30 deaf men and women on Martha's Vineyard were not handicapped, because no one perceived their deafness as a handicap. As one woman said to me, "You know, we didn't think anything special about them. They were just like anyone else." For more than 250 years,
35 deaf Vineyarders were not only encouraged but expected to participate in the community to the fullest extent of their ability.

Today, when the medical, legal, and social service professions are heatedly arguing the advantages and
40 disadvantages of incorporating disabled individuals into mainstream society, the situation that existed on Martha's Vineyard is of particular relevance. The stories these elderly islanders shared with me merit careful consideration.

Passage B by Oliver Sacks

45 Helen Keller believed that her deafness was a far greater hardship than her blindness. "Blindness cuts people off from things," she said. "Deafness cuts people off from people." This is particularly true of deaf children in our society who have never been
50 taught Sign Language. A deaf child who never learns to sign may not acquire any language at all, and this was the case of a child I once met named Joseph.

A boy of eleven who had just entered school for the first time, Joseph had no language whatsoever. He had
55 been born deaf but this had not been realized until he was in his fourth year. His failure to talk or understand speech at the normal age was put down to "retardation," and this diagnosis had clung to him. When his deafness finally became apparent, he was
60 seen as "deaf and dumb," dumb not only literally but metaphorically, and there was never any real attempt to teach him language.

But Joseph longed to communicate. He looked alive and animated, but profoundly baffled; he was
65 attracted to speaking mouths and signing hands — his eyes darted to our mouths and hands, inquisitively and, it seemed to me, yearningly. He perceived that something was "going on" between us, but he could not comprehend what it was. He had, as yet, almost no idea
70 of symbolic communication and was unable to hold abstract ideas in his mind. In the first few months after I met him, he began to acquire some Sign Language and he had some communication with others. This gave him great joy: He wanted to stay at school all day,
75 all night, all weekend, all the time. His distress at leaving school was painful to see, for going home meant returning to silence, to a hopeless communicational vacuum where he could have no commerce with his parents, neighbors, and friends. It
80 meant becoming a non-person again.

Joseph was unable to communicate how he had spent the weekend—one could not really ask him, even in Sign Language. He could not even grasp the idea of a question, much less formulate an answer. But it was
85 not only language that was missing. There was not, it was evident, a clear sense of the past, of "a day ago," as distinct from "a year ago." His life only existed in the moment, in the present. And yet one still felt he was of normal intelligence. It was not that Joseph lacked a
90 mind, but that he was not using his mind fully. He was not mindless or mentally deficient without language, but he was severely restricted in the range of his thoughts—confined, in effect, to an immediate, small world.

1. The passage most strongly suggests that Gale is surprised by the author's question in lines 9-10 of Passage A because:

   A. he thought the answer was obvious.
   B. he was offended by the author's presumptuousness.
   C. he was amazed that the author had been so perceptive.
   D. he was alarmed by the author's tone.

2. The main function of the reporter's quote in lines 21-26 of Passage A is to:

   F. provide a scientific approach to the topic.
   G. present an opposing viewpoint.
   H. highlight a specific example.
   J. add validity to the author's description.

3. According to the passage, why is the author of Passage A so interested in the way deaf people were treated on Martha's Vineyard?

   A. She wants us to recognize how modernization impacts a community.
   B. She believes that Sign Language can be taught to everyone.
   C. She sees it as an example of how the deaf can be insulated from mainstream society.
   D. She considers the community a model for the integration of the disabled into society.

4. The author of Passage B is mainly concerned with conveying how:

   F. different children learn to speak.
   G. the lack of a language can affect a person.
   H. children who cannot read or write can still communicate through pictures.
   J. deaf children may not benefit from learning Sign Language after the age of ten.

5. Which of the following statements best describes the opinion held by the author of Passage B about Joseph's intelligence?

   A. His lack of a sense of sequential time indicated that he was mentally disabled.
   B. His deafness helped him develop an aptitude for the visual arts.
   C. Although his inadequate language acquisition restricted him, his intelligence was self-evident.
   D. He was adept at solving verbal problems, despite his inability to speak.

6. In the context of the passage, the statement that Joseph was "becoming a non-person again" (line 80) most nearly means that:

   F. he took no pleasure in activities at home.
   G. his family refused to learn Sign Language.
   H. his school did not teach him what role to play in his family.
   J. he could not communicate outside of school.

7. Which of the following examples provided in Passage B does the author use to support the claim that Joseph "was unable to hold abstract ideas in his mind" (lines 70-71)?

   A. He was fascinated by communication.
   B. He disliked going home from school.
   C. He did not grasp the concept of time.
   D. He eventually acquired language skills.

8. The authors of Passages A and B would probably agree with all the following statements EXCEPT

   F. hearing people should make an effort to accommodate the needs of deaf people.
   G. people are happier and healthier when they can communicate with others.
   H. the deaf prefer to keep to themselves.
   J. societies have a responsibility to integrate people with disabilities.

9. Which of the following statements best explains why Joseph's experience in Passage B was so different from the experience of the deaf people described in Passage A?

   A. Sign Language puts very restrictive limits on the ability of the deaf to communicate.
   B. Deaf people are often better at visual problems than at verbally-based ones.
   C. Having a language in common with the rest of society reduces the isolation of the deaf.
   D. Deafness, unlike blindness, separates people from people.

10. The experience of the deaf on Martha's Vineyard 100 years ago was similar to Joseph's in that:

    F. they needed to escape from isolation, eventually leaving the island altogether.
    G. they were incapable of developing beyond a rudimentary level of communication.
    H. their sense of the passage of time was seasonal and cyclic rather than chronological.
    J. they demonstrated that they had the capacity to communicate with those around them.

Passage VIII

SOCIAL SCIENCE: This passage is adapted from the essay "Tocqueville's Progression from Politics to History" by Steven Heyman.

Louis Napoleon's *coup d'état* was not six months old when Alexis de Tocqueville was asked by a French academy to give a valedictory speech at an upcoming academic ceremony. In resigning himself to the task,
5 Tocqueville fought the urge to include a passage from a speech that criticized Napoleon Bonaparte for suppressing the Académie.

But Tocqueville's April 1852 speech at the *Académie des Sciences Morales et Politiques* is
10 significant for other reasons. In his speech, he asserts the importance of the academy as a place where political theory is discussed and insists that it is a scholarly and not a political body. He then goes on to make clear the distinction between the theory of
15 politics (a subject for the academy) and the art of government (a subject for politicians). The entire speech reads like a covert declaration of the academy's right—if not duty—to continue thinking and discussing freely, even under despotic rule.

20 The speech, in effect, marked the end of Tocqueville's political career, which had brought him all the way to foreign minister. Tocqueville knew that, in a France of Louis Napoleon, there would be no room for him in politics. This, in a sense, provided a
25 window for Tocqueville to speak more frankly about the pitfalls of juggling politics and history—a practice that, for Tocqueville, in spite of his ardent political aspirations, yielded only scholarly success.

The brusque end to Tocqueville's political career
30 was coupled with a sense of great despair for the future of France. In February of 1852, he wrote that there was nothing for him to do but wait until the liberal spirit was reborn. He took to history, then, intending for it to distract him from the current climate.

35 Tocqueville began his track toward pure history, culminating in *L'Ancien Régime et La Révolution*, amid the backdrop of a political situation that became the embodiment of everything he detested. It seems a quintessential paradox of Tocqueville, how, as his
40 history became purer, it became more politically charged—albeit, at times, implicitly.

Tocqueville belonged to an age when thinkers were not expected to have only one area of academic expertise. His seminal works—*Souvenirs, L'Ancien
45 Régime et La Révolution* and *De la démocratie en Amérique*—are examples of political, historical and sociological writing. Tocqueville used his less-than-complete knowledge of French and English history to enrich *Démocratie*. But this work was far short of a
50 complete history.

When he was 51, *L'Ancien Régime*, the first total history, was written. Eighteen months later, and sixteen away from his death, he produced his first and only example of conventional narrative history.

55 *L'Ancien Régime et La Révolution* never dealt with the French Revolution proper and, more importantly, the outcome of the Revolution, in any comprehensive sense. It was Tocqueville's intention to write about it in a subsequent volume. Had he finished
60 his study on the French Revolution, he would have completed the historical development of his lifelong theme, which in *Democratie* he had treated sociologically. Toward the end of his career, Tocqueville admitted that the heft of his writing on
65 history dwarfed his political writings.

Even while in his political stage, the task of striking a balance between politics and history was a source of continual strain for Tocqueville who, perhaps as a result of his aristocratic pride, was
70 regarded as a straight-laced and stodgy politician. It was of utmost importance to preserve a sense of historical integrity, which, Tocqueville thought, compromised his chance for political success.

It is not my claim that Tocqueville wrote about
75 two essentially different things in his life, or even that he was motivated by different forces. Tocqueville was first a politician whose essays were spurred by ambition and, more importantly, by a dark, illiberal period in France which he took as a call to action. His
80 historical papers show a bookish reverence for facts, as well as a desire—it was always there, really—to treat history with fairness and integrity. If anything, his shift from political writing to the writing of history was caused by his forced removal from politics.
85 History, which was initially only a distraction, became a more apt means for Tocqueville to deal with his *idée mère*.

1. The passage makes the claim that Tocqueville's historical papers:

    A. were inspired by his fondness for facts and his affinity towards treating history fairly.
    B. were revered throughout Europe for their astonishing accuracy.
    C. characterized a dark, illiberal France.
    D. were written at the command of Louis Napoleon himself.

2. The author asserts that Tocqueville's April 1852 speech is significant because:

   F. he insisted that the university was a political, not a scholarly, body.
   G. Tocqueville was regarded as a straight-laced and stodgy politician.
   H. he insisted that the university was a scholarly, not a political, body.
   J. the speech marked the beginning of Tocqueville's illustrious political career.

3. One of the main points the author seeks to make in the passage is that Tocqueville:

   A. saw a fundamental conflict between the quest for historical accuracy and the advancement of one's political career.
   B. was torn between his love of freedom and his desire for political power.
   C. wrote *L'Ancien Régime*, his first total history, when he was 51.
   D. gave a speech at a French Academy six months after Louis Napoleon's *coup d'état.*

4. According to the passage, how does the theory of politics compare to the art of government?

   F. The theory of politics should be studied by politicians, while the art of government should be studied by governmental officials.
   G. Neither the theory of politics nor the art of government is a suitable topic to discuss in an academic setting.
   H. The theory of politics should be discussed in universities, while the art of government should be reserved for politicians.
   J. The theory of politics should be discussed by politicians, while the art of government should be reserved for universities.

5. According to the passage, what was the effect of Tocqueville's realization that, under Louis Napoleon, there would be no room for him in politics?

   A. Tocqueville took the situation as a call to action, and began mobilizing opposition to Napoleon's regime.
   B. Tocqueville sank into despair on account of his aristocratic pride.
   C. Tocqueville first started juggling politics with historical research.
   D. Tocqueville began to speak more freely, no longer constrained by political ambition.

6. When the author asserts that France was *illiberal,* he most likely means that France:

   F. was ungenerous with its resources, causing great poverty.
   G. did not look favorably upon free intellectual thought.
   H. was ruled by Louis Napoleon.
   J. did not allow people of his class into the political realm.

7. The author describes Tocqueville's works in lines 44-49 to make the point that he:

   A. incorporated ideas from a number of disciplines into his multifaceted and diverse theories and works.
   B. displayed knowledge solely in what we today would deem "history."
   C. viewed politics and history as mutually striving for the same ideals.
   D. allowed his preference for politics to skew his views on historical developments.

8. As used in line 73, the word *compromised* means:

   F. settled.
   G. pledged.
   H. increased.
   J. impaired.

9. According to the passage, which of the following are works published by Tocqueville?

   I. *L'Ancien Régime et La Révolution*
   II. *L'Académie des Sciences Morales*
   III. *De la démocratie en Amérique*

   A. I only.
   B. I and III.
   C. III only.
   D. I, II, and III.

10. The "quintessential paradox" that the author references in line 39 is the assertion that:

   F. as his politics became purer, they became more historically charged.
   G. the more power a person has, the better recognized his work will be.
   H. as his history became purer, it became more politically charged.
   J. as literary works become better known, they become more politically useful to the author.

Passage IX

HUMANITIES: This passage is adapted from "Shakespearean Playhouses" by Joseph Quincy Adams.

Before the building of regular playhouses, the itinerant troupes of actors were accustomed to give their performances in any place that chance provided, such as street-squares, barns, churches, and—most
5 frequently of all—the yards of inns. These yards were admirably suited to dramatic representations, consisting as they did of a large open court surrounded by two or more galleries.

One of the earliest moralities, *Mankind*, acted by
10 strollers in the latter half of the fifteenth century, gives us an interesting glimpse of an inn-yard performance. The opening speech makes distinct reference to the two classes of the audience described above as occupying the galleries and the yard: "O ye sovereigns
15 that sit, and ye brothers that stand right up." The "brothers," indeed, seem to have stood up so closely about the stage that the actors had great difficulty in passing to and from their dressing-room. Thus, one character leaves the stage with the request: "Make
20 space, sirs, let me go out!" Language such as this would hardly be appropriate if addressed to the "sovereigns" who sat in the galleries above; but, as addressed to the "brothers," it probably served to create a general feeling of good nature. And a feeling
25 of good nature was desirable, for the actors were facing the difficult problem of inducing the audience to pay for its entertainment.

This problem they met by taking advantage of the most thrilling moment of the plot. The Vice and his
30 wicked though jolly companions, having wholly failed to overcome the hero, Mankind, decide to call to their assistance the great Devil himself. Immediately he roars in the dressing-room, and shouts: "I come, with my legs under me!" There is a flash of powder, and an
35 explosion of fireworks, while the eager spectators crane their necks to view the entrance of this "abhomynabull" personage. But nothing appears; and in the expectant silence that follows the actors calmly announce a collection of money, facetiously making
40 the appearance of the Devil dependent on the liberality of the audience.

And with such phrases as "God bless you, master," "Ye will not say nay," "Let us go by," "Do them all pay," "Well mote ye fare," they pass through
45 the audience gathering their groats, pence, and twopence; after which they remount the stage, fetch in the Devil, and continue their play without further interruption.

In the smaller towns the itinerant players might
50 secure the use of the town-hall, of the schoolhouse, or even of the village church. In such buildings, of course, they could give their performances more advantageously, for they could place money-takers at the doors, and exact adequate payment from all who
55 entered. In the great city of London, however, the players were necessarily forced to make use almost entirely of public inn-yards—an arrangement which, we may well believe, they found far from satisfactory. Not being masters of the inns, they were merely
60 tolerated; they had to content themselves with hastily provided and inadequate stage facilities; and, worst of all, for their recompense they had to trust to a hat collection, at best a poor means of securing money. Often too, no doubt, they could not get the use of a
65 given inn-yard when they most needed it, as on holidays and festive occasions; and at all times they had to leave the public in uncertainty as to where or when plays were to be seen. Their street parade, with the noise of trumpets and drums, might gather a motley
70 crowd for the yard, but in so large a place as London it was inadequate for advertisement among the better classes. And as the troupes of the city increased in wealth and dignity, and as the playgoing public grew in size and importance, the old makeshift arrangement
75 became more and more unsatisfactory.

At last, the unsatisfactory situation was relieved by the specific dedication of certain large inns to dramatic purposes; that is, the proprietors of certain inns found it to their advantage to subordinate their
80 ordinary business to the urgent demands of the actors and the playgoing public. Accordingly they erected in their yards permanent stages adequately equipped for dramatic representations, constructed in their galleries wooden benches to accommodate as many spectators
85 as possible, and were ready to let the use of their buildings to the actors on an agreement by which the proprietor shared with the troupe in the "takings" at the door. Thus there came into existence a number of playhouses, where the actors, as masters of the place,
90 could make themselves quite at home.

1. The primary purpose of this passage is to:

   A. encourage readers to give generously to funds supporting local theater groups.
   B. share new information scholars have learned through observation of historical plays.
   C. convince readers that the services and housing provided to actors is inadequate.
   D. describe the progression of accommodations for actors and how actor groups adjusted.

2. Which of the following best describes the function of the first paragraph in relation to the passage as a whole?

F. It presents an image of actors that is challenged throughout the rest of the passage.

G. It supports the author's belief that audiences should not be divided based on their ability to afford premium seating.

H. It asserts a claim that is the foundation for the author's analysis of playwriting.

J. It establishes a context for the situations described later in the passage.

3. When the writer refers to a "problem" in line 28, he is most likely referring to:

A. actor troupes needing to convince audiences to pay for performances.

B. the difficulty actors had in going from the stage to their dressing room.

C. the separation of the audience into the upper galleries and lower yards.

D. the strained relationship between the characters of Vice and Mankind.

4. The passage's author most likely relates the opening speech of *Mankind* to:

F. illustrate how economics affected the organization of the audience.

G. provide an entertaining interruption to the academic analysis of historical theater.

H. suggest some artists were local citizens with family members in the audiences.

J. encourage the reader to study social structures that influenced 15ᵗʰ century architecture in Europe.

5. Which of the following is most similar to the actions of the actors described in the third paragraph (lines 28-41)?

A. television shows that interrupt climactic events with commercial breaks

B. professional athletes who switch teams based on which is willing to pay the highest salary

C. a local business that decides to expand its market by opening a store in a new location

D. a magician who uses excessive dramatics to disguise a simple illusion

6. The passage mentions actor troupes performing plays in all of the following locations EXCEPT:

F. inn-yards.

G. streets.

H. playhouses.

J. schoolhouses.

7. In the context of the passage, the phrase "a poor means of securing money" (line 63) can most nearly be paraphrased as:

A. an average amount of profits for a showing.

B. a popular profession for people with few assets.

C. a process of debt collection that was too costly and slow.

D. an unreliable method for collecting fees.

8. As it is used in lines 25, *nature* most nearly means:

F. wildlife.

G. landscape.

H. essence.

J. temperament.

9. The main purpose of the last paragraph is to:

A. reveal the lasting impact that theater has had on the architecture of England.

B. acknowledge that fifteenth-century actor troupes never found accommodations that were fully satisfactory.

C. describe the fortunate resolution to actor troupes' need for performance spaces.

D. present an optimistic prediction for the future of theatrical professions.

10. According to the passage, inn owners decided to build playhouses because:

F. they were enthusiastic fans of theater.

G. new laws required them to support London artists.

H. they could profit from taking some of the actors' revenue.

J. more space was needed for large gatherings during holidays and festive occasions.

Passage X

HUMANITIES: This passage is adapted from the article "Discovery or Mockery: The Unknown Origin of *La Bella Principessa*" by Joe Tan.

Perhaps it is fitting that the story of *La Bella Principessa*, a painting that has been the subject of much controversy, begins with a lie. According to art collector Peter Silverman, he was visiting a friend in
5 Switzerland when he opened a drawer and discovered an old drawing of a young woman. Executed in chalk and ink on a sheet of animal skin known as vellum, the delicate profile was of a beautiful, aristocratic, Milanese woman in Renaissance attire. According to
10 Silverman, "My heart started to beat a million times a minute. I immediately thought this could be a Florentine artist. The idea of Leonardo [da Vinci] came to me in a flash." Silverman asked his friend who the artist was, but his friend did not know for certain;
15 he had only bought the piece because he thought it was "a nice pretty thing." Silverman purchased the portrait from his friend, but didn't dare mention that he believed it was a work by the renowned artist da Vinci.

Though Silverman's tale makes for a thrilling
20 story, it is a dramatic fib, one of several fabrications of the story he has told. The truth is, Silverman first saw the portrait at an auction years earlier and he was outbid by Kate Ganz, a New York art dealer who acquired the piece for $21,850. At the time, it was
25 simply called *Head of a Young Girl in Profile to the Left* and classified as "19th-century, possibly German." Nearly a decade later, Silverman found the drawing in Ganz's New York gallery and bought it for only $19,000. During the years Ganz displayed the work,
30 many art experts concurred that the drawing was relatively modern. Ganz labeled it as "obviously based on a number of paintings by Leonardo da Vinci," but certainly not an authentic work by the master artist. If the drawing was by da Vinci, it had been overlooked
35 by some of the world's greatest experts and most respected collectors. It seems very unlikely that such an important discovery could be missed by so many knowledgeable people, and yet this is Silverman's incredible claim.

40 Whenever there is a discovery of a new piece by a renowned artist (and perhaps none are more renowned than da Vinci), the art world is filled with excitement and gossip. This latest discovery is no exception. Ganz stands by her judgment of the work,
45 saying, "I do not believe that this drawing is by Leonardo da Vinci, and nothing I have read or seen has changed my mind." However, Alessandro Vezzosi, director of the Leonardo da Vinci Museum in Vinci, Italy, is of the belief that *La Bella Principessa* is an
50 authentic da Vinci. "There is some embarrassment out there," says Vezzosi in response to critics such as Ganz. "Just looking at it, you know it isn't German." Vezzosi's faith in the authenticity of the drawing is supported by art-forensics specialist Peter Paul Biro,
55 who used sophisticated multispectral imaging technology to analyze the work. Biro discovered the print of an index finger on a corner of the drawing, and he claims the fingerprint is "highly comparable" to another found on da Vinci's painting in the Vatican.
60 "The fingerprint is simply a confirmation of what we believed to be true," Vezzosi says. "Like at a crime scene, it is often the sum of the clues that are gathered to arrive at what I call reasonable certainty." But critics have questioned Vezzosi's faith in Biro. Years earlier,
65 Biro was accused of falsely claiming that a painting was an authentic work by Jackson Pollock. His primary evidence: an alleged fingerprint, which some claim that Biro copied from a paint can in Pollock's studio. If Biro did forge the Pollock print, perhaps it is
70 not his only counterfeit. Presently, the debate over *La Bella Principessa* continues, and with more than 500 years separating the drawing's creation and its recent discovery, it will be a challenge to ever definitively know if it is the product of da Vinci's master hand.

75 You may wonder: Why all the fuss? What is the value of knowing whether or not the portrait is by da Vinci? One matter is money, the difference between a "possibly German" work worth $19,000 and a Renaissance masterpiece worth more than
80 $150,000,000. The other matter is the scholarly obsession with da Vinci, the genius and quintessential "Renaissance Man." Creator of the *Mona Lisa* and *The Last Supper*, he is considered to be one of the greatest painters ever to have lived. As a scientist and inventor
85 in numerous fields, he is also considered by some to be one of the most diversely talented people of all time. For centuries, scholars have sought to understand his skillful art and incredible mind. Every newly discovered work offers more insight, whereas falsely
90 accredited works will only muddy our understanding of the artist.

1. Based on the passage, confirming whether *La Bella Principessa* is by da Vinci is significant because:

   A. it determines whether the painting can provide insights into a great mind.
   B. it would settle the dispute over whether da Vinci is worthy of respect.
   C. it would show the credibility of Peter Silverman's professional expertise.
   D. Ganz should know if the painting was worth more than the price for which she sold it.

2. Which of the following statements best describes the structure of this passage?

   F. It begins with a story, which it discredits, and ends with an assertion of the topic's importance.
   G. It uses a highly detailed anecdote to show how the author's claims which he makes in the first paragraph are incorrect.
   H. It compares and contrasts the author's perspective on an artist with the perspectives of several other people.
   J. It focuses primarily on a story about a recent event in the author's life that he feels taught him an important lesson.

3. Viewed in the context of the passage, the information in lines 64-69 is most likely intended to suggest that:

   A. Jackson Pollock, like da Vinci, was an influential artist.
   B. it is impossible to determine whether a work of art is authentic.
   C. Biro's discovery should not be believed as authentic.
   D. the practice of art forgery is damaging the integrity of researchers and collectors.

4. The main function of the final paragraph (lines 75-91) is to:

   F. contrast the merits of average artists with those of great artists.
   G. offer an explanation for how *La Bella Principessa* might have been lost.
   H. illustrate the difficulty of trying to understand a person who is no longer living.
   J. describe the importance of the topic discussed in the passage.

5. The author develops the second paragraph (lines 19-39) mainly through:

   A. vague philosophical musings on the merits of classic art.
   B. detailed descriptions of his memories of art galleries.
   C. vivid depictions of da Vinci's most controversial art.
   D. personal assessments based on numerous facts.

6. The passage makes it clear that Silverman acquired the *La Bella Principessa* painting:

   F. at a friend's home in Switzerland.
   G. at an auction in New York.
   H. at Kate Ganz's art gallery.
   J. at a museum in Vinci, Italy.

7. The author calls Silverman's claim "incredible" (line 39) to support his argument that:

   A. it is likely false.
   B. it is part of an exciting story.
   C. da Vinci was an extremely talented artist.
   D. Silverman deserves credit for an important discovery.

8. It can be inferred from the passage that the author would most agree with whose judgment of *La Bella Principessa*?

   F. Peter Silverman
   G. Kate Ganz
   H. Alessandro Vezzosi
   J. Peter Paul Biro

9. By his statement in lines 1-3, the author is most nearly asserting that:

   A. it does not matter whether we know the true origins of *La Bella Principessa*.
   B. nothing is known about the history of *La Bella Principessa*.
   C. there are several controversies relating to the history of *La Bella Principessa*.
   D. *La Bella Principessa* has a unique style unlike any other traditional art.

10. The "embarrassment" mentioned in line 50 most directly refers to:

    F. the incorrect claim that da Vinci was German.
    G. the supposed mistake of many art experts who did not recognize a work of da Vinci.
    H. the controversy surrounding Biro's forensics.
    J. the self-consciousness and anxiety of people who are the subjects of portraits.

Passage XI

HUMANITIES: This passage is adapted from the essay "The New Function of Art and the Loss of Human Experience" by Vera Bagnyuk.

While it is rather problematic to define what exactly was or is Modernism, modernity itself exhibits very specific phenomena that continue to alter the notion of human experience. With the rise of
5 technology and industrialization—and, subsequently, the rise of the middle class and leisure time—came the downfall of the self and of human experience. This downfall is particularly evident in the new function that art serves in the modern society, and in the gradual
10 erosions of older forms to make room for newer forms, such as the introduction of photography and film in the case of visual art, and shortening of the average pop music piece to three or four minutes.

These new mediums cater to the new experience
15 of experience, or lack thereof. The commodification of art and the ever-rising tide of information have, in many ways, paved new paths for experiencing boredom. One's instant reaction to the function of art is to relate to the representation of reality, or the
20 popular notion that all art must represent life on some level. However, the new function of art is precisely that it does not focus on representing any sort of truth, but rather serves a decorative or distracting purpose, which is the complete reverse of the very definition of
25 truth or reality.

Broch and Benjamin argue that the function of art changed drastically at the beginning of the nineteenth century due to its escalating concern with decoration and no longer with representation of truth. True art,
30 according to Broch, is "superior to kitsch only because it deals with new representations of reality; not with sole purpose of creating sensation." Broch and Benjamin attribute this to rapid industrialization at the beginning of the 1800s. The sudden increase of leisure
35 time prompted the redefinition of art. Historically, art has been limited to wealthy patrons and the artist himself—the peasants and the artisans were not privy to it. The rise of the bourgeoisie produced an interest in art, but art itself was evaluated for its aesthetic
40 assessment rather than its reality.

Various methods of mass production were developing simultaneously, such as lithography, which enabled art to be produced and reproduced more quickly than a painting or drawing could. In other
45 words, art became more prevalent and its ability to be reproduced rendered the quantity greater than the quality, but even the quality was assessed in decorative terms. Broch termed this a "new religion of beauty"

that was growing among the masses who had the
50 leisure to purchase the status of owning art works but not necessarily enough leisure time to absorb their meaning and non-decorative value.

The search for mere decoration negates the meaning of the object, and yet artworks deemed the
55 most brilliant and meaningful today are ones that were created for ritual use rather than exhibition. The "aura" of the art object is created by the knowledge of its ritual use. Benjamin argues that a reproduction cannot replicate the aura, while it is possible to replicate the
60 shape and the color of the object.

Nevertheless, it is the mere imitation that erases the spiritual, or aural, dimension of the object because it is being taken out of its context that gives it significance. Brush strokes, original size, and the
65 condition of the original work are just a few of the contextual elements lost in a reproduction. Placing a reproduction in one's own bedroom further renders it meaningless. Art that is stripped of its aura, its ritual meaning, its authenticity, and in Broch's terms, of its
70 reality, is art that is only good for reproducibility.

This, Benjamin concludes, is art's new function— solely to exist for its own sake, meaning exhibition. The earlier function as representation of reality is now taken on by the new medium of photography, and
75 later, film. It was the start of the information society, where reality evolved to become purely factual.

The irony of photography and film as new media for representation of reality was that the represented was not reality. The practice of photo captioning, as
80 Benjamin mentions, replaces any remnants of personal interpretation that could be extracted from looking at a photo. Film takes it even further by unfolding the scenes of the storyline so quickly that the mind is dictated the trajectory of the message without the need
85 of caption. Moreover, the existence of photography and film facilitates the effacing of the medium—one does not see the photo or video camera, just the product; and it is the effacing of this medium that removes aura from such art. What remains is the so-
90 called reality without the "contamination" by the medium—that is, the subject of the artist's (or kitsch artist's) choosing, dictated by the consumer's need for a certain reality—and this trend is continuing today.

1. The passage suggests that photography:

    A. is the superior art form of the twentieth century.
    B. is an adequate replacement for classical art.
    C. takes away from the meaning of art.
    D. is impressive in its ability to capture reality.

2. It can reasonably be inferred from the passage that the author believes that art was truer in previous centuries because:

   F. it was created only for wealthy patrons and artists, instead of for a mass audience.
   G. it was the primary source of decoration.
   H. people had more leisure time in previous centuries.
   J. modern people are averse to good art.

3. The passage primarily emphasizes the idea that modernism:

   A. created a higher standard of living in the Western world.
   B. turned art into a meaningless escape from boredom.
   C. gave people more time to appreciate what was truly beautiful.
   D. created photography, a fascinating tool for capturing reality.

4. As it is used in lines 86 and 91, *medium* most nearly means:

   F. middle.
   G. compromise.
   H. moderate.
   J. tool.

5. It can reasonably be inferred from the passage that the author thinks art serving a decorative purpose is:

   A. a trend that had roots long before its outward development at the beginning of the nineteenth century.
   B. a pleasant distraction from the weighty realities and responsibilities that confront us in the modern technological age.
   C. only distantly and weakly related to true art, which delves into deeper human truths.
   D. a natural evolution of artistic styles that fails to serve a practical purpose in modern times.

6. It can reasonably be inferred from the passage that all of the following are considered "inferior" mediums to produce art EXCEPT:

   F. photography.
   G. computer graphics.
   H. watercolors.
   J. print.

7. The "irony" the author refers to in lines 77-79 is that:

   A. film and photography were intended to capture reality more accurately than painting, but what they captured was further from the truth than what classical art portrayed.
   B. classical art was intended to capture reality more accurately than photography, but what it captured was further from the truth than what modern film portrays.
   C. film is supposed to be honest, but it can often be used to create lies.
   D. painted subjects are often imaginary, whereas photographed subjects always exist.

8. When the author describes a "new religion of beauty" (line 48) she is describing:

   F. a new generation of art owners who strive for truth over beauty in art.
   G. a new interpretation of art that has a unique, powerful grasp of truth unfamiliar to artists from previous generations.
   H. an appreciation of art that comes from the status associated with possession rather than from an honest appreciation of the essential meaning of the work.
   J. the current desire to own pieces of art.

9. It can reasonably be inferred from the passage that the author believes that our modern ability to replicate classical pieces of art:

   A. is one of the major advantages of the modern era.
   B. results in a large quantity of inferior pieces.
   C. was influenced by the invention of photography.
   D. will only continue to a greater extent in the future.

10. Broch and Benjamin most attribute the change in the public's attitude towards art to the:

    F. decreasing average intelligence of the modern man.
    G. modern innovations in art media, which led to a greater appreciation of art.
    H. Industrial Revolution of the 1800s.
    J. beauty and naturalness of photography.

Passage XII

HUMANITIES: This passage is adapted from the essay "L'hypocrite Lecteur, Monsieur Sartre? An analysis of Jean-Paul Sartre's Study of Charles Baudelaire" by Steven Heyman.

Most halfway decent biographies of Jean-Paul Sartre begin at his funeral. Such a beginning makes sense for an author and philosopher whose work is almost universally characterized as "a real downer,"
5 "dark," and "depressing." But everyone who was in Paris for Sartre's funeral on April 19, 1980—and there were tens of thousands—spoke of the event as a triumphant moment for western thought, almost a celebration.

10 It was a triumph simply by right of the turnout. Not only for its size—50,000, and countless more watching on television—but also for all the disparate groups which, proud to cite Sartre as a friend, spokesman or avatar, had come to pay their final
15 respects: Insurgents. Algerians. Arabs and Jews. Communists. Freedom Fighters. Petits-bourgeois. Children. Students, of course. Africans. Asians.

The 50,000 souls who passed all of Sartre's smoke-encased haunts down the Boulevard Edgar-
20 Quinet knew then—and even a long while before then—that Monsieur Sartre had left much behind. At the age of 20, when he wrote the short play, *J'aurai Un Bel Enterrement*, Sartre would have been hard-pressed to envision such a spectacle.

25 Earlier, during the wake, three veterans of Sartre's journal, *Les Temps Modernes*, smoked, drank and remembered the philosopher until 5 a.m., when a nurse finally kicked them out of the hospital where his body lay. Charged with organizing the funeral, the trio
30 visited the director of the Montparnasse Cemetery, who, according to one of them, greeted them with much civility. Sartre would be buried in a temporary grave, he said, and then, after his body was disinterred and cremated, he would be moved to the first alley, to
35 the right of the gate. "You'll see it's very peaceful," the funeral director said, "and not too far from Baudelaire. If I remember correctly, Sartre wrote a book on Baudelaire, didn't he?"

In 1946 Jean-Paul Sartre published *Baudelaire*, a
40 stunning caricature of the vaunted nineteenth-century poet which, for all its gusto, is today of little or no critical importance to either scholars of Baudelaire or Existentialism. Sartre himself later called his book "extremely bad."

45 Is *Baudelaire* just a relic? The short answer is, of course, yes—it is too bold, too wide of the mark.

Baudelaire is written with rancor; obviously not wearing kid gloves, Sartre seems to throw punches at the venerable poet with brass knuckles. What fueled
50 his passion? Was it his method, his philosophy that provided him with a rubric for judging Baudelaire? Or was it something deeper, more secret and sinister? Many have suggested that Sartre saw a bit of Baudelaire in his own psyche, and attempted in
55 *Baudelaire* to repudiate his own psychological destiny.

All of Sartre's study flows from what is referred to as Baudelaire's initial choice, made at the age of seven and resulting from the trauma of his mother's
60 second marriage, to flee into a self-imposed exile. Baudelaire's trauma from losing the total affection of his mother— "when one has a son like me, one doesn't remarry"—leads to a flight into the self. Baudelaire sets to affirm himself as different; he is condemned to
65 a separate existence. He prefers himself to everyone else since everyone (at the time, "everyone" was his mother) abandoned him.

Sartre goes on to rebuke Baudelaire for being immature, narcissistic, masochistic, obsessive, and
70 exhibitionistic. What makes these accusations sting— and, in a sense, sing with a completely novel profundity—is Sartre's belief that we choose what we wish to become. As such, Baudelaire is "fully and lucidly responsible" for his financial woes, his
75 syphilis, and his emotional addiction to his mother. Sartre explains how Baudelaire, through a denial of the absolute freedom that he, unlike most of us, knew he possessed, inculcated these psychological problems and sought the torment which marked his anguished
80 existence.

Sartre's great mind washes over the particulars of Baudelaire's life—and his literary creations—with almost a reckless attention to his conclusion: summing up Baudelaire as a superfluous, in many respects
85 useless, poet who deserved his entire lot in life right down to his case of syphilis. So Sartre refuses to track any development in the life of his subject, refuses to delineate a succession of events. The method leads us toward startling relationships but, ultimately, I think,
90 in the wrong direction.

1. The author's attitude toward Sartre's criticism of Baudelaire can best be described as:

    A. insulted anger.
    B. intense dislike.
    C. jealous rivalry.
    D. critical skepticism.

2. The main purpose of the passage is to:

   F. examine Jean-Paul Sartre and his criticism of Baudelaire.
   G. illustrate what French society was like at the time of Sartre's death.
   H. discuss Baudelaire's relationship with his mother.
   J. describe the major tracts of modern philosophy.

3. According to the second paragraph (lines 10-17), Sartre's funeral was a triumph because:

   A. although few people attended, those who paid their respects were influential members of the community.
   B. his funeral symbolized the surprising journey he had made through adversity and hard times.
   C. 50,000 people from many different walks of life attended to pay him their respects.
   D. the European philosophical community saw past Sartre's earlier failures and appreciated him for his later works.

4. When the author talks of Baudelaire's "initial choice" (line 58), he means:

   F. the choice that Baudelaire made to separate himself from those around him, as a result of his mother's rejection.
   G. the choice that Baudelaire made to put himself into debt.
   H. the choice that Baudelaire made to contract syphilis.
   J. the choice that Baudelaire made to be emotionally addicted to his mother.

5. As described in the passage, Sartre's legacy can best be summarized by which of the following statements?

   A. Sartre's impact can be safely overlooked because his book, *Baudelaire*, was "extremely bad."
   B. Sartre made an impact with his first novels, but that impact lessened over time.
   C. Sartre's tremendous impact has been primarily limited to his book, *Baudelaire*.
   D. Sartre's impact was so great that at his death, tens of thousands of people regarded his funeral as a celebration of Western thought.

6. According to the author, Sartre's criticism of Baudelaire's lifestyle is particularly stinging because:

   F. Baudelaire, for all his failings, tried hard to live a noble life.
   G. Baudelaire was jealous of Sartre as a contemporary in the philosophical world.
   H. Sartre believed that we choose what we become.
   J. Sartre's criticisms of Baudelaire are founded more on Sartre's own psychological profile than on any of Baudelaire's actual doings.

7. The passage indicates that Sartre's own appraisal of *Baudelaire* was that it was:

   A. a magnificent work of art.
   B. a work without any merit.
   C. obsessed with repudiating his own psychological destiny.
   D. headed in the wrong direction.

8. It can reasonably be inferred that the author believes that had Sartre seen his own funeral when he was 20 years old, his reaction would have been one of:

   F. disbelief.
   G. satisfaction.
   H. horror.
   J. fury.

9. The author calls *Baudelaire* a "relic" (line 45) because:

   A. it is today of little or no critical importance to scholars of Baudelaire or Existentialism.
   B. it was written so long ago that it can be characterized as ancient art.
   C. the author believes the work is so bad that it should be buried in the sands of time and never considered again.
   D. Baudelaire's emotional attachment to his mother affected his entire existence.

10. According to the passage, Sartre's book on Baudelaire was mentioned after Sartre's death by:

    F. his mother.
    G. the funeral director.
    H. Montparnasse.
    J. Baudelaire himself.

Passage XIII

NATURAL SCIENCE: Passage A is adapted from the article "Dino Theory Flies Out the Window" by Peter Wolfe. Passage B is adapted from the article "It's a Bird! It's a Reptile! It's a Snapshot of Evolution!" by Cecile Erickson.

Passage A by Peter Wolfe

Some over-eager scientists are falsely regarding the Archaeopteryx, which lived 145 million years ago, as not only the first bird but also a theropod, one of the late ground-dwelling dinosaurs. About the size of a
5   crow, Archaeopteryx had many skeletal similarities to certain species of dinosaurs, such as sharp teeth and curving claws. Other features seem distinctively avian—a covering of insulating fuzz, an opposable *hallux,* or big toe, and a *furcula,* or wishbone, formed
10 from fused clavicles. While this fossil shows an interesting set of features, it is only a testament to how distant common ancestors and shared environmental pressures can lead to similar evolutionary paths; it is not proof that birds originated from theropods.

15 Modern birds are descendants of some birdlike species that have yet to be discovered. The evolutionary jump from a ground-dwelling dinosaur like the theropod to flight is just too massive. The Archaeopteryx is an acknowledged early relation to
20 birds, exhibiting many structural features including a clavicle and birdlike feet. Various species of theropods lacked clavicles; it is unlikely that clavicles disappeared from theropods and then reappeared in the Archaeopteryx.

25 Furthermore, the dinofuzz that surrounded Archaeopteryx and species like it covered their bodies entirely; it was an excellent insulator. Yet those who believe that feathers originally developed for insulation, and capacity for flight came as a byproduct,
30 are ignoring the logic of evolution. Feathers are ideally suited for flight and energetically costly to produce, too costly and complex to have developed for the purpose of insulation alone when a coat of fur would suffice. It is illogical to think that feathers were formed
35 for insulation and then flight developed as a result. Rather, feathers were developed for the specific purpose of flight. Some tree-dwelling creatures may have had the need for mobility beyond jumping and thus developed into birds, but it is unlikely that a
40 ground-dweller would suddenly find itself coated with warm feathers and take to the sky.

Passage B by Cecile Erickson

Modern birds are the direct descendants of ancient, meat-eating dinosaurs called theropods, a

famous example of which is Tyrannosaurus Rex.
45 Although there are many differences between modern birds and theropods of the past, these differences are irrelevant from an evolutionary standpoint because they occurred further down the evolution chain. Proof of common ancestry lies in the similarities; there are
50 at least 85 characteristics that link features of birds to their theropod relatives.

The Archaeopteryx is generally accepted as being the oldest known bird; it links dinosaurs and birds in evolutionary history. The Archaeopteryx shares traits
55 with both birds and dinosaurs, and helps us put in context the birdlike traits found in many theropods by giving us an example of a transitory species.

Sinosauropteryx, a theropod approximately 130 million years old, was covered in dinofuzz not unlike
60 that of the Archaeopteryx. Fossils show that theropods also had clavicles as part of their skeletal structure, which would fuse together later to form the *furcula* (wishbone) found in birds. Unenlagia, approximately 88 million years old, was found to hold its arms in the
65 same way that birds fold their wings. Oviraptor sat on its eggs in a bird-like fashion. Various other theropods had hollow bones and three-toed feet; certain types of theropods known as *maniraptorans,* like the Rahona, even had back-facing curved claws on its hind feet just
70 like the ones that allow modern birds to perch on branches.

The flight capacity of birds could actually have been an adapted skill that started as ground-dwelling theropods jumped into the air to hunt insects. It is
75 unclear exactly how the proto-feathers that allowed this developed, but one promising theory is that, in changing climates, they served as insulation, an effective alternative to the scales of other species.

1. The author of Passage A lists all of the following as birdlike features of the Archaeopteryx EXCEPT:

    A. sharp teeth.
    B. insulation.
    C. opposable *hallux.*
    D. fused clavicles.

2. As it is used in line 12, *common* most nearly means:

    F. public.
    G. ordinary.
    H. mutual.
    J. dull.

3. Which of the following statements would the author of Passage A NOT support?

   A. Archaeopteryx was definitely a bird and not a theropod.
   B. Birds were direct descendants of Archaeopteryx, not of theropods.
   C. Many species of theropods lacked clavicles.
   D. Feathers are too complex to have been simply an insulator.

4. Passage B does NOT include the hypothesis that:

   F. feathers formed for a purpose other than flight.
   G. flight evolved from a tree-dwelling creature.
   H. similar traits in two species are important to determining the trail of evolution.
   J. Archaeopteryx was an evolutionary offshoot related to birds.

5. Passage B states that Archaeopteryx, the first bird, helps link birds to dinosaurs. If true, which of the following could be used to counter this argument?

   A. Archaeopteryx was more dinosaur than bird, and therefore not closely related to birds.
   B. Archaeopteryx had traits of both birds and dinosaurs.
   C. Archaeopteryx had a clavicle.
   D. Archaeopteryx ate insects.

6. Which of the following statements best explains why the author of Passage B mentions Rahona?

   F. Rahona shows both theropod and bird qualities.
   G. Rahona shows neither theropod nor bird qualities.
   H. Rahona was clearly a bird.
   J. Rahona was clearly a theropod.

7. Proponents of both theories would agree with which of the following conclusions?

   A. Theropods were the ancestors of modern day birds.
   B. Dinofuzz was an adaptation that led to the capacity for flight.
   C. The *furcula* is a structure unique to birds.
   D. Archaeopteryx was a direct ancestor of modern day birds.

8. Passage A differs from Passage B regarding the clavicle in that:

   F. Passage A states that the clavicle was always present in theropods.
   G. Passage A states that the clavicle would not be needed in theropods to link them to birds.
   H. Passage A states that theropods never had clavicles.
   J. Passage A states that the clavicle was not always present, and it would be impossible for a clavicle to reappear as a *furcula* in modern birds.

9. Compared to the author of Passage A, the author of Passage B provides more information about:

   A. the physical features of the Archaeopteryx.
   B. bird-like traits of specific theropods.
   C. the use of insulating fuzz on dinosaurs.
   D. the location of the discovery of the Archaeopteryx.

10. Suppose that scientists discovered a fossil of a theropod that was similar to the Archaeopteryx, lived on the ground, and had feather-covered wings. This finding would most directly support the argument of the author of:

    F. Passage A, because it indicates that Archaeopteryx is a direct ancestor of birds.
    G. Passage A, because it indicates that Archaeopteryx is not a direct ancestor of birds.
    H. Passage B, because it indicates that Archaeopteryx is a direct ancestor of birds.
    J. Passage B, because it indicates that Archaeopteryx is not a direct ancestor of birds.

Passage XIV

NATURAL SCIENCE: This passage is adapted from the essay "To Each as They Need: An Argument for Life Cycle Assessment" by Alex M. Shapiro.

Does our society fully understand how the materials we manufacture affect the environment? Environmental studies have increased our awareness of the multiple interactions that are played out in the world around us. It is no longer accurate to speak of end-products in isolation.

Industries developing chemicals or any new product have in the past been required to study only the behavior of these materials in relation to their intended use under controlled conditions. But think of a battery or a disposable diaper: the period during which a product is actually used can represent only a small fraction of its life. It must be manufactured, distributed, and then sold. Once it has fulfilled its intended use, it must be disposed of in some fashion. A product can have serious environmental consequences at any one of these stages, both before and after its intended use, and no current state or federal regulations require companies to test for these effects.

A "life-cycle assessment" is exactly such an evaluation. It examines the environmental impact that a product could have at every stage of its life. What raw materials were extracted to make it? How were these materials processed and did this process create any hazardous by-products? Can it be disposed of in a fashion that does not contaminate air, soil, or groundwater?

The life-cycle assessment consists of three distinct phases: inventory analysis, impact analysis, and improvement analysis. The first phase consists of the quantification of all air emissions, waterborne effluents, solid wastes, and other releases into the environment at every stage in the life of the chemical or product. The impact analysis evaluates the quantities compiled during the inventory phase and analyzes the impact that all releases could have on the environment. This is perhaps the most important stage and it can be extremely complex, because it requires the calculation of a wide variety of environmental factors and possible results.

In the final phase, recommendations are made for specific changes to improve environmental effects.

An example of the kind of problem life-cycle assessments would prevent is a phenomenon known to toxicologists as synergism. Pesticides provide a well-known example of synergism. Malathion and Delnav are two organophospate insecticides, which were tested separately for the number of fish deaths they would cause at certain concentrations. When the two chemicals were combined, however, their toxicity was significantly greater than their individual tests allowed scientists to expect. Scientists speculate that there may be many similar occurrences of unpredicted and currently unknown synergistic toxicities operating in the environment.

There is increasing public concern over the disposal of products and the release of chemicals whose effects on the environment are not adequately understood. Life-cycle assessments are objective, fact-based processes designed to meet this need. The U.S. Environmental Protection Agency and other organizations are still involved in developing the scientific basis and technical guidelines for these assessments. But many scientists and policymakers believe that once these guidelines are completed, every manufacturer should be required to file a comprehensive evaluation of environmental impacts similar to the statements, which must be filed by developers on large construction projects. Many expect life-cycle assessments to become an essential component in the field of environmental regulation and a prerequisite for the approval of both new and existing products and chemicals.

Although these arguments primarily concern corporations, we as individuals can perform life-cycle assessments, too. Next time you purchase a product with the intention of helping the environment, consider what will happen to it after you dispose of it. Plastic cups may say they are made of recycled material, but where will they go once you have had your drink? Just as a well-intentioned child plucks a flower to try to grow it in a pot, only finding that he has killed it, you may be harming the environment more than you think. Consider paper cups, which are biodegradable, as an alternative. It is an interesting facet of human nature that we concern ourselves only with the present—or at best, the immediate, visible, future. Don't allow this tendency to detract from the actions you take as an environmentally responsible citizen.

1. The passage states that *synergism* is:

    A. the disposal of products and the release of chemicals whose effects on the environment are not adequately understood.
    B. the symbiosis of biodegradable materials.
    C. the illegal use of pesticides.
    D. the mixing of chemicals that together are more harmful to the environment than any of the individual products.

2. The passage indicates that the life-cycle assessment contains which of the following sequences of events?

   F. The quantification of total releases, then an analysis of the impact of the releases, and then recommendations for specific changes.
   G. An analysis of the impact of the releases, then a quantification of total releases, and then recommendations for specific changes.
   H. The quantification of total releases, then an analysis of the inventory, then recommendations for specific changes.
   J. An analysis of the impact of the releases, then an analysis of the inventory, then an analysis of possible improvement.

3. The author likens the reader to a well-intentioned child because both:

   A. perform life-cycle assessments.
   B. intentionally harm the environment.
   C. use plastic instead of paper cups.
   D. do more damage than they realize when trying to help the environment.

4. The passage indicates that the damage a battery can cause is not controlled by the government because:

   F. many expect life-cycle assessments to become an essential component in the field of environmental regulation.
   G. of a phenomenon known to toxicologists as synergism.
   H. the period during which a product is used can represent only a small fraction of its life.
   J. currently no regulations require companies to test for the effect a battery has on the environment after it has been disposed.

5. It can reasonably be inferred that the author finds the second stage of a life-cycle assessment the most important because:

   A. it consists of the quantification of air emissions, solid wastes, and other releases into the environment at every stage in the life of the chemical or product.
   B. although it is the simplest stage, it produces the most useful results.
   C. it is the step that actively calls on companies to effect change.
   D. it is the most complex stage, and yields results that illustrate a product's impact.

6. The passage indicates that once guidelines are completed by the U.S. Environmental Protection Agency, many expect life-cycle assessments will:

   F. become virtually unnecessary.
   G. be necessary for all companies either putting a new product on the market or making the case for an existing product.
   H. become the cause of many expensive lawsuits.
   J. replace recycling as the most important action to take in order to protect the environment.

7. The author calls life-cycle assessments "objective" in line 59 because they are:

   A. designed with specific goals in mind.
   B. not biased by liberal or conservative views.
   C. fact-based.
   D. based on the opinion of the tester.

8. When the author says, "It is no longer accurate to speak of end-products in isolation" (lines 5-6), she means that:

   F. placing products in an area where they are far away from humans is no solution to the environmental problem they pose.
   G. new scientific data shows that end-products are less deadly to the environment than was originally assumed.
   H. a discussion of the environmental soundness of a product should no longer begin and end with the way it is sold, as the rest of its life should be considered, too.
   J. former scientific data exaggerated the significance of the manufacturing process.

9. The author favors paper cups over plastic cups because:

   A. plastic cups are biodegradable.
   B. paper cups aren't biodegradable.
   C. plastic cups aren't biodegradable.
   D. paper cups are equal to plastic cups in environmental soundness.

10. As it is used line 25, *hazardous* most closely means:

    F. dangerous.
    G. producing a warning.
    H. confusing.
    J. random.

Passage XV

NATURAL SCIENCE: This passage is adapted from the article "Cooking Up Science" by Anne Williams.

Laboratory science has always shared similarities with the art of cooking. Both require the careful use of techniques and chemicals. In both, precise temper-atures and sterile environments are often necessary.
5 Many culinary techniques, such as the baking of bread or making of cheese, rely on chemical processes that have been studied and perfected by scientists. In some cases, major scientific discoveries have relied on the innovations and expertise from the world of cooking.
10 It should come as no surprise that when microbiologist Walther Hesse conducted his studies on bacteria, the key to his research would be based on techniques from the kitchen.

Many common foods rely on bacteria. Without
15 these hungry microbes, we would not have yogurt, sauces, or pickles. Sourdough bread relies on bacterial colonies, known as "mother doughs," some of which have been carefully cultivated by families of bakers for over a hundred years. But despite their prevalence,
20 bacteria were little understood by the scientific community. Throughout much of the nineteenth century, scientists were unable to differentiate between strains of bacteria. On pieces of spoiled food, such as moldy bread, it was clear that different
25 organisms were growing because they were different colors, sizes, and textures. In order to study and understand these microbe colonies, scientists would have to isolate and cultivate them. In the simplest terms, this is analogous to separating and planting
30 different types of plant seeds in order to study how they grow differently. However, this is much more complicated with bacteria. Walther Hesse was a brilliant pioneer of the idea that microorganisms exist everywhere, even within the air we breathe, but he
35 struggled to prove his theory because these organisms are too small to see and too plentiful to separate.

Early attempts to cultivate bacteria proved ineffective, but showed the usefulness of food in these studies. A very basic experiment might involve
40 removing a spoiled portion of fruit and inserting it into unspoiled fruit monitored in a sterile environment. Hesse's laboratory partner, Robert Koch, used slices of potato to grow bacterial colonies. By boiling a potato and cutting it in half with a heated blade, he
45 could create a sterile environment that could be used to grow specific bacteria. This method was used to find the cause of anthrax, which marked the first time that a bacterium was proven to cause disease. However, Koch's experiments were limited because only certain
50 bacteria could thrive on the nutrients in potatoes. In Hesse's own experiments, he used filters to capture airborne microorganisms, which he then cultivated in gelatin. Different nutrients, such as beef broth, could be mixed in the gelatin in order to encourage or
55 prohibit growth of certain bacteria. However, the gelatin would melt at the warm temperatures needed to grow many bacteria, and some bacteria would consume and degrade the gelatin. Hesse was frustrated by his search for a medium that would be stable,
60 adaptable, and hospitable to microbial life.

The solution to Walther Hesse's problem came from his wife's knowledge of food. One story says that Walther and his wife Angelina were enjoying a summer picnic when he noticed that her desserts were
65 not melting in the heat. She explained that her jellies and puddings were made with agar, an algae-based gelatinous substance commonly used in many Asian cuisines. A more likely story is that Angelina, who often assisted Walther in the laboratory, recognized
70 that the gelatin he was using, which was derived from animal collagen, was not as stable as agar, which she had used in making Indonesian dishes. With Angelina's guidance, Walther created a gel of agar and meat broth which proved perfect for his experiments.

75 The combined work of the Hesses led to the creation of Petri dishes (Julius Petri worked with Hesse and Koch), which are commonly used in microbiology research today. With the use of agar plates, Walther Hesse continued his study of diseases,
80 laying the foundation for the battle against tuberculosis, cholera, and typhoid fever. It is thanks to the innovation of the Hesses that we have been able to develop preservatives and vaccinations which protect us from disease.

1. The passage can best be described as an exploration of:

   A. several unexpected events that have led to scientific discoveries throughout history.
   B. the health benefits of different cuisines.
   C. the natural processes by which strains of bacteria develop and spread.
   D. the origin of a useful scientific tool.

2. The passage mentions all of the following as materials used to cultivate bacteria EXCEPT:

   F. dough.
   G. fruit.
   H. potatoes.
   J. collagen.

3. The author's overall tone when discussing Hesse's work can best be described as:

    A. doubtful.
    B. indifferent.
    C. admiring.
    D. critical.

4. Which of the following best states how the last paragraph functions in the passage as a whole?

    F. It explains the significance of the experiments discussed in the passage.
    G. It transitions the focus of the passage from cooking techniques to scientific research.
    H. It makes a comparison between Hesse's rudimentary work and the more advanced methods used now.
    J. It restates the central point made in the first paragraph.

5. The passage suggests that, before Hesse's experiments, scientists struggled to study bacteria because:

    A. bacteria are rare and therefore hard to find.
    B. researchers lacked the necessary ingredients to create Petri dishes.
    C. it was not understood that bacteria can cause disease.
    D. it was difficult to create controlled environments with single strains of bacteria.

6. It can be logically inferred from the passage that Koch used a heated blade in his experiments because:

    F. the heat would kill any bacteria that might otherwise contaminate the experiment.
    G. it would be easier to cut through the potatoes than if he used a cold blade.
    H. the heat would melt any gelatin that might degrade the bacteria.
    J. he was testing the reaction of bacteria to certain temperatures and therefore needed to match the heat of the blade to that of the boiled potato.

7. The author uses the example of dividing and growing plant seeds in order to:

    A. emphasize the connection between culinary ingredients and subjects of scientific research.
    B. demonstrate the many food-based environments in which bacteria grow.
    C. explain the aims of certain scientists studying bacteria.
    D. illustrate how much simpler it is to cultivate bacteria than it is to cultivate plants.

8. As it is used in line 24, the word *clear* most nearly means:

    F. pure.
    G. flawless.
    H. evident.
    J. transparent.

9. The main point of the fourth paragraph (lines 61-74) is that:

    A. the commonly known story about Hesse's creation of the Petri dish is false.
    B. Angelina Hesse deserves more respect for her role in Walther's research.
    C. a technique used for cooking served as a practical solution in scientific research.
    D. scientists' understanding of bacteria may help them develop more complex cooking techniques.

10. Which of the following questions is NOT answered in the third paragraph (lines 37-60)?

    F. What types of nutrients did scientists use to cultivate bacteria?
    G. What was the outcome of the research on bacteria?
    H. What were the scientific explanations for diseases before the role of bacteria was proven?
    J. What factors complicated early research on bacteria?

Passage XVI

NATURAL SCIENCE: This passage is adapted from the essay "Neurological Disorders" by Scott Keonig.

Prosopagnosia, or face-blindness, is a neurological condition that renders a person incapable of recognizing faces. A person may be perfectly capable of seeing a face, but unable to recognize the person it
5 belongs to.

Prosopagnosia is strong evidence that the brain specializes in notions more complex than basic shapes or colors. In patients with prosopagnosia, a vital part of the brain is missing or damaged. Prosopagnosia
10 patients, like most people, can "see" faces perfectly well, but what is missing is the ability to identify them upon seeing the same ones again. Prosopagnosiacs have great difficulty recognizing the faces of people they have met many times, including even their
15 spouses and children in extreme cases. Furthermore, they often cannot picture someone's face when that person is not there. These instances illustrate just how complex the process of recognizing a face can be: the ability to "recognize" a face comes down to much
20 more than just the ability to "see" the face.

Capgras' delusion—the belief that a close relative or friend has been replaced by an impostor, an exact double, despite recognition of familiarity in appearance and behavior—is arguably the reverse of
25 prosopagnosia. It points to the existence of yet another place in the brain, though a rather abstract one: an area that, given certain sensory input (a loved one's face, for example), provides a sense of "properness," that all is right in the world. Lacking this, the world could get
30 very creepy. Indeed, it's much more chilling to see a doppelganger masquerading as a family member than to simply see a dangerous-looking stranger.

So it seems that even if the visual system is functioning just fine—i.e., one is conscious and aware
35 of a situation—it is apparently not enough to satisfy the mind.

Neuroscience focuses not only on the unity of the brain, but also on how unique and independent each area of the brain can be. A parallel phenomenon to the
40 separateness of the seeing and recognizing of a face comes from our understanding of sentences. Certain sentences, called "garden path" sentences, show how the same sequence of words can mean two different things depending on where the mental breaks are
45 placed. In the sentence "the coffee cup was placed by the man on the table," for example, the word "on" is what is called a "fork" word, in that it could apply to either the man or the coffee cup. When people hear the

sentence, they have to retrace their steps, as along the
50 garden path, back through the sentence to see what the fork word should apply to. Given how quickly a person can adjust his or her comprehension of the sentence to ensure that it makes sense, this tendency is indicative of high-level thinking—the man was not
55 likely standing on the table.

This technique can be used to test the mental awareness of someone who appears to be in a persistent vegetative state. Assuming the subject's auditory system is functioning properly, he should
60 respond precisely the same way when read the sentences. Despite total paralysis—the subject alluded to above could not even blink—he was able to demonstrate, albeit with the aid of some sophisticated equipment, that he was still "in there," and very much
65 conscious of his surroundings (how horrible it must have been to hear his doctor discussing his dire prognosis and being unable to signal his awareness to anyone!).

Another example of a brain's faulty interpretation
70 of accurate stimulus is the "phantom limb" phenomenon. Consciousness of a limb does not require its physical presence. Indeed, patients with phantom limbs report that the sensation of a limb's existence can linger past its amputation.

75 The foil to phantom limbs, anosognosia, presents another interesting case study. An elderly woman looks at her arm and claims that it belongs to someone else, as sternly as would you or I when asked about an arm belonging to someone clear across the room. The
80 rationalizations for this are difficult to fathom, but at the same time, they are understandable, given the brain's response when it faces discrepancies in reality. The left brain can only tweak so much; one can only stubbornly decide against a simple action so many
85 times. Eventually, the mind will no longer be able to ignore the fact that the arm is, in fact, still attached to the body. That's where the right brain comes in, and conveniently persuades the person that, OK, you were just asked to raise your hand… and now you've done
90 it!

1. According to the passage, what is anosognosia?

   A. The sensation of a limb that does not exist
   B. The sense that another person's limb is one's own
   C. The sense that another person's limb does not exist
   D. The sense that one's own limb belongs to someone else

2. The author suggests that Capgras' delusion is the opposite of prosopagnosia because:

    F. patients with Capgras' delusion can recognize people.
    G. patients with Capgras' delusion cannot recognize people.
    H. patients with prosopagnosia cannot recognize a person's face, whereas patients with Capgras' delusion recognize the person's face, but not the person.
    J. prosopagnosia is treatable whereas Capgras' delusion is not.

3. What does the passage offer as evidence that understanding "garden path" sentences is a sign of mental awareness?

    A. They elicit an "N400" reaction in one's brain.
    B. They suggest a doppelganger masquerading as a family member.
    C. They are indicative of mental illness.
    D. They can cause a reaction in people who appear to otherwise be in a vegetative state.

4. In the context of the passage, what does the author mean when he says, "the world could get very creepy" (lines 29-30)?

    F. To believe that family members are impostors could be a very frightening experience.
    G. Knowing that so many neurological disorders exist could make human life seem quite eerie.
    H. The idea that we can see things that might not actually exist is very frightening.
    J. It is disturbing to consider that the sensation of the limb's existence could linger past its amputation.

5. The passage implies that a "fork" word:

    A. tests one's ability to derive different meanings from the same sequence of words.
    B. signifies a strong break in the idea that the author is trying to present.
    C. is a concept with too much ambiguity to be considered scientifically legitimate.
    D. was conceived long after "garden path" sentences were first suggested by psychological studies.

6. What does the author suggest when he says in lines 33-36, "even if the visual system is functioning just fine…it is apparently not enough to satisfy the mind?"

    F. We need several visual cues to confirm that what we see does indeed exist.
    G. Optical illusions can confuse the mind into seeing something that isn't real.
    H. Even if what we see is correct, the brain needs assurance that what we see does in fact exist.
    J. Even if what we see is not correct, the brain can think that what we see does exist.

7. In the context of the passage, "on" is used as an example of a:

    A. word that a prosopagnosiac would not recognize.
    B. "garden path."
    C. "fork" word in a "garden path" sentence.
    D. doppelganger that appears to be something else.

8. Which of the following are examples of the brain incorrectly interpreting correct data?

    I.   Anosognosia
    II.   Phantom limbs
    III. Garden path sentences
    IV.   Capgras' Delusion

    F. II and IV only
    G. I and IV only
    H. I, II, and IV only
    J. I, II, III, and IV

9. The author implies that "phantom limb" phenomenon is similar to Capgras' delusion because both involve:

    A. an incorrect interpretation of senses.
    B. a loss of senses.
    C. an irrational sense of fear.
    D. confusion due to a lack of recognition.

10. As it is used in lines 70 and 73, the word *phantom* most nearly means:

    F. ghostly.
    G. creepy.
    H. imaginary.
    J. secret.

SUMMIT
EDUCATIONAL
GROUP

Writing Overview

- ❏ The Writing Test
- ❏ Format and Scoring
- ❏ Working Through the Writing Test
- ❏ General Tips

The Writing Test

❑ The ACT Writing Test measures your skill at analyzing situations, evaluating arguments, and effectively developing ideas through writing. You will evaluate three perspectives on a complex issue and create an argument supported by your reasoning and experience.

❑ The Writing Test is optional, and therefore it appears at the end of the exam.

❑ You have 40 minutes to complete the Writing Test.

Format and Scoring

❑ You are given a single Writing score on a 1-36 scale, as well as four subscores.

The Writing score is **not** factored into the 1-36 ACT Composite score.

❑ The four Writing subscores focus on specific skills you must display in your essay.

- Ideas and Analysis

    Scores in this category represent a student's ability to comprehend the rhetorical situation; generate productive ideas in response; think critically about the task; evaluate and analyze multiple perspectives; and employ effective rhetorical strategies.

- Organization

    Scores in this category indicate a student's ability to structure an argument logically, sequence ideas strategically, and organize writing clearly.

- Development and Support

    Scores in this category reflect a student's ability to illustrate, explain, and substantiate claims and ideas. Strong writers discuss and explore their ideas, making clear their pertinence by way of detailed, persuasive examples and sound reasoning. They bolster their claims by marshaling evidentiary support, drawing from their knowledge and relevant experience.

- Language Use and Conventions

    Scores in this category denote a student's ability to use standard written English in service of a persuasive purpose. Competent writers demonstrate control over the conventions of grammar, syntax, word usage, and mechanics. Stronger writers make effective rhetorical choices in voice and tone, and express nuanced ideas by way of precise word choice.

❑ Learn the instructions before you take the test.

The instructions are the same on every ACT. Memorize the format and instructions before you take the test. At test time, you can skip the instructions and focus on the questions.

Essay Task

Write a unified, coherent essay in which you evaluate multiple perspectives on the (*prompt topic*). In your essay, be sure to:

- analyze and evaluate the perspectives given
- state and develop your own perspective on the issue
- explain the relationship between your perspective and those given

Your perspective may be in full agreement with any of the others, in partial agreement, or wholly different. Whatever the case, support your ideas with logical reasoning and detailed, persuasive examples.

Planning Your Essay
Your work on these prewriting pages will not be scored.

Use the space below and on the back cover to generate ideas and plan your essay. You may wish to consider the following as you think critically about the task:

Strengths and weaknesses of the three given perspectives

- What insights do they offer, and what do they fail to consider?
- Why might they be persuasive to others, or why might they fail to persuade?

Your own knowledge, experience, and values

- What is your perspective on this issue, and what are its strengths and weaknesses?
- How will you support your perspective in your essay?

Working Through the Writing Test

❑ Take the time to analyze the prompt.

Do not rush to begin writing; this will lead to a rambling, unfocused essay. Instead, carefully read the prompt and consider each perspective.

❑ Plan and outline your essay.

Make sure you have a strong sense of your thesis and arguments. This will ensure that you can work quickly and efficiently as you write.

❑ Save a minute or two to review.

When you are finished writing, look back over your essay and try to spot any minor errors you can correct. It's important to manage your time to eliminate obvious errors.

❑ Allocating Your Time

3-5 minutes	Reading	Read the issue in the prompt and brainstorm relevant topics about which you are knowledgeable. These topics will be used as examples to support your arguments in your essay. Read the three perspectives and consider how they relate to the issue and each other.
5-8 minutes	Planning	Decide on a perspective you will defend. Develop an outline that plans what examples you will use to support your argument and how you will discuss each of the three perspectives in the prompt.
25-30 minutes	Writing	Write your essay. Pay attention to how much time you have remaining and adjust the depth of your analysis accordingly.
1-3 minutes	Review and Editing	Quickly look back over your essay for any errors or weaknesses. Correct spelling or grammar mistakes, and make quick improvements.

General Tips

❑ Write legibly.

Essay scorers need to be able to read your writing, so do not rush so much that it negatively impacts your handwriting.

❑ Longer essays are not necessarily better. Do not be unnecessarily wordy for the sake of making your essay seem longer. Prioritize creating strong arguments.

❑ While planning and writing your essay, it may help to imagine you are in a debate. Develop a convincing argument that cannot be countered, and anticipate how an opponent might try to argue against you.

Writing

- Analyzing the Issue

- Assessing Perspectives

- Preparing to Write

- Introduction

- Supporting Paragraphs

  - Prove

  - Disprove

  - Compare

- Conclusion

- Proofread

- Writing Effectively

Analyzing the Issue

❑ Before you begin your essay, read the assignment carefully and consider the issue and perspectives.

❑ The issue is designed to be complex, with no clear answer. Resist the urge to judge the issue presented in the writing prompt with your own opinions. You may realize that you have more examples to defend an argument with which you don't personally agree.

❑ As you read the issue, try to think of relevant information or events related to the topic.

You may have seen the issue discussed in news articles and books, or you may have had a personal experience that relates to the issue. The topics are common, modern subjects for debate and discussion.

❑ By brainstorming examples before you look at the perspectives, you keep your views broad and creative. If you look at the perspectives first, your thoughts are more likely to be limited to the scope of these perspectives.

TRY IT OUT

Read the following essay prompts. Consider the issues presented and list any specific examples you could use to discuss them.

Soda Tax

Sumptuary taxes are levied on goods and services that a society considers undesirable or unhealthy. Historically, tobacco, alcohol, and gambling have been heavily taxed in the United States. Lawmakers in support of sumptuary taxes have argued that these industries make large profits but do not make positive contributions to society. Following this reasoning, these taxes would allow some of the profit generated from these goods and services to be used for more socially beneficial investments. Recently, as dietary problems have become a growing concern, some people have called for new taxes on unhealthy foods. In particular, sugary soft drinks have been targeted because of the proven connection between their consumption and health problems such as diabetes and obesity.

Examples: _____

_____

_____

_____

_____

_____

Estate Tax

The United States estate tax is a tax on the value of the estate of a deceased person. Assets included in a will or granted as an insurance benefit are included in this tax. The percent of taxation can vary depending on the value of the assets, and the tax only applies to estates above $5 million in value. The tax does not apply to assets that are left to a spouse. Also, expenses for funeral services or charitable contributions are not taxed.

There are many policies that are designed to prevent avoidance of the estate tax. For example, a person cannot transfer his or her estate to others shortly before death in order without being taxed. However, it is still common that people with large estates will find ways to circumvent these tax laws in order to prevent their assets from being taxed.

Examples: _____

_____

_____

_____

_____

_____

Assessing Perspectives

❑ Read each perspective and determine how it relates to the issue presented in the prompt.

Some perspectives will directly support or criticize the issue. Others will bring up a related issue that further complicates the main issue.

❑ Consider whether you have any examples that argue for or against these perspectives.

❑ An effective way to develop your thesis is to determine which viewpoint you can thoroughly defend or debate. Keep in mind that your entire essay needs to focus on supporting your thesis.

Think of how you will disprove, discredit, or surpass the other viewpoints. By showing the weaknesses of these viewpoints, you will make your own thesis seem stronger.

TRY IT OUT

Read the following essay prompt. Consider the issue and perspectives. Write a brief response in support of or in opposition to each perspective.

Genetically Modified Foods

Genetically modified foods are organisms that have had their DNA altered. Through genetic engineering, scientists modify organisms to be more resilient, nutritious, and appealing. Plants are common subjects of genetic modification, which allows scientists to have more control over plant traits than traditional methods of selective breeding. Many crops have been genetically modified to be more resistant to disease and less vulnerable to parasites. Even milk-producing animals have been modified to produce proteins used in medical treatments. Because genetic modification is a modern practice made possible by recently discovered techniques, there is still controversy over the labeling and regulation regarding genetically modified foods. Many of these policies are not yet finalized because there are no long-term studies on the effects of producing or consuming these foods.

Read and carefully consider these perspectives. Each suggests a particular way of thinking about the problems or benefits associated with genetically modified foods.

Perspective One	Perspective Two	Perspective Three
As the human population rises, there is an immediate need for more food. By making food sources more available and productive, genetic modification is the solution to world hunger.	Modified foods should not be made available to consumers until more testing is done. Such modifications can create new diseases or other problems. We should not potentially endanger consumers.	Scientists have an ethical obligation to honor and preserve the natural world. A change made for humanity's sake may harm systems of nature, which must be preserved for our existence.

Perspective One: _____

_____

_____

Perspective Two: _____

_____

_____

Perspective Three: _____

_____

_____

Preparing to Write

❑ Before you begin writing, take a minute to plan your essay. Make a simple outline of the points you want to cover in your essay.

❑ Organize your brainstorming examples into an outline. This will ensure that each portion of your essay is focused and effective.

❑ Because you must address each of the three viewpoints in the prompt, you should focus on one viewpoint per body paragraph.

❑ Make sure that you can develop strong arguments relating to the prompt's viewpoints. Your arguments are effective if they support your central thesis and if they can be defended with specific details.

❑ It is usually best to have four or five paragraphs in your essay: the introduction, two or three supporting paragraphs, and a conclusion.

A simple way to organize your essay is to create three body paragraphs: one for defending your thesis, and the other two for assessing the other viewpoints presented in the prompt.

❑ Use the template below as a general guide for the purpose of each part of your essay:

Introduction:

  Address the issue being discussed

  Make your thesis statement

  State your supporting points

Supporting Paragraph 1:

  Write a topic sentence stating your first supporting point.

  Support the point with details (facts, examples, etc.)

> One supporting paragraph should prove your thesis. At least one supporting paragraph should address the perspectives that don't agree with your thesis.

Supporting Paragraph 2:

  Write a topic sentence stating your second supporting point.

  Support the point with details (facts, examples, etc.)

Supporting Paragraph 3 (if needed):

  Write a topic sentence stating your third supporting point.

  Support the point with details (facts, examples, etc.)

> Two fully developed examples are better than three "thin" examples.

Conclusion:

  Conclude by restating your thesis.

  Summarize how the supporting paragraphs proved your thesis.

TRY IT OUT

Read the following essay prompt. Consider the issue and perspectives. Write your ideas for each portion of the outline on the following page.

Gender-Divided Classrooms

In recent years, the debate over whether boys and girls should be educated separately has intensified. Traditionally, public school classrooms consisted of both girls and boys. Some schools offered gender-specific classes, such as woodworking for boys and home economics for girls, but most core classes were co-ed. In the past few decades, there has been a shift away from dividing classes based on traditional gender roles. However, there have also been new views on learning styles and development which have led to new types of gender division. Because research shows males and females mature at different rates, more people have chosen to put their children in gender-divided classrooms.

Read and carefully consider these perspectives. Each suggests a particular way of thinking about whether classrooms should be divided based on gender.

Perspective One	Perspective Two	Perspective Three
American history shows that classrooms should not be segregated by race, and this lesson should be extended to gender segregation. Whether we make divisions based on race or gender, segregation will always promote stereotypes, prejudice, and inequality.	If gender-divided classrooms provide the best education, all schools should offer them. A school's primary duty is to provide and promote a strong education, which is not possible when students are constantly distracted by social pressures.	We cannot organize our classes based on outdated and restrictive views on gender. Some students would not be comfortable being grouped according to biological sex rather than gender identity. By integrating classrooms, we promote acceptance and allow people to develop freely.

Introduction

    Issue being discussed: _____

_____

    Thesis statement: _____

_____

    Supporting points: _____

_____

Supporting Paragraph 1

    Topic sentence: _____

_____

    Supporting details: _____

_____

Supporting Paragraph 2

    Topic sentence: _____

_____

    Supporting details: _____

_____

Supporting Paragraph 3

    Topic sentence: _____

_____

    Supporting details: _____

_____

Conclusion

    Restate thesis: _____

_____

    Summarize arguments: _____

_____

Introduction

❑ The purpose of the introduction is to address the topic and state your viewpoint on that topic. You can also use the introductory paragraph to mention your supporting points or summarize your main arguments.

❑ The introductory paragraph states your main idea and establishes what you will be discussing in your essay. This helps your reader understand what your focus is and to know what to expect in your essay.

❑ There are three essential elements to an introduction:

- A strong **opening** that relates to your main idea and grabs the attention of the reader.

- Your **thesis statement**, which states the argument that is central to your essay.

- The **arguments** or **examples** you will be using to prove and defend your thesis.

These examples will be expanded upon in your supporting paragraphs. You can mention these examples in your thesis statement or in a sentence that relates them back to your thesis.

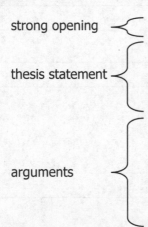

strong opening

thesis statement

arguments

    Education brings freedom. It is better to teach people how to make good decisions than it is to simply take away their ability to make decisions. For this reason, our government must not enforce taxes targeting unhealthy foods. Instead, we should focus on creating a better-educated, more health-conscious society. Certainly, unhealthy diets are a large concern of the modern world, but the government needs to attack this problem in our schools rather than our wallets. History has shown that taxes are ineffective at regulating industries and that our education system can strengthen our social values and practices. A foundation of learned behaviors, instilled at a young age, can keep the public away from unhealthy products far more effectively than any punishing tax can.

❑ It is essential to plan before you write. Your introduction should mention the examples that will appear later in your essay, so you must have your examples prepared in advance.

❑ It can be helpful to have a great opening sentence, or "hook," but this can be hard to come up with while facing the time pressures of the test. It may be helpful to create a basic structure for a type of opening sentence that you enjoy using.

Do not get stuck on your opening sentence. In order to finish your essay on time, you must be efficient and quick.

Below are some types of sentences that can make effective introductions to your essay:

- **Broad statements** and **generalizations** introduce the general theme or the context of the essay's main idea.

  "Public health is a major concern in both government legislation and social values."

- **Contradictions** begin with a perspective you don't support and state its weaknesses, as well as reasons why your own position is correct.

  "Although it is tempting to regulate health, people will always be able to choose what they want to eat. Rather, it is better to educate citizens about healthy eating."

- **Questions** make the reader consider an answer, which you should provide with your thesis statement. Make sure your question is phrased in a way that could only be reasonably answered in support of your perspective.

  "Whose responsibility is it to ensure that people live healthily?"

- **Quotations** provide a context and can support your thesis through a respected authority. However, quotations are difficult to use when you must rely on memory.

  "On the topic of taxes," respected author Robert Heinlein wrote, "There is no worse tyranny than to force a man to pay for what he does not want merely because you think it would be good for him."

❑ Don't begin your essay by bluntly saying "I agree" or "I disagree." Your essay will have a more fluid beginning if you start with a more general statement about the issue being discussed.

Similarly, avoid using "I believe" or "In my opinion" when making your argument. These types of phrases limit your argument by making it seem more judgmental than factual. Also, since you are writing the essay, it's understood that it is your opinion.

TRY IT OUT

Write an introduction for an essay addressing this prompt.

Globalization

Globalization is the process of integration among nations. As communication and transportation technologies progress, people become more connected across the world. Goods and services are traded worldwide. Ideas and ideologies are rapidly spread. Cultures that were once confined to specific geographic areas are now widespread and widely known. Globalization is often viewed as an unavoidable consequence of modern advancements, but can its effects be regulated or limited? Given the increasing pace of globalization, it is worth examining its impact on the modern world.

Read and carefully consider these perspectives. Each suggests a particular way of thinking about the effects of globalization.

Perspective One	Perspective Two	Perspective Three
As companies from different countries are thrust into the same markets, they become more competitive. This results in better products and lower prices. Globalization encourages the strongest companies to grow even stronger.	Global companies have exploited other nations, taking advantage of cheaper labor and lower business regulations. This has led to loss of jobs in more developed nations and poor working conditions in less developed nations.	As more nations become economically and politically connected, new policies are created that ensure greater equality and acceptance. Also, the sharing of technologies and knowledge ensures that all nations can prosper.

_____

_____

_____

_____

_____

_____

_____

_____

TRY IT OUT

Write an introduction for an essay addressing this prompt.

Internet Censorship

Censorship refers to the control of access to ideas and information. Typically, censorship is performed by some authority in order to protect itself or citizens from certain media considered offensive, harmful, or immoral. As the vast amount of information on the internet has become more accessible, several groups have expressed interest in controlling what can be published or viewed online. Some schools and parents restrict access to media that is deemed inappropriate for their students and children. Some countries block information that is deemed dangerous or subversive. Some internet service providers will reduce the speed of access to certain websites in order to give themselves an advantage over competitors. As the internet becomes increasingly influential and vital to modern society, it is critical that we determine how it should be utilized and regulated.

Read and carefully consider these perspectives. Each suggests a particular way of thinking about censorship and regulation of internet services and information.

Perspective One	Perspective Two	Perspective Three
Unrestricted access to all internet services is essential to promoting global equality. Just as all people have a human right to free speech, they have a right to view and share the wealth of human knowledge. This allows all people to prosper and advance together.	Not all media is positive or beneficial. The internet contains much information that is vulgar or offensive, and people should be protected against this. By default, internet users should have access to only unbiased and inoffensive material.	Through the control of information, an authority may misrepresent itself and others in order to maintain control. All people of the world should have unregulated access to the internet so they can be informed and empowered.

_____

_____

_____

_____

_____

_____

_____

_____

SUMMIT
EDUCATIONAL
GROUP

Supporting Paragraphs

❑ The body of your essay is typically made up of two or three paragraphs that support your thesis. Each supporting paragraph should focus on one argument.

The body is where you will need to use logic and reasoning to prove the strength of your thesis.

❑ Supporting paragraphs are organized like mini-essays.

The first sentence of a supporting paragraph is the **topic sentence**. The topic sentence should mention what example will be discussed in the paragraph and the main argument that the paragraph will focus on.

The majority of a supporting paragraph is used to describe your example, develop it with specific evidence and details, and explain how it proves your thesis.

The final sentence of a supporting paragraph summarizes your example by relating it back to your main idea.

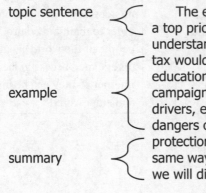

topic sentence ⎰ The essentials of healthy living, diet, and exercise, should be a top priority of our educational system. If we help people understand how and why they should eat healthily, a sumptuary tax would be unnecessary. A prime example of the benefits of education is the Mothers Against Drunk Driving group. Their

example ⎰ campaign, which began with a crusade against intoxicated drivers, evolved into a movement for public education about the dangers of alcohol. This has led to new laws, better police protection, and a significant reduction in harmful drinking. In the

summary ⎰ same way, if we teach people the importance of healthy living, we will directly support better eating habits.

❑ Explain the logic of how your examples prove your arguments. It is not enough to simply mention facts or details and expect your reader to figure out how they work. Your supporting paragraph should fully explain how and why the example is proof that your main argument is correct.

Keep your reader in mind. Imagine that your reader would not be able to understand your argument without you explaining every logical step.

❑ Specific details and evidence should be used to explain how your example proves your thesis.

Vague statements and hypothetical situations ("If _____ would happen, then…") create weak arguments. Examples need to be developed with concrete details.

> This is an entrenched problem, one that has its grasping fingers wrapped tightly around the very roots of our free-market culture. Punishing the consumer undermines the ideals which make this culture virtuous, without even casting light on the underlying problem. What if the government made all of the choices for people, telling them what they should buy all the time?

1. What statements in this paragraph are too vague?

2. What additional information is needed in order to strengthen these statements?

❑ An easy way to organize your supporting paragraphs is to have each focus on one of the perspectives supplied in the prompt.

One paragraph should focus on proving your thesis, which will usually be in support or opposition of one perspective. Another two body paragraphs can be based on the other two perspectives, disproving their arguments by showing that they are weaker than the main argument of your thesis.

TRY IT OUT

Write a supporting paragraph for an essay addressing this prompt.

Globalization

Globalization is the process of integration among nations. As communication and transportation technologies progress, people become more connected across the world. Goods and services are traded worldwide. Ideas and ideologies are rapidly spread. Cultures that were once confined to specific geographic areas are now widespread and widely known. Globalization is often viewed as an unavoidable consequence of modern advancements, but can its effects be regulated or limited? Given the increasing pace of globalization, it is worth examining its impact on the modern world.

Read and carefully consider these perspectives. Each suggests a particular way of thinking about the effects of globalization.

Perspective One	Perspective Two	Perspective Three
As companies from different countries are thrust into the same markets, they become more competitive. This results in better products and lower prices. Globalization encourages the strongest companies to grow even stronger.	Global companies have exploited other nations, taking advantage of cheaper labor and lower business regulations. This has led to loss of jobs in more developed nations and poor working conditions in less developed nations.	As more nations become economically and politically connected, new policies are created that ensure greater equality and acceptance. Also, the sharing of technologies and knowledge ensures that all nations can prosper.

_____

_____

_____

_____

_____

_____

_____

_____

TRY IT OUT

Write a supporting paragraph for an essay addressing this prompt.

Internet Censorship

Censorship refers to the control of access to ideas and information. Typically, censorship is performed by some authority in order to protect itself or citizens from certain media considered offensive, harmful, or immoral. As the vast amount of information on the internet has become more accessible, several groups have expressed interest in controlling what can be published or viewed online. Some schools and parents restrict access to media that is deemed inappropriate for their students and children. Some countries block information that is deemed dangerous or subversive. Some internet service providers will reduce the speed of access to certain websites in order to give themselves an advantage over competitors. As the internet becomes increasingly influential and vital to modern society, it is critical that we determine how it should be utilized and regulated.

Read and carefully consider these perspectives. Each suggests a particular way of thinking about censorship and regulation of internet services and information.

Perspective One	Perspective Two	Perspective Three
Unrestricted access to all internet services is essential to promoting global equality. Just as all people have a human right to free speech, they have a right to view and share the wealth of human knowledge. This allows all people to prosper and advance together.	Not all media is positive or beneficial. The internet contains much information that is vulgar or offensive, and people should be protected against this. By default, internet users should have access to only unbiased and inoffensive material.	Through the control of information, an authority may misrepresent itself and others in order to maintain control. All people of the world should have unregulated access to the internet so they can be informed and empowered.

_____

_____

_____

_____

_____

_____

_____

_____

Prove

❑ At least one supporting paragraph should focus on proving your thesis correct.

❑ You will need to use specific facts and details to defend your argument.

Try to think of events, books, articles, or personal experiences that relate to the topic and confirm your thesis.

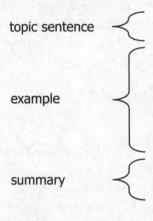

topic sentence — The success of the "driver's education" program proves the effectiveness of public education for solving social problems.

example — Driver's education courses have proven to be an effective solution to a major concern. Teen drivers have always been the group most prone to traffic accidents, and this has been largely corrected by classes that teach them to be more careful and considerate of their driving behavior. Studies in several states show that students who have attended these classes have half as many driving-related injuries or fatalities. Since these classes

summary — have shown such significant improvements in teen behavior, similar education about healthy eating will promote better behavior.

❑ Some arguments can be proven by explaining that the alternative would be unsuccessful or problematic. For example, if you are proposing a solution to a problem, you can explain the negative consequences that would result if your solution is not used.

This type of argument supports your thesis by suggesting that it is the only effective option.

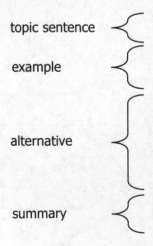

topic sentence — Without proper education, people will not know how to live healthily. This is demonstrated by the global advancement of sex education.

example — In our nation, the administration of sex ed classes in schools has been directly connected to the decrease of sexually transmitted diseases and unwanted pregnancies. In Africa, the importance of this education has been made very clear. Early efforts to solve the crisis of AIDS in Africa included making condoms easily available to all people. However, this was not

alternative — effective when people did not understand the importance of "safe sex" practices or the dangers of STDs. With better sex education, there has been a significant reduction in the spread of AIDS and other diseases. In the same way, we cannot trust

summary — people to eat more healthily unless we better educate them on the benefits of proper diet and nutrition.

❑ An effective way to organize your essay is to use your first body paragraph to directly prove your argument. This will create a strong support for your thesis and give your essay a clear focus.

You can also use your first body paragraph to show why another argument is incorrect, and then use your second body paragraph to prove your own argument is superior. This will create a problem-solution structure that emphasizes how your thesis solves a challenging problem.

TRY IT OUT

Write a paragraph proving one of the perspectives in this prompt.

Globalization

Globalization is the process of integration among nations. As communication and transportation technologies progress, people become more connected across the world. Goods and services are traded worldwide. Ideas and ideologies are rapidly spread. Cultures that were once confined to specific geographic areas are now widespread and widely known. Globalization is often viewed as an unavoidable consequence of modern advancements, but can its effects be regulated or limited? Given the increasing pace of globalization, it is worth examining its impact on the modern world.

Read and carefully consider these perspectives. Each suggests a particular way of thinking about the effects of globalization.

Perspective One	Perspective Two	Perspective Three
As companies from different countries are thrust into the same markets, they become more competitive. This results in better products and lower prices. Globalization encourages the strongest companies to grow even stronger.	Global companies have exploited other nations, taking advantage of cheaper labor and lower business regulations. This has led to loss of jobs in more developed nations and poor working conditions in less developed nations.	As more nations become economically and politically connected, new policies are created that ensure greater equality and acceptance. Also, the sharing of technologies and knowledge ensures that all nations can prosper.

_____

_____

_____

_____

_____

_____

_____

_____

TRY IT OUT

Write a paragraph proving one of the perspectives in this prompt.

Internet Censorship

Censorship refers to the control of access to ideas and information. Typically, censorship is performed by some authority in order to protect itself or citizens from certain media considered offensive, harmful, or immoral. As the vast amount of information on the internet has become more accessible, several groups have expressed interest in controlling what can be published or viewed online. Some schools and parents restrict access to media that is deemed inappropriate for their students and children. Some countries block information that is deemed dangerous or subversive. Some internet service providers will reduce the speed of access to certain websites in order to give themselves an advantage over competitors. As the internet becomes increasingly influential and vital to modern society, it is critical that we determine how it should be utilized and regulated.

Read and carefully consider these perspectives. Each suggests a particular way of thinking about censorship and regulation of internet services and information.

Perspective One	Perspective Two	Perspective Three
Unrestricted access to all internet services is essential to promoting global equality. Just as all people have a human right to free speech, they have a right to view and share the wealth of human knowledge. This allows all people to prosper and advance together.	Not all media is positive or beneficial. The internet contains much information that is vulgar or offensive, and people should be protected against this. By default, internet users should have access to only unbiased and inoffensive material.	Through the control of information, an authority may misrepresent itself and others in order to maintain control. All people of the world should have unregulated access to the internet so they can be informed and empowered.

_____

_____

_____

_____

_____

_____

_____

_____

_____

Disprove

❑ Because your essay must address all perspectives of the issue presented in the prompt, you will likely need to discuss arguments that conflict with your thesis. Your essay should not just mention a counter-argument but disprove it as well. By weakening the opposing argument, your own argument becomes stronger.

❑ You can disprove an argument by pointing out false information or assumptions. Such an argument may have effective reasoning but a weak basis of facts.

> By implementing sumptuary taxes, we hope that people will be discouraged from buying things that are not good for them. However, people will not always make their decision based on costs. Our nation already has "sin taxes" on tobacco, alcohol, and gambling in order to discourage the usage or practice of these things. But people still smoke, drink, and bet, despite the expense. The problem with these taxes, and the flaw of the proposed soda tax, is that they do not directly address the main problem: cultural values and lack of knowledge.

1. What is the argument that this paragraph is disproving?

2. How does this paragraph prove that the argument uses false assumptions?

❑ An argument may be disproven because it uses poor logic. Such an argument may have a strong basis on facts, but its reasoning is flawed.

> We must not try to solve one problem by creating another. While it is true that people make poor dietary choices and that the government relies on much-needed tax revenue, these are separate issues that must be addressed in different ways. If the government is in need of money, it should not try to solve this problem by creating a tax on unhealthy products because this tax creates a conflict of interest. If such a tax existed, it would actually benefit the government to support the sale of sodas, because this sale would bring more tax revenue. If the government wants to solve the problem of an unhealthy population, it should seek to alleviate the ignorance that leads to bad decisions.

1. What is the argument that this paragraph is disproving?

2. How does this paragraph prove that the argument uses poor logic?

❑ An argument may be disproven because it is not true in all cases. Such an argument may have a strong basis of facts and effective reasoning, but it only applies in certain circumstances.

Any sumptuary tax, including the soda tax, will not be entirely effective because not all people will allow themselves to be restricted. In the 1920s in the United States, the Prohibition movement banned the sale of alcoholic beverages. While this ban did promote greater health and reduced alcoholism, it also led to a very high increase in criminal activity. The public demand for illegal alcohol caused the rise of large gangs in major cities. A "black market" of alcohol was created, and because it was not regulated, the alcohol products were sometimes dangerous due to improper distillation or the addition of cheap chemicals. If we place a high tax on unhealthy foods, such as soda, we may see a similar criminal underground that starts dealing junk food. A soda tax will only benefit people who follow the laws, and it may lead to new opportunities for those who disregard the law.

1. How does this paragraph prove that the argument would not be true in all cases?

TRY IT OUT

Write a paragraph disproving one of the perspectives in this prompt.

Globalization

Globalization is the process of integration among nations. As communication and transportation technologies progress, people become more connected across the world. Goods and services are traded worldwide. Ideas and ideologies are rapidly spread. Cultures that were once confined to specific geographic areas are now widespread and widely known. Globalization is often viewed as an unavoidable consequence of modern advancements, but can its effects be regulated or limited? Given the increasing pace of globalization, it is worth examining its impact on the modern world.

Read and carefully consider these perspectives. Each suggests a particular way of thinking about the effects of globalization.

Perspective One	Perspective Two	Perspective Three
As companies from different countries are thrust into the same markets, they become more competitive. This results in better products and lower prices. Globalization encourages the strongest companies to grow even stronger.	Global companies have exploited other nations, taking advantage of cheaper labor and lower business regulations. This has led to loss of jobs in more developed nations and poor working conditions in less developed nations.	As more nations become economically and politically connected, new policies are created that ensure greater equality and acceptance. Also, the sharing of technologies and knowledge ensures that all nations can prosper.

_____

_____

_____

_____

_____

_____

_____

_____

SUMMIT
EDUCATIONAL
GROUP

TRY IT OUT

Write a paragraph disproving one of the perspectives in this prompt.

Internet Censorship

Censorship refers to the control of access to ideas and information. Typically, censorship is performed by some authority in order to protect itself or citizens from certain media considered offensive, harmful, or immoral. As the vast amount of information on the internet has become more accessible, several groups have expressed interest in controlling what can be published or viewed online. Some schools and parents restrict access to media that is deemed inappropriate for their students and children. Some countries block information that is deemed dangerous or subversive. Some internet service providers will reduce the speed of access to certain websites in order to give themselves an advantage over competitors. As the internet becomes increasingly influential and vital to modern society, it is critical that we determine how it should be utilized and regulated.

Read and carefully consider these perspectives. Each suggests a particular way of thinking about censorship and regulation of internet services and information.

Perspective One	**Perspective Two**	**Perspective Three**
Unrestricted access to all internet services is essential to promoting global equality. Just as all people have a human right to free speech, they have a right to view and share the wealth of human knowledge. This allows all people to prosper and advance together.	Not all media is positive or beneficial. The internet contains much information that is vulgar or offensive, and people should be protected against this. By default, internet users should have access to only unbiased and inoffensive material.	Through the control of information, an authority may misrepresent itself and others in order to maintain control. All people of the world should have unregulated access to the internet so they can be informed and empowered.

_____

_____

_____

_____

_____

_____

_____

_____

Compare

❑ Your thesis may partially agree with another perspective. In this case, you don't want to fully disprove that argument, because it would weaken your own. Instead, you should compare that perspective to your thesis in order to show that yours is stronger.

❑ An argument may be valid, but be less effective than your own. In describing such an argument, make sure to explain clearly why your argument is better. If you can, provide specific details that demonstrate your argument's superiority.

> We must consider the political consequences of creating a soda tax. There are some who argue that consumers of unhealthy foods should be forced to pay more for this food because they are not just harming themselves; they are a burden on all of society. By knowingly ruining their own health, these people are creating unnecessary expenses for the rest of us through higher insurance rates and healthcare taxes. A soda tax would help pay back these expenses. However, there is a larger concern here. The creation of a soda tax establishes a precedent for making more laws that would control people's behaviors. Is it more important that we save some money or that we protect our personal freedoms? The problem of poor public health may be a consequence of having natural rights, which must be defended.

1. What is the argument that this paragraph is addressing?

2. How does this paragraph compare this argument to the essay's main argument?

❑ An argument may be valid but won't work well without additional components from your own argument. If you can prove that another argument cannot be effective without first implementing your own ideas, your argument will seem stronger.

> Regardless of whether there are companies which are taxed for unhealthy foods, they will certainly continue to sell these products. For this reason, people argue that companies should have to advertise when products are unsafe. This would help ensure that consumers can get nutritious foods and avoid unhealthy ones. The issue with this idea, however, is that it only works if we first educate consumers. Companies can display that they include an ingredient, but consumers need to know what that means. If we do not know how to identify what is healthy, we cannot make educated decisions. Therefore, a system of public health education is still necessary.

1. What is the argument that this paragraph is addressing?

2. How does this paragraph show that the argument relies on the essay's argument?

❑ An argument may be valid, but be strengthened by your own argument. If you can prove that another argument will not be effective unless it also includes your own ideas, your argument will seem stronger.

> People respond better to rewards than to punishments. Businesses have a long history of bending the laws in order to avoid regulations. Offshore accounts, undocumented labor, and personal expense accounts are common examples of when businesses illegally evade paying taxes, and it is likely that businesses will be compelled to find similarly unlawful methods in order to not pay a soda tax. So how can we encourage the production of healthier foods? The answer is simple: give positive incentives. If companies recognize that there are more potential profits in healthy foods, they will logically follow this market demand. This solution would be most effective if consumers have more desire for healthy foods than unhealthy ones. In order to create this demand, we must show all people the benefits of a healthy lifestyle, and these benefits can be revealed by providing public education on healthy living.

1. What is the argument that this paragraph is addressing?

2. How does this paragraph show that the argument would be strengthened by the essay's argument?

TRY IT OUT

Write a paragraph comparing one of the perspectives in this prompt to your own thesis.

Globalization

Globalization is the process of integration among nations. As communication and transportation technologies progress, people become more connected across the world. Goods and services are traded worldwide. Ideas and ideologies are rapidly spread. Cultures that were once confined to specific geographic areas are now widespread and widely known. Globalization is often viewed as an unavoidable consequence of modern advancements, but can its effects be regulated or limited? Given the increasing pace of globalization, it is worth examining its impact on the modern world.

Read and carefully consider these perspectives. Each suggests a particular way of thinking about the effects of globalization.

Perspective One	Perspective Two	Perspective Three
As companies from different countries are thrust into the same markets, they become more competitive. This results in better products and lower prices. Globalization encourages the strongest companies to grow even stronger.	Global companies have exploited other nations, taking advantage of cheaper labor and lower business regulations. This has led to loss of jobs in more developed nations and poor working conditions in less developed nations.	As more nations become economically and politically connected, new policies are created that ensure greater equality and acceptance. Also, the sharing of technologies and knowledge ensures that all nations can prosper.

_____

_____

_____

_____

_____

_____

_____

_____

TRY IT OUT

Write a paragraph comparing one of the perspectives in this prompt to your own thesis.

Internet Censorship

Censorship refers to the control of access to ideas and information. Typically, censorship is performed by some authority in order to protect itself or citizens from certain media considered offensive, harmful, or immoral. As the vast amount of information on the internet has become more accessible, several groups have expressed interest in controlling what can be published or viewed online. Some schools and parents restrict access to media that is deemed inappropriate for their students and children. Some countries block information that is deemed dangerous or subversive. Some internet service providers will reduce the speed of access to certain websites in order to give themselves an advantage over competitors. As the internet becomes increasingly influential and vital to modern society, it is critical that we determine how it should be utilized and regulated.

Read and carefully consider these perspectives. Each suggests a particular way of thinking about censorship and regulation of internet services and information.

Perspective One	Perspective Two	Perspective Three
Unrestricted access to all internet services is essential to promoting global equality. Just as all people have a human right to free speech, they have a right to view and share the wealth of human knowledge. This allows all people to prosper and advance together.	Not all media is positive or beneficial. The internet contains much information that is vulgar or offensive, and people should be protected against this. By default, internet users should have access to only unbiased and inoffensive material.	Through the control of information, an authority may misrepresent itself and others in order to maintain control. All people of the world should have unregulated access to the internet so they can be informed and empowered.

_____

_____

_____

_____

_____

_____

_____

_____

Conclusion

❑ The conclusion of an essay summarizes the arguments of the essay and brings the focus back to the essay's central argument or idea.

The conclusion should give your reader a sense of what is most important in your essay.

❑ A conclusion should restate the essay's thesis. You should not repeat the thesis from your introduction word-for-word. Instead, find a way to reword your thesis.

❑ Effective conclusions show how the supporting paragraphs proved the essay's thesis. The examples of the supporting paragraphs should be noted or briefly summarized, and you should explain how these examples prove your main argument.

❑ Think of the conclusion as a restatement of your essay's introductory paragraph. Just as the introduction establishes the essay's central argument and what examples will be used to support it, the conclusion reaffirms the essay's argument and reviews how the examples proved it.

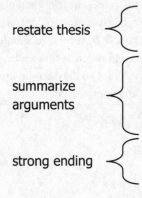

restate thesis

summarize arguments

strong ending

The soda tax is an itchy band-aid on a complex social issue; it doesn't help to heal the patient and just hides the unsightly wound. The problem with unhealthy foods is not that they are so affordable. Rather, the problem is that people do not understand the risk of eating these foods or know healthy alternatives. Trying to solve this with politics or economics will be ineffective or cause even more issues. Until we treat the underlying problem, we will continue to have an unhealthy society. This is why we must better utilize our educational systems to promote a culture of health awareness that includes proper diet.

❑ The conclusion should not introduce new material or new ideas. You want to make sure that your conclusion ties everything together, rather than bringing up new topics that would need further discussion.

Make sure you end with a strong, definitive statement about your essay's argument.

❑ If you are low on time, try to quickly summarize any unfinished supporting paragraphs and get at least two sentences written for the conclusion.

This summary can be easily done by taking phrases from the introduction's thesis statement or supporting paragraphs' topic sentences and using synonyms for key words.

TRY IT OUT

Write a conclusion for an essay addressing this prompt.

Globalization

Globalization is the process of integration among nations. As communication and transportation technologies progress, people become more connected across the world. Goods and services are traded worldwide. Ideas and ideologies are rapidly spread. Cultures that were once confined to specific geographic areas are now widespread and widely known. Globalization is often viewed as an unavoidable consequence of modern advancements, but can its effects be regulated or limited? Given the increasing pace of globalization, it is worth examining its impact on the modern world.

Read and carefully consider these perspectives. Each suggests a particular way of thinking about the effects of globalization.

Perspective One	Perspective Two	Perspective Three
As companies from different countries are thrust into the same markets, they become more competitive. This results in better products and lower prices. Globalization encourages the strongest companies to grow even stronger.	Global companies have exploited other nations, taking advantage of cheaper labor and lower business regulations. This has led to loss of jobs in more developed nations and poor working conditions in less developed nations.	As more nations become economically and politically connected, new policies are created that ensure greater equality and acceptance. Also, the sharing of technologies and knowledge ensures that all nations can prosper.

_____

_____

_____

_____

_____

_____

_____

_____

SUMMIT
EDUCATIONAL
GROUP

TRY IT OUT

Write a conclusion for an essay addressing this prompt.

Internet Censorship

Censorship refers to the control of access to ideas and information. Typically, censorship is performed by some authority in order to protect itself or citizens from certain media considered offensive, harmful, or immoral. As the vast amount of information on the internet has become more accessible, several groups have expressed interest in controlling what can be published or viewed online. Some schools and parents restrict access to media that is deemed inappropriate for their students and children. Some countries block information that is deemed dangerous or subversive. Some internet service providers will reduce the speed of access to certain websites in order to give themselves an advantage over competitors. As the internet becomes increasingly influential and vital to modern society, it is critical that we determine how it should be utilized and regulated.

Read and carefully consider these perspectives. Each suggests a particular way of thinking about censorship and regulation of internet services and information.

Perspective One	Perspective Two	Perspective Three
Unrestricted access to all internet services is essential to promoting global equality. Just as all people have a human right to free speech, they have a right to view and share the wealth of human knowledge. This allows all people to prosper and advance together.	Not all media is positive or beneficial. The internet contains much information that is vulgar or offensive, and people should be protected against this. By default, internet users should have access to only unbiased and inoffensive material.	Through the control of information, an authority may misrepresent itself and others in order to maintain control. All people of the world should have unregulated access to the internet so they can be informed and empowered.

_____

_____

_____

_____

_____

_____

_____

_____

Proofread

☐ Take time during the last two minutes to read through your essay. You won't have time to make major changes, but you can make some minor improvements. It's easy to skip or misspell words when you're trying to write quickly, so this step is very important.

☐ Reread your thesis statement and topic sentences for each paragraph. Make sure that they are clear. Rewrite them, if necessary.

Since the graders won't spend a long time reading your essay, it's important that the structure and organization are clear. A strong, well-written thesis statement and topic sentences that stay focused will help the graders, and your essay, stay on track.

☐ Read through your essay looking for spelling and grammar errors.

Catching glaring errors will pay off. It's important that careless mistakes don't distract the readers from the content of your essay.

☐ You can save time by crossing out and rewriting words rather than erasing. Your essay does not need to look perfect; it's more important that you have time to develop strong arguments. That said, your writing must still be legible and clear.

TRY IT OUT

Proofread the following essay. Underline or circle any errors. Use the space provided to explain what corrections need to be made.

If we seperate students based on gender, we will undermine the primary goal of modern education, which is a free and unbiased sharing of information. When a student body is confined by outdated ideas of gender, the information that this student body has access to is similarly confined.

There exists already a social stigma that discourages people from pursuing certain careers, and this would only be further strengthened by such segregation. For too long, our society has promoted the view that the fields of math and science are made for men, because of this social pressure, women have typically had much lower enrollment in these areas. By separating students, we further promote the division of education by gender. Which unfairly restricts students' interests. This is similar to "separate but equal" laws that segregated students based on race. Such laws did not openly support racist hate, but they did create systems to enforce racism. In the same way, gender-divided classroom would not be created to openly promote sexism, but they would create a more sexist society. Just as schools needs to be racially integrated, they must also be gender integrated in order to promote social and educational equal.

The only way to combat prejudice is through social exposure. And the earlier the better. Some supporters of gender-divided classrooms point to social distractions as the great evil of quality education. But, far from being a distraction, socialization is one of most important parts of a well-rounded education. Furthermore, diversity is essential to an affective classroom. More student perspectives will offer the possibility of more questions and more answers. Segregated classrooms create uniformity, which means students are not expanding there minds by being exposed to new ideas.

It is understandable that some people believe gender-divided classrooms are the best fit for theirselves, but this should not be a system that is forced on all students. If we want to promote equality and diverse knowledge, we must defend our right to have classrooms that anyone can attend.

Writing Effectively

❑ In general, you will improve your writing by paying attention to the grammar and usage skills covered in the English Test.

Additionally, you can improve your writing by making sure that your language is efficient and precise and that every sentence is relevant and advances your arguments.

❑ Make sure each sentence is necessary. Do not try to stuff your essay with irrelevant facts. Your writing will have more impact if it is focused.

Cross out unnecessary details in the following paragraph, which describes the controversy surrounding a book:

The Chocolate War, by Robert Cormier, who also wrote *I Am the Cheese*, has been a surprisingly controversial book. It tells the tale of a high school freshman named Jerry who goes to a fictional school called Trinity School and who is struggling with understanding himself. Robert Cormier wrote numerous short stories about adolescence. In the book, the central character, Jerry, decides to resist peer pressure from a clique known as the Vigils, a group of students at Jerry's school. The goal of this book was to encourage young adults to be strong and moral when they are facing bullying. Cormier often wrote his books in order to help young people work through the hardships of growing up. However, *The Chocolate War* has been one of the most commonly banned books in America because of its harsh language and sexual themes. While some critics and educators have shown great appreciation for the book's writing and messages, others have been more worried about the mature ideas it contains. It's not the only book that has stirred such controversy.

❑ Avoid wordiness. Do not try to sound more intelligent by making your sentences overly complex. Your writing will have a stronger effect if it is concise.

Rewrite:

He acted in a certain way that truly may have seemed to be unnatural.

_____

It is very clearly evident that the one and only correct choice is to change this policy.

_____

❑ Use appropriate language. Avoid the use of clichés and slang.

    Rewrite:

       You should take his opinion with a grain of salt.

       _____

       The novelist Dostoyevsky was often spotted hanging out in gambling halls.

       _____

TRY IT OUT

Cross out the unnecessary details or sentences in the paragraph below.

1. History has shown the social importance of art. Art is extremely significant. Near the beginning of the Civil War, Abraham Lincoln met Harriet Beecher Stowe and remarked, "So this is the little lady who started this great war." Who was this influential woman? Stowe wrote the anti-slavery novel *Uncle Tom's Cabin*, an account of the hardships of slaves that was so moving it sparked a revolution that led to the end of American slavery. This novel gained her a lot of fame. Stowe was born in 1811 and began her writing career as a contributor to religious periodicals. Before her novel was published, the problems of slavery were ignored by many people. This work of art helped spread the ideas of abolition that inspired the Civil War.

Eliminate the wordiness in the following sentences. Rewrite the improved sentences in the space provided.

2. We need to cooperate together in order to get this project fully completed.

   _____

3. It is necessary to see that there are four reasons why this scene is very critically important.

   _____

4. The reason Mr. Henderson arrived late for work was due to the fact that he stopped at very many traffic lights that were red in color.

   _____

   _____

Eliminate the clichés, jargon, and colloquialisms in the following sentences. Rewrite the sentence in the space provided.

5. If you check out Seattle's famous Space Needle, it might blow your mind to think this thing was supposed to be a real masterpiece of the architecture kind.

   _____

   _____

6. In cities that've got lots of history, there's so much trouble when trying to make good roads or sidewalks because there's plenty of people who don't want to screw up all the old stuff that's always been there.

   _____

   _____

Writing Summary

❑ Before you begin your essay, read the assignment carefully and consider the issue and perspectives.

❑ Take a minute to plan your essay. Make a simple outline of the points you want to cover in your essay.

❑ It is usually best to have four or five paragraphs in your essay: the introduction, two or three supporting paragraphs, and a conclusion.

❑ A simply way to organize your essay is to create three body paragraphs: one for defending your thesis, and the other two for assessing the other viewpoints presented in the prompt.

❑ Take time during the last two minutes to read through your essay. You won't have time to make major changes, but you can make some minor improvements. It's easy to skip or misspell words when you're trying to write quickly, so this step is very important.

❑ Make sure each sentence is necessary. Do not try to stuff your essay with irrelevant facts.

Writing Practice

Read the essay assignment below, and evaluate the essay that follows.

Estate Tax

The United States estate tax is a tax on the value of the estate of a deceased person. Assets included in a will or granted as an insurance benefit are included in this tax. The percent of taxation can vary depending on the value of the assets, and the tax only applies to estates above $5 million in value. The tax does not apply to assets that are left to a spouse. Also, expenses for funeral services or charitable contributions are not taxed.

There are many policies that are designed to prevent avoidance of the estate tax. For example, a person cannot transfer his or her estate to others shortly before death in order to avoid being taxed. However, it is still common that people with large estates will find ways to circumvent these tax laws in order to prevent their assets from being taxed.

Read and carefully consider these perspectives. Each suggests a particular way of thinking about the estate tax.

Perspective One	Perspective Two	Perspective Three
An essential feature of our capitalist system is progressive taxation, which prevents the consolidation of wealth. Without progressive taxes, most of the nation's wealth would be held by a select few.	The expense of investigating and preventing estate tax evasion is nearly as high as the funds received from the estate tax. This is not an efficient source of government revenue.	Allowing people to simply inherit great wealth from past generations discourages hard work and a true entrepreneurial spirit. Inheritance should be limited so future generations do not become idle and unappreciative.

The estate tax should only increase as our economy continues to grow. An economy is a living thing, and money is the lifeblood in its veins. The United States cannot afford to let wealth build up in its arteries. Too often it seems that the Reagan-era definition of capitalism has put this great nation into cardiac arrest. A steady flow of money is healthy, but the lifeblood of the United States's economy has been reduced to a fickle trickle. Far too many honest citizens struggle to survive in a nation that prides itself on prosperity. That prosperity does not reach the people who need it most when it's locked away in a stagnant pool of private assets.

Sometimes it feels that labor has taken a backseat to buying power in this country. We say that the customer is always right, but I've witnessed where this sentiment leads. I was finishing a shift at the restaurant where I had worked for the better part of a year. An older woman and her friend sat down at one of my tables, and I was hoping they would quickly order and finish so I could get my last tip of the night. Much to my frustration and despite my earnest efforts, these customers started out rude and only got worse. Everything I did or didn't do for this table was a personal insult. The older woman was complaining loudly about the state of our floors, which in all fairness were certainly disgusting in places but no more so than you'd expect from a family-style restaurant at the tail-end of a long lunch rush. When I went to sweep the floors, she started yelling at me from across the restaurant that she had dust allergies. I couldn't do anything right. These two customers chased every other guest out of our restaurant, and the punchline is that my general manager spent fifteen minutes apologizing to them and compensated their entire meal. This was a valuable lesson: a business should always cater its service to the needs of its clients, but that doesn't mean that the business should value the customer's comforts over those of the employees. Sometimes the customer has unreasonable expectations. Sometimes the customer is wrong.

The gap between wealth and poverty in this country is already far too great. We don't like to talk about it, but history tells us that for every Roman Republic there is a Julius Caesar just waiting in the wings to turn the labor class against its so-called patrons. This country has a proud history of dissent, but I don't think that another revolution is what our founders had in mind when they signed the constitution into law. If the estate tax does little to redistribute the vast resources of this country then the estate tax should be increased, not abolished. Even as it now stands, the estate tax does some good simply by creating jobs for the public servants who uphold this measure. If there is even a slight profit to the taxpayer, so much the better.

The estate tax is a crucial part of our nation's founders' grand experiment, because it puts old money in the pockets of all our children, not just the fortunate few. Like so many things in this country, this measure is a product of compromise and should rightfully be under constant scrutiny, but that does not mean that the estate tax is broken or unrighteous, only that it must always be evolving to meet the ever dynamic needs of this country. Without the estate tax to keep old money flowing in its veins, our struggling economy will inevitably choke on all its prodigious wealth, and we will all be buried alive like the slaves in a pharaoh's lavish tomb.

1. Is the writer's position clearly stated and developed?

2. Does the writer address and analyze each of the perspectives in the prompt?

3. Does the writer use effective examples or reasoning to support his/her position?

4. Do any examples have too much or too little detail?

5. Does the writer skillfully use language and vocabulary?

Read the essay assignment below, and evaluate the essay that follows.

Trade Unions

Trade unions, or labor unions, are organizations of workers who have banded together to achieve common goals. These unions are created in order to balance the power between employers and employees. By threatening to collectively "go on strike" and stop working, employees are able to bargain for better working conditions, such as increased pay or benefits. Trade unions were first created during the Industrial Revolution, when employers took advantage of the unregulated economy and treated their employees unfairly by reducing wages and creating unsafe work environments. Today, trade unions exist in many forms and have different goals and levels of influence.

Read and carefully consider these perspectives. Each suggests a particular way of thinking about the problems or benefits associated with trade unions.

Perspective One	Perspective Two	Perspective Three
Government policies prevent the exploitation of workers, which eliminates the need for trade unions. Unlike benefits from unions, these policies benefit all workers equally and therefore don't create unfair advantages for unionized companies.	People have a natural right to peaceful assembly. As long as there is a balance of power, with neither the employer nor employees gaining an unfair advantage over the other, unions are a helpful assertion of our rights.	Trade unions enable employees to give each other undeserved benefits. If workers are protected by their fellow union members, employers have more difficulty firing or reprimanding employees, which reduces the incentive for better work.

Trade unions have been around for centuries, and although their practices have changed over time they have continued act as the middle man between employers and employees. The Industrial Revolution created new jobs for many, but it also created the need for representation for employees who worked long hours, often in poor conditions, for little pay. When trade unions were formed, they worked to improve these conditions. In the modern era, trade unions are no longer the only system in place to protect the worker's rights; the government has passed laws that do so. However, the law can only do so much. When it comes to negotiating a contract or bargaining for wage increase, a labor union still holds the bargaining power. Immigration, reform policies, decreased labor demand, and the use of technology to perform certain jobs are all issues that employees, employers, and unions have had to contend with in the modern era. Unions have become increasingly more involved in politics, but they have not always tackled political issues correctly, such as education reform, which greatly affects teachers in schools today.

Even if employees and employers are understanding of each other, they will have different perspectives on the roles that each play in the work place. The owners of a large petroleum corporation, such as Hess or ExxonMobil, are aware of what the job requires of their oil rig workers, but they cannot feel the daily physical toll this type of job can take on an employee. Long hours, cold temperatures, dangerous equipment, and hard physical labor are part of the job. Having a middle man, a union leader, to set up meetings with the employer helps to give the employee a sense of security and a belief that if work conditions get worse, they will be protected. If negotiations do not work and a strike is necessary, the union leaders are there to plan and organize the strike for the workers. Without the help of a union, strikes could easily turn violent or become unorganized and chaotic.

On the other hand, union strikes do not always work and can lead to further frustration between employers and employees. It can also affect those who work in the industry and are not affiliated with the union or the strike. With government policies and laws in place for the work place, such as safety regulations, working conditions, and minimum wages, one could argue that unions are unnecessary and do not equally benefit all workers, union and non-union. When nurses go on strike, hospitals cannot shut down or hold off on patient care until the strike is over. Therefore, other employees who continue to work in the hospital and the patients are affected.

With any kind of organization of a group, there exists a type of group dynamic where there are those who lead and those who follow. In a school, there are tenured teachers and teachers who have taught for many years there. These teachers might have strong opinions on education and the role of the union. If a new employee does not want to join a teacher's union, he or she may be asked to do so by other employees or still have to pay union dues. Opponents against teachers' unions argue that these unions keep "bad" teachers from getting fired and only have the interests of the teacher in mind and not those of the many students they teach every day.

As trade unions have changed over the decades, the opinion of society on them has also changed. Trade unions have always stood as a voice for the weaker majority, the employee, and have helped to keep business thriving for the powerful minority, the employer. In the past, society has worked against unions and tried to ban them. In other times, they have embraced the union as a necessary part of the work place. In the modern era, there seems to be mixed opinions. Unions have adapted to meet society's changing opinion and will most likely continuing doing so.

1. Is the writer's position clearly stated and developed?

2. Does the writer address and analyze each of the perspectives in the prompt?

3. Does the writer use effective examples or reasoning to support his/her position?

4. Do any examples have too much or too little detail?

5. Does the writer skillfully use language and vocabulary?

Read the essay assignment below, and write an essay on the following pages.

Genetically Modified Foods

Genetically modified foods are organisms that have had their DNA altered. Through genetic engineering, scientists modify organisms to be more resilient, nutritious, and appealing. Plants are common subjects of genetic modification, which allows scientists to have more control over plant traits than traditional methods of selective breeding. Many crops have been genetically modified to be more resistant to disease and less vulnerable to parasites. Even milk-producing animals have been modified to produce proteins used in medical treatments. Because genetic modification is a modern practice made possible by recently discovered techniques, there is still controversy over the labeling and regulation regarding genetically modified foods. Many of these policies are not yet finalized because there are no long-term studies on the effects of producing or consuming these foods.

Read and carefully consider these perspectives. Each suggests a particular way of thinking about the problems or benefits associated with genetically modified foods.

Perspective One	Perspective Two	Perspective Three
As the human population rises, there is an immediate need for more food. By making food sources more available and productive, genetic modification is the solution to world hunger.	Modified foods should not be made available to consumers until more testing is done. Such modifications can create new diseases or other problems. We should not potentially endanger consumers.	Scientists have an ethical obligation to honor and preserve the natural world. A change made for humanity's sake may harm systems of nature, which must be preserved for our existence.

Essay Task

Write a unified, coherent essay in which you evaluate multiple perspectives on genetically modified foods. In your essay, be sure to:

- analyze and evaluate the perspectives given
- state and develop your own perspective on the issue
- explain the relationship between your perspective and those given

Your perspective may be in full agreement with any of the others, in partial agreement, or wholly different. Whatever the case, support your ideas with logical reasoning and detailed, persuasive examples.

Read the essay assignment below, and write an essay on the following pages.

Soda Tax

Sumptuary taxes are levied on goods and services that a society considers undesirable or unhealthy. Historically, tobacco, alcohol, and gambling have been heavily taxed in the United States. Lawmakers in support of sumptuary taxes have argued that these industries make large profits but do not make positive contributions to society. Following this reasoning, these taxes would allow some of the profit generated from these goods and services to be used for more socially beneficial investments. Recently, as dietary problems have become a growing concern, some people have called for new taxes on unhealthy foods. In particular, sugary soft drinks have been targeted because of the proven connection between their consumption and health problems such as diabetes and obesity.

Read and carefully consider these perspectives. Each suggests a particular way of thinking about whether a tax should be placed on unhealthy foods such as soda.

Perspective One	Perspective Two	Perspective Three
Consumers of unhealthy foods are a burden on all of society. By knowingly ruining their own health, these people are creating unnecessary expenses through higher insurance rates and healthcare taxes. A soda tax would pay back these expenses.	We can discourage people from unhealthy eating by educating the public. If we help people understand how and why they should eat healthily, a tax on unhealthy foods would be unnecessary.	Many people enjoy unhealthy foods but lead healthy lives because they exercise regularly and get proper nutrients. These people should not be penalized. Rather than taxing unhealthy products, we must tax those with unhealthy lifestyles.

Essay Task

Write a unified, coherent essay in which you evaluate multiple perspectives on a soda tax. In your essay, be sure to:

- analyze and evaluate the perspectives given
- state and develop your own perspective on the issue
- explain the relationship between your perspective and those given

Your perspective may be in full agreement with any of the others, in partial agreement, or wholly different. Whatever the case, support your ideas with logical reasoning and detailed, persuasive examples.

SUMMIT
EDUCATIONAL
GROUP

Read the essay assignment below, and write an essay on the following pages.

Gender-Divided Classrooms

In recent years, the debate over whether boys and girls should be educated separately has intensified. Traditionally, public school classrooms consisted of both girls and boys. Some schools offered gender-specific classes, such as woodworking for boys and home economics for girls, but most core classes were co-ed. In the past few decades, there has been a shift away from dividing classes based on traditional gender roles. However, there have also been new views on learning styles and development which have led to new types of gender division. Because research shows males and females mature at different rates, more people have chosen to put their children in gender-divided classrooms.

Read and carefully consider these perspectives. Each suggests a particular way of thinking about whether classrooms should be divided based on gender.

Perspective One	Perspective Two	Perspective Three
American history shows that classrooms should not be segregated by race, and this lesson should be extended to gender segregation. Whether we make divisions based on race or gender, segregation will always promote stereotypes, prejudice, and inequality.	If gender-divided classrooms provide the best education, all schools should offer them. A school's primary duty is to provide and promote a strong education, which is not possible when students are constantly distracted by social pressures.	We cannot organize our classes based on outdated and restrictive views on gender. Some students would not be comfortable being grouped according to biological sex rather than gender identity. By integrating classrooms, we promote acceptance and allow people to develop freely.

Essay Task

Write a unified, coherent essay in which you evaluate multiple perspectives on gender-divided classrooms. In your essay, be sure to:

- analyze and evaluate the perspectives given
- state and develop your own perspective on the issue
- explain the relationship between your perspective and those given

Your perspective may be in full agreement with any of the others, in partial agreement, or wholly different. Whatever the case, support your ideas with logical reasoning and detailed, persuasive examples.

Read the essay assignment below, and write an essay on the following pages.

Globalization

Globalization is the process of integration among nations. As communication and transportation technologies progress, people become more connected across the world. Goods and services are traded worldwide. Ideas and ideologies are rapidly spread. Cultures that were once confined to specific geographic areas are now widespread and widely known. Globalization is often viewed as an unavoidable consequence of modern advancements, but can its effects be regulated or limited? Given the increasing pace of globalization, it is worth examining its impact on the modern world.

Read and carefully consider these perspectives. Each suggests a particular way of thinking about the effects of globalization.

Perspective One	Perspective Two	Perspective Three
As companies from different countries are thrust into the same markets, they become more competitive. This results in better products and lower prices. Globalization encourages the strongest companies to grow even stronger.	Global companies have exploited other nations, taking advantage of cheaper labor and lower business regulations. This has led to loss of jobs in more developed nations and poor working conditions in less developed nations.	As more nations become economically and politically connected, new policies are created that ensure greater equality and acceptance. Also, the sharing of technologies and knowledge ensures that all nations can prosper.

Essay Task

Write a unified, coherent essay in which you evaluate multiple perspectives on globalization. In your essay, be sure to:

- analyze and evaluate the perspectives given
- state and develop your own perspective on the issue
- explain the relationship between your perspective and those given

Your perspective may be in full agreement with any of the others, in partial agreement, or wholly different. Whatever the case, support your ideas with logical reasoning and detailed, persuasive examples.

Read the essay assignment below, and write an essay on the following pages.

Internet Censorship

Censorship refers to the control of access to ideas and information. Typically, censorship is performed by some authority in order to protect itself or citizens from certain media considered offensive, harmful, or immoral. As the vast amount of information on the internet has become more accessible, several groups have expressed interest in controlling what can be published or viewed online. Some schools and parents restrict access to media that is deemed inappropriate for their students and children. Some countries block information that is deemed dangerous or subversive. Some internet service providers will reduce the speed of access to certain websites in order to give themselves an advantage over competitors. As the internet becomes increasingly influential and vital to modern society, it is critical that we determine how it should be utilized and regulated.

Read and carefully consider these perspectives. Each suggests a particular way of thinking about censorship and regulation of internet services and information.

Perspective One	Perspective Two	Perspective Three
Unrestricted access to all internet services is essential to promoting global equality. Just as all people have a human right to free speech, they have a right to view and share the wealth of human knowledge. This allows all people to prosper and advance together.	Not all media is positive or beneficial. The internet contains much information that is vulgar or offensive, and people should be protected against this. By default, internet users should have access to only unbiased and inoffensive material.	Through the control of information, an authority may misrepresent itself and others in order to maintain control. All people of the world should have unregulated access to the internet so they can be informed and empowered.

Essay Task

Write a unified, coherent essay in which you evaluate multiple perspectives on internet censorship. In your essay, be sure to:

- analyze and evaluate the perspectives given
- state and develop your own perspective on the issue
- explain the relationship between your perspective and those given

Your perspective may be in full agreement with any of the others, in partial agreement, or wholly different. Whatever the case, support your ideas with logical reasoning and detailed, persuasive examples.

Read the essay assignment below, and write an essay on the following pages.

Estate Tax

The United States estate tax is a tax on the value of the estate of a deceased person. Assets included in a will or granted as an insurance benefit are included in this tax. The percent of taxation can vary depending on the value of the assets, and the tax only applies to estates above $5 million in value. The tax does not apply to assets that are left to a spouse. Also, expenses for funeral services or charitable contributions are not taxed.

There are many policies that are designed to prevent avoidance of the estate tax. For example, a person cannot transfer his or her estate to others shortly before death in order to avoid being taxed. However, it is still common that people with large estates will find ways to circumvent these tax laws in order to prevent their assets from being taxed.

Read and carefully consider these perspectives. Each suggests a particular way of thinking about the estate tax.

Perspective One	Perspective Two	Perspective Three
An essential feature of our capitalist system is progressive taxation, which prevents the consolidation of wealth. Without progressive taxes, most of the nation's wealth would be held by a select few.	The expense of investigating and preventing estate tax evasion is nearly as high as the funds received from the estate tax. This is not an efficient source of government revenue.	Allowing people to simply inherit great wealth from past generations discourages hard work and a true entrepreneurial spirit. Inheritance should be limited so future generations do not become idle and unappreciative.

Essay Task

Write a unified, coherent essay in which you evaluate multiple perspectives on the estate tax. In your essay, be sure to:

- analyze and evaluate the perspectives given
- state and develop your own perspective on the issue
- explain the relationship between your perspective and those given

Your perspective may be in full agreement with any of the others, in partial agreement, or wholly different. Whatever the case, support your ideas with logical reasoning and detailed, persuasive examples.

Read the essay assignment below, and write an essay on the following pages.

Trade Unions

Trade unions, or labor unions, are organizations of workers who have banded together to achieve common goals. These unions are created in order to balance the power between employers and employees. By threatening to collectively "go on strike" and stop working, employees are able to bargain for better working conditions, such as increased pay or benefits. Trade unions were first created during the Industrial Revolution, when employers took advantage of the unregulated economy and treated their employees unfairly by reducing wages and creating unsafe work environments. Today, trade unions exist in many forms and have different goals and levels of influence.

Read and carefully consider these perspectives. Each suggests a particular way of thinking about the problems or benefits associated with trade unions.

Perspective One	Perspective Two	Perspective Three
Government policies prevent the exploitation of workers, which eliminates the need for trade unions. Unlike benefits from unions, these policies benefit all workers equally and therefore don't create unfair advantages for unionized companies.	People have a natural right to peaceful assembly. As long as there is a balance of power, with neither the employer nor employees gaining an unfair advantage over the other, unions are a helpful assertion of our rights.	Trade unions enable employees to give each other undeserved benefits. If workers are protected by their fellow union members, employers have more difficulty firing or reprimanding employees, which reduces the incentive for better work.

Essay Task

Write a unified, coherent essay in which you evaluate multiple perspectives on trade unions. In your essay, be sure to:

- analyze and evaluate the perspectives given
- state and develop your own perspective on the issue
- explain the relationship between your perspective and those given

Your perspective may be in full agreement with any of the others, in partial agreement, or wholly different. Whatever the case, support your ideas with logical reasoning and detailed, persuasive examples.

SUMMIT
EDUCATIONAL
GROUP

Answer Key

TEST-TAKING FUNDAMENTALS

Attractors – p. 17
1. C
2. G
3. C

ENGLISH

USAGE AND MECHANICS

Pronouns
p. 24
  a passenger
  Pearls
  He
  who
  who
  whom
  who

p. 26 Put It Together
1. C
2. J
3. C
4. F
5. D

Subject-Verb Agreement
p. 28
  was
  is
  want
  is
  are

p. 29 Put It Together
1. C
2. J
3. B
4. J
5. B

Verb Tense
p. 30
  has been
  had been

p. 31 Put It Together
1. C
2. H
3. A
4. H

Adjectives versus Adverbs / Idioms
p. 32
  delightfully
  careful
  with
  from

p. 33 Put It Together
1. C
2. G
3. A
4. J

Diction
p. 34
  except
  accept
  affect
  effect
  than
  then
  loose
  lose
  lay
  lie
  lead
  led
  principle
  principal
  number
  amount
  fewer
  less
  between
  among

p. 35 Put It Together
1. C
2. H
3. C
4. J

Checkpoint Review – p. 36
1. A
2. J
3. B
4. H
5. D
6. F
7. B
8. H
9. C
10. G

Fragments
p. 38
Cape Cod <u>provides</u> …
The journalist <u>traveled</u> …
The editor, a stern man, <u>censored</u> …
Achilles' mother held him by the <u>heel and</u> …

p. 39 Put It Together
1. C
2. J
3. B
4. H

Run-On Sentences
p. 40
… <u>and</u> I've learned a lot from her

p. 41 Put It Together
1. A
2. H
3. B

Parallelism
p. 42
elegant, stylish, and <u>expensive</u>
drab, awkward, and <u>cheap</u>
<u>being</u> aware …
… Tanya <u>does</u>.

p. 43 Put It Together
1. B
2. J

Modifiers
p. 44
<u>Mike felt that his</u> vacation…
<u>As I looked at the horizon</u>, ominous clouds…

p. 45 Put It Together
1. B
2. H
3. B
4. H
5. B
6. H

Checkpoint Review – p. 46
1. D
2. J
3. D
4. J
5. B
6. H
7. D
8. H
9. B
10. H

Periods
p. 48
My cat Moxie likes chasing the laser pointer.
Yesterday she ran into a wall.

p. 49 Put It Together
1. B
2. J

Semicolons and Colons
p. 50
Mark's job was <u>monotonous; it</u> …

p. 51 Put It Together
1. C
2. H

Commas

p. 52

At the end of the <u>street, I</u> saw...

After a leisurely <u>breakfast, we</u> took...

...want to <u>play, but</u> really...

...my parents, <u>Elvis, and</u> Michael Jackson

Mr. Kamin's speech was <u>profound, reflective, and</u>

p. 54 Put It Together

1. B
2. F
3. C
4. H
5. B
6. H
7. A
8. H

Apostrophes

p. 56

Children's

hers

theirs

It's

its

p. 58 Put It Together

1. C
2. F
3. B
4. J
5. C

Checkpoint Review – p. 60

1. B
2. J
3. D
4. J
5. A
6. F
7. D
8. F
9. A
10. H

RHETORICAL SKILLS

Main Idea

p. 66

Steroid use in baseball has led to negative views of the sport and the players.

C

p. 67 Put It Together

1. B
2. F
3. D

Intent

p. 68

Steroid use has led to controversy from people who view the sport in different ways.

No, it is more about the steroid controversy regarding the sport as a whole.

C

p. 69 Put It Together

1. D
2. J
3. D

Organization

p. 70

Some players have been kept out of the Hall of Fame. Other controversial players were allowed in the Hall of fame.

The first idea

B

p. 71 Put It Together

1. D
2. H
3. B

Addition

p. 72

Not suitable: A

No explanation: C, D

Correct: B

p. 73 Put It Together

1. B
2. J
3. A

Deletion

p. 74

Provides an example to represent previous sentence.

D

p. 75 Put It Together

1. B
2. G
3. B

Transitions

p. 77

First: increase of homeruns and steroid usage

Second: other factors cause rising homerun numbers

Not relevant: B, D

Correct: A

p. 78 Put It Together

1. C
2. J
3. A
4. F
5. D
6. G

Style

p. 80

B

G

p. 81 Put It Together

1. C
2. F

Wordiness

p. 82

D

J

p. 83 Put It Together

1. D
2. G
3. D

English Practice – p. 88

PASSAGE I

1. A
2. G
3. C
4. F
5. B
6. J
7. C
8. J
9. D
10. F
11. B
12. G
13. D
14. F
15. C

PASSAGE II

1. D
2. G
3. C
4. J
5. D
6. J
7. A
8. J
9. D
10. H
11. C
12. J
13. C
14. G
15. C

PASSAGE III

1. A
2. G
3. D
4. J
5. A
6. J
7. A
8. H
9. C
10. J
11. C
12. J
13. A
14. H
15. B

PASSAGE IV

1. D
2. H
3. C
4. H
5. A
6. H
7. C
8. G
9. B
10. H
11. C
12. G
13. D
14. F
15. D

PASSAGE V

1. D
2. G
3. D
4. H
5. D
6. G
7. B
8. G
9. D
10. G
11. C
12. H
13. A
14. G
15. C

PASSAGE VI

1. C
2. H
3. B
4. F
5. D
6. H
7. C
8. H
9. A
10. J
11. B
12. H
13. D
14. J
15. A

PASSAGE VII

1. D
2. H
3. B
4. G
5. D
6. H
7. A
8. G
9. C
10. J
11. D
12. G
13. C
14. H
15. C

PASSAGE VIII

1. B
2. G
3. A
4. J
5. B
6. J
7. B
8. F
9. B
10. G
11. C
12. G
13. D
14. J
15. B

PASSAGE IX

1. C
2. H
3. C
4. H
5. A
6. H
7. C
8. J
9. C
10. J
11. C
12. F
13. C
14. G
15. A

PASSAGE X
1. C
2. F
3. C
4. F
5. C
6. G
7. B
8. J
9. C
10. H
11. C
12. F
13. C
14. H
15. D

READING

Attractors – p. 132
1. D
2. H

Active Reading

p. 141 Try It Out
1. The laws of nature prevent the existence of science-fiction scale organisms.
2. Giant-scale animals could not survive the physical pressures of their own bodies.
3. Tiny-scale animals would starve and/or freeze to death.
4. Despite this scientific knowledge, the author still enjoys sci-fi films.
5. Although giant/tiny sci-fi creatures are entertaining, they are physiologically impossible.

Paired Passages

p. 144 Put It Together

1. A
2. G
3. D
4. H
5. C
6. J
7. D
8. G
9. B
10. G

Literary Narrative or Prose Fiction Passages

p. 146
Narrator respects Bill and sees him as a father-figure.
Bill doesn't feel as attached. Sees narrator as just an employee.
Pickfords are very conservative and perhaps uptight.
Hiddles are likely more informal and wild.

Social Science Passages

p. 147
In the 18th century, thinkers like Kant supported new ideas about individuality and rights. This led to people wanting more freedom from the people who traditionally ruled their lives.

Humanities Passages

p. 148
We know little of Robert Johnson. Stories depict him as secretive and talented.
Part of his fame is due to his mystery. The lack of information allows for interesting stories to explain his life.

Natural Science Passages

p. 149
Scientists did not know how Egyptians had iron beads at such an early time.
Dates of iron beads and Iron Age, nickel-rich alloy, meteoric.

Checkpoint Review – p. 150

1. D
2. H
3. C
4. H
5. C
6. J
7. B
8. F
9. B
10. J

Anticipating the Answer

p. 153

Bad design can make it hard to tell how something should be operated.

C

p. 154 Try It Out

1. The Cavendish is relatively unpalatable and inconsistent.
2. Tastier
3. "Panama Disease"
4. Branch, sprout
5. The advantages/disadvantages of the Cavendish
6. Cavendish is hardy; Gros Michel is soft, creamy, and fragrant.
7. Genetically modified crops could "spread potential mutations."
8. N/A

p. 156 Put It Together

1. A
2. G
3. C
4. G
5. A
6. J
7. D
8. F

Process of Elimination

p. 159

A – it's not about the user's abilities, but about how the device "converses" with the user

B – it's not about simpler tools, but making it easier for the user to use complex tools

C – too extreme

D - correct

p. 160 Put It Together

1. C
2. J
3. A
4. J
5. C

Detail

p. 163 Put It Together

1. B

Generalization

p. 165 Put It Together

1. A
2. H
3. B

Main Idea

p. 167 Put It Together

1. C
2. F

Comparative Relationships

p. 169 Put It Together

1. B
2. J

Cause-Effect

p. 171 Put It Together

1. A
2. H

Voice

p. 173 Put It Together

1. D
2. J
3. D

Method

p. 175 Put It Together

1. C
2. G
3. D

Contextual Meaning

p. 177 Put It Together

1. D
2. H
3. A
4. J

Inference

p. 179 Put It Together

1. B
2. J

Reading Practice – p. 184

Passage I – Prose Fiction
1. D
2. J
3. B
4. H
5. B
6. G
7. B
8. H
9. D
10. G

Passage II – Prose Fiction
1. C
2. G
3. C
4. J
5. C
6. G
7. A
8. G
9. D
10. G

Passage III – Literary Narrative
1. C
2. J
3. B
4. G
5. A
6. G
7. A
8. G
9. A
10. F

Passage IV – Prose Fiction
1. D
2. J
3. C
4. J
5. B
6. H
7. C
8. H
9. B
10. H

Passage V – Social Science
1. D
2. F
3. C
4. H
5. C
6. H
7. A
8. H
9. C
10. J

Passage VI – Social Science
1. D
2. F
3. B
4. J
5. B
6. F
7. D
8. G
9. D
10. F

Passage VII – Social Science
1. A
2. J
3. D
4. G
5. C
6. J
7. C
8. H
9. C
10. J

Passage VIII – Social Science
1. A
2. H
3. A
4. H
5. D
6. G
7. A
8. J
9. B
10. H

Passage IX – Humanities
1. D
2. J
3. A
4. F
5. A
6. G
7. D
8. J
9. C
10. H

Passage X – Humanities
1. A
2. F
3. C
4. J
5. D
6. H
7. A
8. G
9. C
10. G

Passage XI – Humanities
1. C
2. F
3. B
4. J
5. C
6. H
7. A
8. H
9. B
10. G

Passage XII – Humanities
1. D
2. F
3. C
4. F
5. D
6. H
7. B
8. F
9. A
10. G

Passage XIII – Natural Science
1. A
2. H
3. B
4. G
5. A
6. F
7. C
8. J
9. B
10. H

Passage XIV – Natural Science
1. D
2. F
3. D
4. J
5. D
6. G
7. C
8. H
9. C
10. F

Passage XV – Natural Science
1. D
2. F
3. C
4. F
5. D
6. F
7. C
8. H
9. C
10. H

Passage XVI – Natural Science
1. D
2. H
3. D
4. F
5. A
6. H
7. C
8. H
9. A
10. H

WRITING

Proofread

p. 259 Try It Out

If we **separate** students based on gender, we will undermine the primary goal of modern education, which is a free and unbiased sharing of information. When a student body is confined by outdated ideas of gender, the information that this student body has access to is similarly confined.

There exists already a social stigma that discourages people from pursuing certain careers, and this would only be further strengthened by such segregation. For too long, our society has promoted the view that the fields of math and science are made for men**. B**ecause of this social pressure, women have typically had much lower enrollment in these areas. By separating students, we further promote the division of education by gender**, w**hich unfairly restricts students' interests. This is similar to "separate but equal" laws that segregated students based on race. Such laws did not openly support racist hate, but they did create systems to enforce racism. In the same way, gender-divided classroom would not be created to openly promote sexism, but they would create a more sexist society. Just as schools **need** to be racially integrated, they must also be gender integrated in order to promote social and educational **equality**.

The only way to combat prejudice is through social exposure**, a**nd the earlier the better. Some supporters of gender-divided classrooms point to social distractions as the great evil of quality education. But, far from being a distraction, socialization is one of most important parts of a well-rounded education. Furthermore, diversity is essential to an **effective** classroom. More student perspectives will offer the possibility of more questions and more answers. Segregated classrooms create uniformity, which means students are not expanding **their** minds by being exposed to new ideas It is understandable that some people believe gender-divided classrooms are the best fit for **themselves**, but this should not be a system that is forced on all students. If we want to promote equality and diverse knowledge, we must defend our right to have classrooms that anyone can attend.

p. 262 Try It Out

1. History has shown the social importance of art. ~~Art is extremely significant.~~ Near the beginning of the Civil War, Abraham Lincoln met Harriet Beecher Stowe and remarked, "So this is the little lady who started this great war." Who was this influential woman? Stowe wrote the anti-slavery novel *Uncle Tom's Cabin*, an account of the hardships of slaves that was so moving it sparked a revolution that led to the end of American slavery. ~~This novel gained her a lot of fame. Stowe was born in 1811 and began her writing career as a contributor to religious periodicals.~~ Before her novel was published, the problems of slavery were ignored by many people. This work of art helped spread the ideas of abolition that inspired the Civil War.

2. We need to cooperate to complete this project.

3. There are 4 reasons this scene is important.

4. Mr. Henderson was late for work because he had to stop at many red lights.

5. If you look at Seattle's famous Space Needle, it might be surprising to think it was supposed to be an architectural masterpiece.

6. In cities with lots of history, it is difficult make good roads or sidewalks because many people don't want to ruin the historical sites.

Writing Practice

p. 269

1. Yes, the introduction clearly states the writer's position.

2. The writer addresses Perspective One, but not the other two perspectives.

3. No, the examples are only vaguely related to the main topic.

4. The example of Rome is not developed thoroughly enough.

5. Yes, the language is strong, with good vocabulary and clever lines.

p. 271

1. No, it is not clear whether the writer supports unions.

2. Yes, the writer addresses all perspectives.

3. Examples are relevant and effective.

4. Examples have too little detail. Descriptions should be more thorough and specific.

5. Yes, the language is strong and consistent.

Test Week Checklist

Week of the Test

❑ By now, you know what you know. Cramming won't help you learn anything new, and it will only add to your test anxiety. If you want to study, review the Chapter Summaries.

❑ Take it easy, and try to get a week's worth of good sleep. You want to be well rested for test day.

❑ If you are not testing at your own school, make sure you know where you're going. Don't rely on an online mapping program the morning of the test. If you need to, take a test run the weekend before.

Friday night

❑ Again, you know what you know. Do something relaxing and fun.

❑ Lay out everything you need to bring with you:

- Your admission ticket
- Official photo ID
- 3 or 4 sharpened No. 2 pencils with erasers
- Calculator with new batteries
- Watch
- A drink and a small snack that won't get your hands sticky

❑ Visualize success. See yourself solving question after question. Envision completing the last question, putting your pencil down, and closing the test booklet. Let yourself feel the good feeling of a job well done.

❑ Go to sleep at the same time you've been going to sleep all week. Otherwise, you'll just toss and turn. Don't worry if you have trouble sleeping. You'll have plenty of adrenaline to keep your brain going during the test.

Morning of the Test

❑ Have a backup alarm – either another clock or a parent.

❑ Eat a good breakfast. Make sure to avoid heavy, fatty foods.

❑ Do something easy that you enjoy (take a walk or listen to music). You want to go into the test awake and upbeat.

At the Test

❏ Arrive about fifteen minutes early to the test center to find your room and settle in.

❏ Make sure to use the bathroom before you start the test. You only have a few short breaks during the test; you don't want to have to worry about a line at the restroom.

❏ Find your seat and sit for a minute. Continue to visualize yourself working successfully through the test, using all of the skills and strategies you've learned.

❏ During breaks, stand up and walk around. It helps you to stay focused.

❏ Pace yourself and keep your eye on the clock.

❏ If you start losing focus, try this concentration exercise: Every five questions, put down your pencil, stare at the ceiling, blink a few times, take several deep, slow breaths and then continue with the next five questions.

After the Test

❏ Plan to do something positive and fun. You deserve it!